The Ashantee Campaign

The Ashantee Campaign

An Account of the Third Anglo-Ashanti War
by an Eyewitness West Africa, 1873-4

Winwood Reade

LEONAUR

The Ashantee Campaign
An Account of the Third Anglo-Ashanti War by an Eyewitness West Africa, 1873-4
by Winwood Reade

First published under the title
The Ashantee Campaign

Leonaur is an imprint of Oakpast Ltd

Copyright in this form © 2012 Oakpast Ltd

ISBN: 978-0-85706-968-9 (hardcover)
ISBN: 978-0-85706-969-6 (softcover)

http://www.leonaur.com

Contents

Preface

As five other books on the Ashantee War have been announced or have already appeared, the preface to a work on that subject ought to be apologetic; and my apology for writing on an over-written subject is this, that it was my fortune to see more fighting than anyone else in the Expedition, excepting a few officers in the native regiments. Moreover no other writer, military or civil, witnessed either of these three events—the storming of Amoaful by the Black Watch; the storming of Ordahsu by the Rifle Brigade; or the taking of Coomassie by Sir Archibald Alison and Col. McLeod. I witnessed all three events, and therefore venture to believe that my personal experiences ought to be recorded as a contribution to the history of the Campaign.

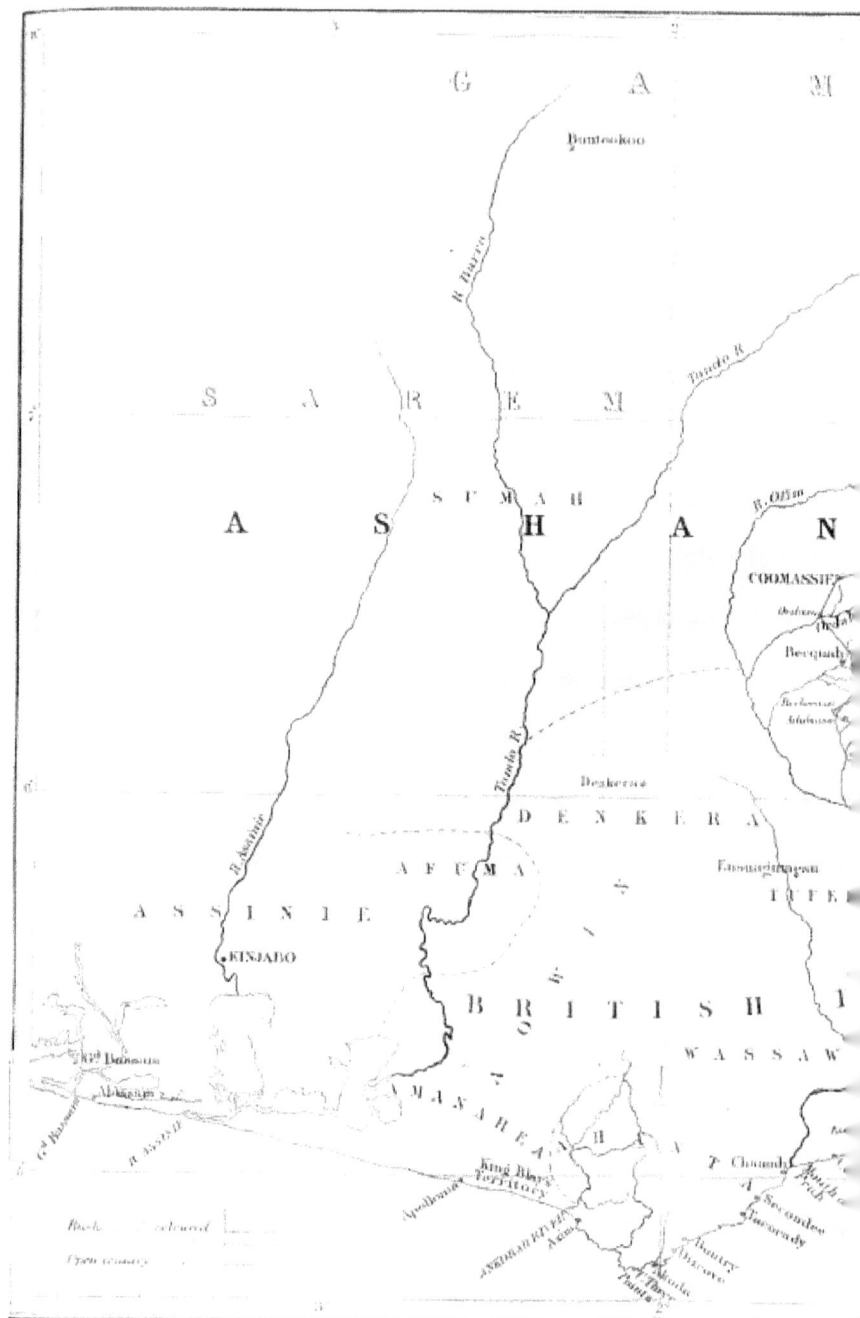

G A M

Buntookoo

R. Barra

Tando R.

S A R E M

A S H A N

SUMAH

COOMASSIE

R. Offin

Ordah

Bercquah

Barbarassa
Afsinassa

DENKERA

Denkerassa

Tando R.

AFUMA

Enssagintagan

TUFE

R. Assinie

ASSINIE

KINJABO

BRITISH

WASSAW

AMANAHEA

Kʳᵈ Bassam

Abossam

King Blay's
Territory

Apollonia

Chamah

Secondee
Tacorady

Axim

R. ASSINEE

Anda

Boutry

Dixcove

Takorady
Pocket

Rock covered

Open country

MAP
to illustrate the story of
THE ASHANTEE CAMPAIGN
by
WINWOOD READE.

English Statute Miles

Chapter 1

The Gold Coast

In 1870 I was staying at Odumassie, near the Volta, with one of the Basle missionaries. My host belonged to a type not uncommon, perhaps, in Germany, but rarely to be met with elsewhere. Before he was inspired by that impulse of religion and romance which decided his career, he had exercised the calling of a *baker*: yet not only was he a Greek and Hebrew scholar, but he had also the manners of a man of the world, and took an ardent interest in the problems of the day. I often look back to that visit with pleasure. In the morning we breakfasted early, somewhat in the country fashion, to which, as an old African traveller, I was thoroughly accustomed. Our beverage was a kind of coffee, prepared from the pods of a seed-bearing plant, the virtues of which my excellent host had discovered. We then went to our books. After dark we used to chat over a bottle of red Rhine wine on such subjects as the future union of Germany, the conversion of Africa, or the Darwinian theory.

On the manners and customs of the natives, my friend possessed rich stores of information, which he poured forth in clear and eloquent English an hour at a time. Sometimes he spoke of his brethren who had been taken captive to Coomassie.

One morning he brought me a stone which had evidently been shaped by human hands into the image of an axe. It was so small as rather to resemble a toy or model than a real implement of work; yet such in past ages it had been. With these miserable tools the ancestors of the white men, the yellow men, the red men, and the black men, had hewed down the oaks of Europe, the cedars of Asia, the pines of America, and the huge silk-cotton trees of Negroland. Not only are these stone implements dug up all over the world, but all over the world they are supposed by the common people to be thunderbolts.

As regards West Africa this belief is easily explained.

The Stone Age is there comparatively recent, and many axes are merely covered by the upper soil. After heavy storms of rain, which are usually accompanied by thunder and lightning, this upper soil being washed away, the stone implements are found lying on the ground, and so seem to have fallen from the sky. However, the stone which Mr. Zimmermann showed me had been dug up in his yard at some little depth below the surface. He informed me that he had sent specimens to the missionary museum at Basle, and I afterwards discovered that two specimens from Christiansborg (while that fort was under the Danes) had been sent to the Copenhagen collection, which is unrivalled in the world for its relics of the Age of Stone. But I was the first to bring stone implements from Western Africa to England; and being thus put upon the scent, obtained large numbers at two other missionary stations—Akropong and Aburé.

The next time I saw a stone implement was in the tent of Mr. Kühne, at Prahsu. He had found it on an Ashantee altar, or shrine, as he was on his way from Coomassie to the camp. I asked my interpreter if he had ever seen one before; he replied they were 'found everywhere,' and I made a small collection during the march through Ashantee. When the troops took a village, I always hunted for this kind of plunder. Sometimes I found the stone hanging before doorways at the end of a string, like a plummet, and often it would be daubed over with chalk. The natives regard these stones with superstitious reverence, call them *God-axes*, and believing that all things sacred are medicinal, grind from them a powder which they use for rheumatism and other complaints.

It may be assumed that the Africans of the Stone Age were of a low order in the human scale. Perhaps they lived on nests or platforms in the trees, dressed their bodies with dirt in the daytime, slept in a nightgown of warm ashes, hunted and fought with stakes, the points of which were hardened in the fire, and dined on roots, shellfish, snails, caterpillars, grasshoppers, white ants and prisoners of war. Even a knowledge of iron, and skill in its manufacture, is not incompatible with the still extant practices mentioned above. Mohammed-el-Tounsy, an intelligent Arab traveller (whose works, translated into French, should be carefully studied by ethnologists), gives some description of those forest-tribes of the equator which are hunted every year by the slave-catchers of Waday, and, as he justly observes, it is a most singular fact that these people, so savage and debased, nevertheless produce beautiful iron weapons and tools, which can only be compared with those that are made by the English. The finest specimens of native cutlery that I have seen myself, came from some low bush-tribe behind Monrovia; the knife-blades were engraved with tasteful designs, and were purchased at a heavy price by the other native tribes as works of art.

The cannibal Fans of the Gaboon, who are primitive enough in their habits, wearing only small aprons of goat-skin or bark, are exceedingly skilful as blacksmiths, and have even an iron currency. It is impossible to say where and how this art originated. The African bellows are different from the Asiatic kind, and are found all over, the continent; it is therefore not unreasonable to suppose that the Africans discovered for themselves the art of smelting iron ore, and that the art was conveyed, by means of tribal migrations and wandering guilds of blacksmiths, from one part of Negroland to another. Certain it is that wherever iron exists in Africa it is worked; and so abundant is it on the Gold Coast, that the slugs used by the Ashantees were chiefly bits of iron stone. Now, the discovery of iron would soon be followed by the discovery of gold in countries where that metal might exist, and in such countries gold-dust, instead of iron, would become the currency. Gold-dust on the Gold Coast is the money of the land: a *periguin* is 46 dollars, nearly 10*l*: an ounce is 3*l*. 12*s*.: an *ackie* is half-a-crown. But the natives are so well acquainted with the precious metal, that I have seen them buy plantains with less than a farthing's worth of gold, putting one or two grains on the tip of a knife.

I have shown that the knowledge of iron does not do much by itself to raise the condition and culture of the savage: but it is very different with gold. From Cape Palmas to Accra it is all one great forest; the physical features are everywhere identical; and there is no reason to doubt that the natives of this forest tract had the same origin. Yet the natives to the west of Assinie (where the gold ceases) are ages behind the natives of the Gold Coast. The villages of the seaboard contribute the *kroos*, a useful class of labourers, to the ships and factories. Everybody knows what uncouth savages they are when they first go to sea; but these villagers of the beach, savage as they are, look with contempt on their brethren of the bush.

I have travelled among these people (they would not let me go very far), and found them no better than the bush-tribes of Gaboon. Every village was a kingdom; at every thirty miles another dialect was spoken—that surest sign of barbarism: prisoners of war were eaten, but not women, 'because they were tough;' it was forbidden by the fetish to kill the chimpanzee, because he was 'too near;' considered in fact as a man and a brother. I found that warfare was chronic, that no man travelled more than a day's journey from his village, that commerce, except within such limits, did not exist, and that exploration was impossible. Even the Moslem traders who inhabit the open country beyond the forest-belt, have never penetrated into that poor and inhospitable land. But on the Gold Coast the natives are not uncivilised; it is scarcely correct to call them savages; one language, the Oji, is spoken over a vast area; organised kingdoms exist. In the forest of the Kroos iron is in use, but gold is unknown; and it is doubtless the knowledge of gold which by means of commerce has raised the people of the Gold Coast from that early and rude condition in which their neighbours still remain.

We have a strange but sure proof that even in very ancient times the Gold Coast was indirectly connected with the civilised world. It is the custom in Western Africa to bury articles of value with the dead; and certain beads or bugles are often disinterred upon the Gold Coast.

These *aggry* beads are of Egyptian or Phoenician manufacture, and are probably glass mosaics. The artists of Birmingham cannot imitate them with success, an attempt which has been frequently made, for they are the precious stones of the country, and sell for their weight in gold. It is a law of Ashantee that if an *aggry* bead is broken in a scuffle, seven slaves must be paid to the owner. [1] As these beads are usually found at some distance from the sea, it may be inferred that they were brought by the overland route; and in fact it never could have paid the Carthaginians to traffic with Guinea by sea, though undoubtedly they had sailed along its shores. With a land trade it was very different: the Egyptians and Phoenicians themselves had no occasion to cross the continent; they sold their goods to the Berbers, who sold them to the blacks south of the Sahara, and so they were passed on from tribe to tribe.

Just as English calicoes penetrate into parts of Africa which are quite inaccessible to English travellers; so the linen of Egypt, the scarlet cloth of Carthage, and the beads manufactured in both countries, found their way to the Gold Coast; and as a tusk of ivory obtained in the unknown land to the west of Lake Tanganyika, or behind the Fans of the Gaboon, finally arrives at Liverpool or Hamburg, so the gold of

1. Bowdich.

Guinea was transported across the regions watered by the Niger and the Nile, across the fiery desert, and at last, worked up into ornaments, flashed' upon the brow of a Sophonisba or Rhodopis

The *aggry* beads, though only to be found by accident, are yet very plentiful, which proves that in those days the trade of the Gold Coast was flourishing and active. Such a trade would destroy the spirit of non-intercourse prevailing to the present day among the bush-tribes on the west. There would be a tendency to centralise: the clans would gather into tribes, the tribes into nations: the market-places would grow into cities colonised from different regions: the language of trade would become dominant Then again, the access of wealth from commerce would produce an important revolution. The owners of the gold-land would purchase slaves in large numbers; thus a Patrician order would be formed, and the descendants of the slaves, becoming freedmen, would constitute the people.

The wives of the former class being no longer compelled to work in the plantations, would become more refined in feature and in form, while slaves who displayed an aptitude for art would be encouraged by their masters to cultivate the talents they possessed. Those mural arabesques and crimson basements which we found in the best houses at Fomana and Coomassie, do not exist in the semi-oriental cities— Timbuctoo, Kano, Sokoto, and Kukawa. They seem to be original, and were possibly prior to that civilising movement, which must now be described.

The Egyptians did not travel beyond the limits of their valley; the world came to them. The Greeks of Alexandria penetrated into Abyssinia, but never reached Central Africa, and Ptolemy must have obtained his materials from negro traders and captured slaves. The Carthaginians merely occupied Algeria; the Romans and their successors, the Byzantine Greeks, did not invade the lands beyond the Desert. But when the Arabs conquered Egypt and Northern Africa, they not only occupied those countries and converted its natives to the Faith, they also navigated the great Dry Ocean on their camels, discovered the Niger and settled in Timbuctoo. At first they were merely missionaries: they preached the *Koran*, and worked miracles, [2] but chiefly spread their religion by means of the school. After a time, in all the great negro cities, a Moslem quarter was established under its own *sheik*; and when the converts were numerous enough the *sheik* proclaimed a Holy War.

2. *Notices et Extraits de la Bibliothèque du Roi, tom. xii.*

In the same manner negroes went forth to other negro lands wearing the turban and the *tobe*, Arabs in all but their colour and their name. In a few centuries the vast prairie plateau of the Niger was conquered or converted to the Moslem creed, and, what was of far more consequence, adopted the manners and customs of the East. The negro nations of the Niger lands dwell in walled towns, cultivate and manufacture cotton, ride on horseback, read and write their own languages, using the Arab character, and also study Arabic, which is to them what Latin was to Europe in the Middle Ages; partly a sacred language, partly a means of intercourse between nations far apart. Thousands of negroes make every year the pilgrimage to Mecca; negro prophets have often arisen and founded military empires. The conversion of Soudan, it is needless to say, has greatly facilitated commerce; intercourse became more frequent and familiar among nations who worshipped the same God, and were governed by the same code of laws.

Now it is to be remarked that the Moslems have never been able to conquer except where cavalry can be used. They have scarcely entered the country lying west of the Niger (in its lower course), for there begins that vast and unknown forest which probably extends without an oasis of open land to the Great Lakes of the equator. In the same manner the marshy delta of the Niger and the bush-regions of the Guinea Coast are still in the hands of pagan chiefs, (as at time of first publication).

The natives of the Gold Coast, secure in their, stronghold, the Forest, preserved their independence and their barbarism. But still they were not uninfluenced by the great revolution of Central Africa. The increase of trade augmented their wealth, and the art of cotton-weaving was introduced among them. Henceforth they discarded the apron and assumed the robe.

I apply the term Gold Coast to that forest belt which extends inland from the sea rather more than two hundred miles. Formerly those tribes which dwelt on the border of the Plain possessed a commercial advantage and were probably more civilised than the people of the seaboard. Moreover the gold mines were also situated at some days' journey from the shore. But the sea had also its wealth. Salt is an ingredient of life: people who eat no salt sicken and die. The 'beachmen' enjoyed the monopoly of this precious mineral and boiled it in large quantities for the inland trade. They also had smoked fish to sell, and certain shells prized as ornaments. But a time was at hand when those salt-boilers and fishermen would become the merchant princes of the land.

We now reach the European period of Gold Coast history; and here its true history begins. The pagan nations have no written chronicles, and savage traditions are fabulous or modern. As yet my only guides have been analogy and inference; but now we step forth into the light. We open a book, composed in the fifteenth century—*Azurara, Chronica da Guiné*. We see before us a native village, afterwards called *Elmina*; we see the caravels at anchor in the roadstead, and a boat passing through the surf, and knights in armour landing, followed by men with *harquebusses* on their shoulders, and natives covered with gold ornaments coming down to meet them on the sandy beach.

CHAPTER 2

The Ashantees

Take up Strabo and Diodorus of Sicily, Pliny, Ptolemy, Pomponius Mela, read what they say about Africa, and it will clearly be perceived that they knew very little about the countries south of the Sahara. At the best they had a vague notion that there was an inhabited region beyond the Great Desert, and that it was watered by a river called the Niger, which some supposed to be a tributary of the Nile. It was almost universally believed that the equator was a *torrid zone,* or fiery belt girdling the earth, and dividing by an impassable barrier the people of the north from the people of the south. The negroes dwelt on the borders of this burning land; and it could plainly be seen how their skin was blackened and their hair frizzled by the heat. This theory of a torrid zone was inherited by mediaeval Europe, and in the fifteenth century everyone supposed that the inhabited world came to an end at the Sahara.

Yet Arabs and Spanish Moors, some of them men of culture and learning, had crossed the Sahara, and had found great negro kingdoms existing, on the banks of the Niger. Ibn Batuta, one of the greatest travellers who ever lived, had given some chapters of his book to Negroland. But such authorities were not accessible to the Christians of Portugal and Spain; the Peninsular Crusade had opened a gulf between the learned men of the East and of the West, and by war alone the existence of Guinea was finally revealed. In 1415 the Portuguese took Ceuta, and a young prince who was present at the siege questioned some of the prisoners about the geography of Africa. He then learnt to his astonishment that beyond the Sahara to the south was a fertile and well-populated country, rich in ivory and gold. It was called the *Land of the Blacks*, and could be reached either by sea or land.

The Portuguese dwelling on the shores of the Atlantic were excluded from that Indian trade which the merchants of Pisa, Genoa, Florence, Barcelona, Marseilles, and above all, Venice, carried on with Egypt and the Black Sea. *Finding is keeping* was the proverb of the day, applied to continents and oceans; and though it was not till some time afterwards that the prince had the idea of seeking a sea-route to the Indies along the coast of Africa, he at once saw the advantage of finding a golden land which Portugal might monopolise. He was also a man of piety and zeal, by profession a military monk, Grand Master of the Order of Christ; he believed in the dogma (since then abandoned by the Church) that no heathen could be saved; and his heart yearned towards that unknown multitude of nations doomed to eternal torments unless they were baptised. He determined to devote his life to the discovery of Guinea.

Those who sail in the P. and O. steamers to Gibraltar may observe, if they pass it by daylight, a cape called Sagres, with a lighthouse and telegraph station. There the prince, in a lonely castle, took up his abode. No spot could be more bleak and desolate. The sea dashing furiously against the base of the cliff flung spray across the land and withered up all vegetation. Only a few junipers with rusted foliage grew upon the cape. But there the prince lived in seclusion and peace; there 'the sight of the ocean continually inflamed his thoughts.' In his castle was formed a strange kind of court: Italian cosmographers, German mathematicians, knights seeking peril and adventure, weather-beaten pilots, were those by whom he was surrounded. He built an observatory and laid the foundations of nautical science: from Lagos, the neighbouring port, he sent forth vessels with the cross of the order painted on their sails. But the priests and people protested against his enterprise; they declared that the revenues of the order were being wasted on the dreams of a madman, and that his expeditions were fit for nothing except to make widows and orphans.

The king, however, supported the views of his brother, and the discovery of Madeira was followed by that of the river Senegal, which divides the brown men of the desert from the black men of Soudan. Before the prince died his vessels had reached Sierra Leone; a regular trade with Guinea was established; every year new regions were added to the Crown; a bull had been obtained granting to the Portuguese all lands they might discover to the Indies, *inclusive*; and the prince had received the gratitude of his country, with the illustrious title of *Henry the Navigator*.

The Portuguese had purchased some gold-dust from the Moors on the coast of the Sahara, probably brought from the mines of Bambouk, Upper Senegal. But they found no gold on the Guinea coast till they came to a village called Chamah. At another village twelve miles eastward of Chamah, the natives had so much gold that the Portuguese gave it the name of El Mina or The Mine. There they established their first settlement, and built a noble fort which yet remains. It has been consecrated by the footsteps of Columbus, who once sailed in the Portuguese service to Elmina: it was taken from the Portuguese by the famous Admiral De Ruyter; and its recent cession to Great Britain by the Dutch was a cardinal cause of the Ashantee war.

The Portuguese bought gold, with velvets, hawks' bells, knives, and woollen cloths. They also bought slaves in the Bight of Benin and sold them at a profit to the wealthy natives of Elmina. But the discovery of India was fatal to Guinea; and no attempt was made to conquer or colonise the country. On the other hand, the discovery of America created a demand for slave labour, and this demand was enormously increased when the northern nations invaded the monopoly of Portugal and Spain. In the semi-piratical wars of the tropics the Portuguese were driven from the Gold Coast, which then was divided between the Dutch, the English, the Danes, and the French.

Even the Electorate of Brandenburgh had its African Company and Coast settlements. Between Assinie and the Volta the seaboard was lined with factory forts under the flags of these powers, which thus supplied with slaves their respective American plantations. The slaves were brought down to the seaboard in coffles or chained companies: they were stored in the dungeons of the fort until a vessel arrived; they were then brought forth and carefully examined by the surgeon of the ship: the sound men were marked with a red-hot iron which stamped the Company's arms upon their skin; and they were then shipped for the New World.

There was also an active commerce in gold-dust; and the word *guinea* is derived from that part of Africa. As time went on, the natives became completely dependent on Europe for all luxuries, and even some necessaries of life, for the rum which they drank, the tobacco they smoked, the clothes they wore, and the weapons they used in the battle and the chase. Two hundred years ago the bow and arrow had gone out of vogue, and flintlocks alone were in use; they also celebrated their funerals, their weddings, and all important ceremonies and events with the firing of muskets, sometimes continued for days without intermission. Gunpowder became necessary to them.

The slaves that were sold to the European forts were prisoners of war, and it will therefore be understood that a commerce so gigantic as that of the West Indies was favourable to the growth of war-making tribes. Dahomey was created by the slave-trade, and now that the slave-trade is over is rapidly falling to decay. The Elminas, Fantees, and Accras were merely middle-men; the slaves were hunted, as the gold was mined, in the interior. Two great inland empires arose, Denkera and Akim. The first obtained Elmina as its port; the second obtained Accra, and each took from its port the Note or 'custom' which the Europeans had originally paid to the owners of the soil for permission to settle and trade. But at an early date in Gold Coast history both these powers were conquered by another military kingdom which has since gained by its ambition and audacity a European reputation.

At the close of the seventeenth century Ashantee was already a powerful state and enjoyed access to the coast. At that time the King of Denkera, according to Bosman, 'sent some of his wives to compliment Zay the *King of Asiante*, who not only received and entertained them very civilly, but sent them back, charged with very considerable presents, to express his obliging resentment of the grateful embassy.' Soon afterwards the King Zay (probably the Sai Tootoo of Bowdich) sent some of his wives in the same manner to compliment the King of Denkera, who fell in love with one of them and gratified his passion.

On the Gold Coast women are often employed by their virtuous husbands to allure rich men into intrigues for the sake of damages, and Bowdich relates that in his time the King of Ashantee had a handsome wife whose sole conjugal duty was to inveigle the chiefs her lord desired to ruin; it is, therefore, just possible that the lady ambassador had received her 'instructions' from the king. Be that as it may, she reported the matter on her return, and Zay at once declared war. The King of Denkera offered a large indemnity; but Zay only waited to bring up large quantities of powder from the coast. The Denkeras obtained the alliance of Akim, and the Dutch lent them two or three pieces of cannon. But the two armies were routed, Denkera completely laid waste, and the cannon carried off to Coomassie, where Bowdich afterwards saw them adorning one of the streets of the town.

A Dutch officer was sent to the Ashantee camp and was there when Bosman was writing his letter; he therefore could not mention the result; but we learn from Ashantee sources that Denkera became tributary, and gave to Ashantee the pay-note of Elmina. From that time to the present day the Dutch and the natives of Elmina remained faithful allies of Ashantee.

Colonel Festing's interpreter at Dunquah, a most intelligent native, afterwards attached to Sir Garnet's staff, informed me that the Ashantees were originally vassals of Denkera, and that being badly treated they rebelled and won their independence. As this legend is not mentioned by Bowdich, it will no doubt be disputed. It is not, however, in itself improbable, for at that time Denkera was a powerful kingdom, 'the object of common hatred,' and ruling three other states, one of which was Wassaw. There is also a passage in Bosman which seems to support my informant:

> Thus you see the towering pride of *Dinkira* in ashes, they being forced to fly before those whom they not long before thought no better than their slaves, and themselves being now sold for slaves.

Bowdich derived his history of Ashantee from the Ashantees themselves, and they perhaps were too proud to acknowledge that they had once been a tributary state.

The Ashantees, supplied with powder and arms from Elmina, pursued their conquests for a hundred years: war became the profession of the country: and it was made a law that no king should receive the full honours of a royal burial unless he had himself conducted a campaign. At the beginning of the present century their power had reached its culminating point. The open country to the north had been invaded; Gaman was subdued; the golden stool of Buntookoo had been surrendered by the king; Dutch, Danish, and British flags were displayed at Coomassie; the Notes of all the forts were paid to Ashantee. From Assinie to the Volta the whole coast was in their hands. They had besieged the fort of Annamaboe, 'fighting up to the muzzles of the guns;'[1] the English governor, Colonel Torrane, had basely purchased peace by surrendering Cheboo, a rebel chief. At a later date Cape Coast Castle had been blockaded, and the governor, 'to avert imminent danger,' had paid a heavy sum of gold.

This last event was in 1816. At that time the forts on the Gold Coast belonged to the Royal African Company, and were governed by a committee in London. It was thought advisable to send an embassy to Coomassie 'to deprecate these repeated calamities, and to conciliate so powerful a monarch, and to propitiate an extension of commerce.' On the 22nd of April, 1817, the mission left Cape Coast Castle. Mr.

---

1. Meredith's account of the Gold Coast.

Bowdich, one of its junior, members, a clerk or writer in the Company's service, wrote a work on his return, which excited much attention in England: it was reviewed by Sydney Smith in the *Edinburgh*, bitterly attacked in the *Quarterly*, and still remains the chief authority upon the manners and customs of the land. We in the late campaign saw nothing of the Ashantees except in battle, and we saw very little of them there.

Bowdich started from Annamaboe, but soon struck into that road which has now become historical. Everywhere the villages had been destroyed, and almost every night he had to bivouac. At Mansu, the great slave-market of Fantee, only a few sheds were standing. But when he had crossed the Prah, the beauties of which he painted with a gorgeous hand, he entered the country of Ashantee-Assin, and slept every night in a neatly built village, surrounded by plantations. He ascended the Moinsey or Adansi Hills, and so entered Ashantee Proper. He passed through Quisah and Fomana, the chief of which town, guilty of some misdemeanour, was calmly waiting his death-warrant from the king.

> He conversed cheerfully with us, congratulated himself on seeing white men before he died, and spread his cloth over the log with an emotion of dignity rather than shame; his head arrived at Coomassie the day after we had.

He then passed through Doompassee and Datiasoo and Dadawissa, Dadawassie, and Amafou (Amoaful), crossed the Dah (Ordah) River and 'the marsh which insulates Coomassie.' At two o'clock on May 15 he entered that famous town, passing under a fetish or sacrifice of a dead sheep wrapped up in red silk and suspended between two lofty poles. The description which follows was compared by Sydney Smith to a chapter of the *Arabian Nights*, and it is worth giving as it stands, for probably no Englishman will see the like again. The 42nd regiment when it entered Coomassie was not honoured with a pageant, and gold ornaments instead of being displayed with ostentation were carefully concealed. Bowdich writes as follows:—

> Upwards of 5,000 people, the greater part warriors, met us with awful bursts of martial music, discordant only in its mixture; for horns, drums, rattles, and gong-gongs were all exerted with a zeal bordering on frenzy to subdue us by the first impression. The smoke which encircled us, from the incessant discharges of musketry, confined our glimpses to the foreground; and we

23

were halted whilst the captains performed their Pyrrhic dance, in the centre of a circle formed by their warriors, where a confusion of flags, English, Dutch, and Danish, were waved and flourished in all directions; the bearers plunging and springing from side to side, with a passion of enthusiasm only equalled by the captains, who followed them, discharging their shining blunderbusses so close that the flags now and then were in a blaze; and emerging from the smoke with all the gesture and distortion of maniacs. Their followers kept up the firing around us in the rear.

The dress of the captains was a war-cap, with gilded rams' horns projecting in front, the sides extended beyond all proportion by immense plumes of eagles' feathers, and fastened under the chin with bands of cowries. Their vest was of red cloth covered with fetishes and *saphies* [2] in gold and silver, and embroidered cases of almost every colour, which flapped against their bodies as they moved, intermixed with small brass bells, the horns and tails of animals, shells, and knives; long leopards' tails hung down their backs over a small bow covered with fetishes.

They wore loose cotton trousers, with immense boots of a dull red leather, coming half-way up the thigh, and fastened by small chains to their cartouche or waist-belt; these were also ornamented with bells, horses' tails, strings of amulets, and innumerable shreds of leather; a small quiver of poisoned arrows hung from their right wrist, and they held a long iron chain between their teeth, with a scrap of Moorish writing affixed to the end of it. A small spear was in their left hands, covered with red cloth and silk tassels; their black countenances heightened the effect of this attire, and completed a figure scarcely human.

This exhibition continued about half an hour, when we were allowed to proceed, encircled by the warriors, whose numbers, with the crowds of people, made our movement as gradual as if it had taken place in Cheapside; the several streets branching off to the right presented long *vistas* crammed with people, and those on the left hand being on an acclivity, innumerable rows of heads rose one above another: the large open porches of the houses, like the fronts of stages in small theatres, were filled with the better sort of females and children, all impatient to behold white men for the first time; their exclamations were drowned

2. Scraps of Moorish writing, as charms against evil.

in the firing and music, but their gestures were in character with the scene.

When we reached the palace, about half a mile from the place where we entered, we were again halted, and an open file was made, through which the bearers were passed, to deposit the presents and baggage in the house assigned to us. Here we were gratified by observing several of the *caboceers* pass by with their trains, the novel splendour of which astonished us. The bands, principally composed of horns and flutes, trained to play in concert, seemed to soothe our hearing into its natural tone again by their wild melodies; whilst the immense umbrellas, made to sink and rise from the jerkings of the bearers, and the large fans waving around, refreshed us with small currents of air, under a burning sun, clouds of dust, and a density of atmosphere almost suffocating. We were then squeezed, at the same funereal pace, up a long street, to an open-fronted house, where we were desired by a royal messenger to wait a further invitation from the king.

Here our attention was forced from the astonishment of the crowd to a most inhuman spectacle, which was paraded before us for some minutes; it was a man whom they were tormenting previous to sacrifice; his hands were pinioned behind him; a knife was passed through his cheeks, to which his lips were noosed like the figure of 8; one ear was cut off and carried before him, the other hung to his head by a small bit of skin; there were several gashes in his back, and a knife was thrust under each shoulder-blade; he was led with a cord passed through his nose, by men disfigured with immense caps of shaggy black skins, and drums beat before him; the feeling this horrid barbarity excited must be imagined. We were soon released by permission to proceed to the king, and passed through a very broad street, about a quarter of a mile long, to the market-place.

Our observations *en passant* had taught us to conceive a spectacle far exceeding our original expectations; but they had not prepared us for the extent and display of the scene which here burst upon us: an area of nearly a mile in circumference was crowded with magnificence and novelty. The king, his tributaries, and captains, were resplendent in the distance, surrounded by attendants of every description, fronted by a mass of warriors which seemed to make our approach impervious. The sun was reflected, with a glare scarcely more supportable than the heat, from the massive gold ornaments which glistened in every direction. More than a hundred bands burst at once on our arrival, with the peculiar airs of their several chiefs; the horns flourished their defiances, with the beating of innumerable drums and metal instruments, and then yielded for awhile to the soft breathings of their long flutes, which were truly harmonious; and a pleasing instrument, like a bagpipe without the drone, was happily blended.

At least a hundred large umbrellas, or canopies, which could shelter thirty persons, were sprung up and down by the bearers with brilliant effect, being made of scarlet, yellow, and the most showy cloths and silks, and crowned on the top with crescents, pelicans, elephants, barrels, and arms and swords of gold; they were of various shapes, but mostly dome; and the valances (in some of which small looking- glasses were inserted) fantastically scalloped and fringed; from the fronts of some, the proboscis and small teeth of elephants projected, and a few were roofed with leopards' skins, and crowned with various animals naturally stuffed. The state hammocks, like long cradles, were raised in the rear, the poles on the heads of the bearers; the cushions and pillows were covered with crimson taffeta, and the richest cloths hung over the sides. Innumerable small umbrellas, of various coloured stripes, were crowded in the intervals, whilst several large trees heightened the glare by contrasting the sober colouring of nature.

Discolor unde auri per ramos aura refulsit.

The king's messengers, with gold breastplates, made way for us, and we commenced our round, preceded by the canes and the English flag. We stopped to take the hand of every *caboceer*, which, as their household suites occupied several spaces in advance, delayed us long enough to distinguish some of the ornaments in the general blaze of splendour and ostentation.

The *caboceers*, as did their superior captains and attendants, wore Ashantee cloths of extravagant price, from the costly foreign silks which had been unravelled to weave them in all the varieties of colour as well as pattern; they were of an incredible size and weight, and thrown over the shoulder exactly like the Roman *toga*: a small silk fillet geneally encircled their temples, and massy gold necklaces, intricately wrought, suspended Moorish charms, dearly purchased, and enclosed in small square cases of gold, silver, and curious embroidery. Some wore necklaces reaching to the waist entirely of *aggry* beads; a band of gold and beads encircled the knee, from which several strings of the same depended; small circles of gold, like guineas, rings, and casts of animals, were strung round their ankles; their sandals were of green, red, and delicate white leather; *manillas*, and rude lumps of rock gold, hung from their left wrists, which were so heavily laden as to be supported on the head of one of their handsomest boys.

Gold and silver pipes and canes dazzled the eye in every direction. Wolves' and rams' heads as large as life, cast in gold, were suspended from their gold-handled swords, which were held around them in great numbers; the blades were shaped like round bills, and rusted in blood; the sheaths were of leopard-skin, or the shell of a fish like *shagreen*. The large drums supported on the head of one man, and beaten by two others, were braced around with the thigh-bones of their enemies, and ornamented with their skulls. The kettle-drums resting on the ground were scraped with wet fingers, and covered with leopard's skin. The wrists of the drummers were hung with bells and curiously-shaped pieces of iron, which jingled loudly as they were beating. The smaller drums were suspended from the neck by scarves of red cloth; the horns (the teeth of young elephants) were ornamented at the mouth-piece with gold and the jaw-bones of human victims.

The war-caps of eagles' feathers nodded in the rear, and large fans of the wing feathers of the ostrich played around the dignitaries. Immediately behind their chairs (which were of a black wood, almost covered by inlays of ivory and gold embossment) stood their handsomest youths, with corselets of leopard's skin covered with gold cockle-shells, and stuck full of small knives, sheathed in gold and silver, and the handles of blue agate; cartouche boxes of elephant's hide hung below, ornamented in the same manner; a large gold-handled sword was fixed behind the left shoulder, and silk scarves and horses' tails (generally white) streamed from the arms and waist-cloth: their long Danish muskets had rims of gold at small distances, and the stocks were ornamented with shells.

Finely-grown girls stood behind the chairs of some, with silver basins. Their stools (of the most laborious carved work, and generally with two large bells attached to them) were conspicuously placed on the heads of favourites; and crowds of small boys were seated around, flourishing elephants' tails curiously mounted. The warriors sat on the ground close to these, and so thickly as not to admit of our passing without treading on their feet, to which they were perfectly indifferent; their caps were of the skin of the pangolin and leopard, the tails hanging down behind; their cartouche belts (composed of small gourds which hold the charges, and covered with leopard or pig's skin) were embossed with red shells, and small brass bells thickly hung to them; on their hips and shoulders was a cluster of knives; iron chains and collars dignified the most daring, who were prouder of them than of gold; their muskets had rests affixed of leopard's skin, and the locks a covering of the same; the sides of their faces were curiously painted in long white streaks, and their arms also striped, having the appearance of armour.

We were suddenly surprised by the sight of Moors, who afforded the first general diversity of dress; there were seventeen superiors, arrayed in large cloaks of white satin, richly trimmed with spangled embroidery; their shirts and trousers' were of silk, and a very large turban of white muslin was studded with a border of different-coloured stories: their attendants wore red caps and turbans, and long white shirts which hung over their trousers; those of the inferiors were of dark blue cloth: they slowly raised their eyes from the ground as we passed, and with a most malignant scowl.

The prolonged flourishes of the horns, a deafening tumult of drums, and the fuller concert of the intervals, announced that we were approaching the king: we were already passing the principal officers of his household; the chamberlain, the gold horn-blower, the captain of the messengers, the captain for royal executions, the captain of the market, the keeper of the royal burial-ground, and the master of the bands, sat surrounded by a retinue and splendour which bespoke the dignity and importance of their offices. The cook had a number of small services covered with leopard's skin held behind him, and a large quantity of massy silver plate was displayed before him—punchbowls, waiters, coffee-pots, tankards, and a very large vessel with heavy handles and clawed feet, which seemed to have been made to hold incense. I observed a Portuguese inscription on one piece, and they seemed generally of that manufacture.

The executioner, a man of an immense size, wore a massy gold hatchet on his breast; and the execution stool was held before him, clotted in blood, and partly covered with a caul of fat. The king's four linguists were encircled by a splendour inferior to none, and their peculiar insignia, gold canes, were elevated in all directions, tied in bundles like fasces. The keeper of the treasury added to his own magnificence by the ostentatious display of his service; the blow-pan, boxes, scales, and weights were of solid gold.

A delay of some minutes, whilst we severally approached to receive the king's hand, afforded us a thorough view of him. His deportment first excited my attention. Native dignity in princes we are pleased to call barbarous was a curious spectacle. His manners were majestic, yet courteous; and he did not allow his surprise to beguile him for a moment. of the composure of the monarch.

He appeared to be about thirty-eight years of age, inclined to corpulence, and of a benevolent countenance; he wore a fillet of *aggry* beads round his temples, a necklace of gold cockspur-shells strung by their largest ends, and over his right shoulder a red silk cord, suspending three *saphies* cased in gold; his bracelets were the richest mixtures of beads and gold, and his fingers covered with rings; his cloth was of a dark green silk; a pointed diadem was elegantly painted in white on his forehead; also a pattern resembling an epaulette on each shoulder, and an ornament like a full-blown rose, one leaf rising above another until it covered his whole breast; his knee-bands were of *aggry* beads, and his ankle-strings of gold ornaments of the most delicate workmanship, small drums, stools, swords, guns, and birds, clustered together; his sandals, of a soft white leather, were embossed across the instep-band with small gold and silver cases of *saphies*; he was seated in a low chair, richly ornamented with gold; he wore a pair of gold *castanets* on his finger and thumb, which he clapped to enforce silence.

The belts of the guards behind his chair were cased in gold, and covered with small jaw-bones of the same metal; the elephants' tails, waving like a small cloud before him, were spangled with gold, and large plumes of feathers were flourished amid them. His eunuch presided over these attendants, wearing only one massy piece of gold about his neck: the royal stool, entirely cased in gold, was displayed under a splendid umbrella, with drums, *sankos*, horns, and various musical instruments, Cased in gold, about the thickness of cartridge paper: large circles of gold hung by scarlet cloth from the swords of state, the sheaths as well as the handles of which were also cased; hatchets of the same were intermixed with them: the breasts of the Ocrahs and various attendants were adorned with large stars, stools, crescents, and gossamer wings of solid gold.

We pursued our course through this blazing circle, which afforded to the last a variety exceeding description and memory; so many splendid novelties diverting the fatigue, heat, and pressure we were labouring under. We were almost exhausted, however, by the time we reached the end; when, instead of being conducted to our residence, we were desired to seat ourselves under a tree at some distance, to receive the compliments of the whole in our turn.

The swell of their bands gradually strengthened on our ears, the peals of the warlike instruments bursting upon the short but sweet responses of the flutes; the gaudy canopies seemed to dance in the distant view, and floated broadly as they were springing up and down in the foreground; flags and banners waved in the interval, and the chiefs were eminent in their crimson hammocks, amidst crowds of musketry. They dismounted as they arrived within thirty yards of us; their principal captains preceded them with the gold-handled swords, a body of soldiers followed with their arms reversed, then their bands and gold canes, pipes, and elephants' tails. The chief, with a small bodyguard under his umbrella, was generally supported around the waist by the hands of his favourite slave, whilst captains holla'd, close in his ear, his warlike deeds and (strong) names, which were reiterated with the voices of Stentors by those before and behind; the larger party of warriors brought up the rear.

Old captains of secondary rank were carried on the shoulders of a strong slave; but a more interesting sight was presented in the minors, or young *caboceers*, many not more than five or six years of age, who, over-weighed by ornaments, were carried in the same manner (under their canopies), encircled by all the pomp and parade of their predecessors. Amongst others, the grandson of Cheboo was pointed out, whom the king had generously placed on the stool of his perfidious enemy. A band of Fetish men, or priests, wheeled round and round as they passed with surprising velocity.

Manner was as various as ornament; some danced by with irresistible buffoonery, some with a gesture and carriage of defiance; one distinguished *caboceer* performed the war dance before us for some minutes, with a large spear, which grazed us at every bound he made; but the greater number passed us with order and dignity, some slipping one sandal, some both, some turning round after having taken each of us by the hand; the attendants of others knelt before them, throwing dust upon their heads; and the Moors, apparently, vouchsafed us a blessing. The king's messengers who were posted near us, with their long hair hanging in twists like a thrum mop, used little ceremony in hurrying by this transient procession; yet it was nearly eight o'clock before the king approached.

It was a beautiful starlight night, and the torches which preceded him displayed the splendour of his regalia with a chastened lustre, and made the human trophies of the soldiers more awfully imposing. The skulls of three Banda *caboceers*, who had been his most obstinate enemies, adorned the largest drum: the vessels in which the boys dipped their torches were of gold. He stopped to enquire our names a second time and to wish us goodnight; his address was mild and deliberate: he was followed by his aunts, sisters, and others of his family, with rows of fine gold chains around their necks. Numerous chiefs succeeded, and it was long before we were at liberty to retire. We agreed in estimating the number of warriors at 30,000.

We were conducted to a range of spacious but ruinous buildings, which had belonged to the son of one of the former kings, and who had recently destroyed himself at a very advanced age, unable to endure the severity of disgrace. Their forlorn and dreary aspect bespoke the fortune of their master, and they required much repair to defend us from the wind and rain, which frequently ushered in the nights.

Bowdich remained some months at Coomassie, and, though politely treated by the king, was evidently regarded with suspicion, and at first was not allowed to take walks in the forest for the purpose of making botanical collections. His return was also delayed and postponed in the usual manner of the Africans, and an attempt to leave the town brought on a scuffle with the mob. However, at last he obtained license to depart, and took with him a treaty which the king had signed, but which was not ratified by the local government; and another treaty was made by a Mr. Dupuis, who shortly afterwards visited Coomassie with the appointment of Resident or Consul. These two treaties contained little or nothing in the way of concession from the king; he consented to encourage trade, but that was to his own advantage: he promised also to let his subjects of Gaman come down to the coast to trade, but that promise he did not keep. The king could scarcely have esteemed the English after all that had occurred, and there is a subtle irony in the remark he made to Dupuis:

> From the time Torrane delivered up Cheboo I took the English for my friends because I saw their object was trade only, and they did not care for the people.

However, even at that early date the English had begun to regard Fantee Land as their Protectorate. It was arranged that in case of rebellion or outrage the king should not resort to arms until he had first applied for redress to the English governor. This suited the king very well: he supposed that the English would govern for him his newly-conquered lands, give up all fugitives, malcontents and rebels, and collect whatever fines he thought fit to impose. But he had soon to discover that all Englishmen did not resemble that 'man of sense' as he called him, the governor-in-chief, Colonel Torrane.

CHAPTER 3

The First Ashantee War

What Volney says of the Arabs is true of the Ashantees: '*They could conquer, but they could not govern.*' They were proficient in all the arts of war; their 'flanking tactics' in the field, their feigned retreats, their ambuscades, were supported by similar movements of diplomacy. When the King of Ashantee invaded a tribe he sent envoys with rich presents to the neighbouring powers, justifying his aggression, representing the wrongs he had sustained, and assuring them of his friendship and affection. Yet often he attacked those same tribes in the course of the campaign, and so took them completely unawares. The ideal *Prince* of Machiavelli has never been more nearly realised than in the humble palace at Coomassie. Moreover, the craft of the council was rivalled by the courage of the people. There was no standing army; the nation itself was the army, and the king its commander-in-chief.

As soon as war was proclaimed every man took up his firelock, tied his cartouche-belt round his waist, put some corn-meal and kola-nuts into his bag, and joined his company under the chief or captain to whom he belonged. As soon as the army had marched, the women, stripping themselves naked, or wearing the clothes of their husbands, daubed their bodies with white clay, marched in procession through the streets beating a drum and any man who had ventured to remain behind. The army was accompanied by corps of carpenters, blacksmiths, and other artisans; by sutlers selling provisions; by money-lenders advancing gold-dust at 10 *per cent,* a month; by women who carried pots, calabashes, and other cooking utensils.

In battle these women stood behind their husbands, supplying them with powder, and animating them with songs. The advance skirmishers were slaves; the secondary captains fought in the front; the king and his generals remained in the rear seated on their stools beneath red umbrellas. They were surrounded by their young men, who cut down those that attempted to retreat. It was the fashion for the commander-in-chief to play at some kind of game during the battle, as if to show that he was confident of victory; and in case of defeat it was the custom for the chiefs and captains to commit suicide. Seated on barrels of powder they blew themselves up into the air, according to the Ashantee proverb, '*It is shame which causes the chief to die.*'

It is true that in Akim and Denkera the kings were also absolute, that women, parading the streets, forced all able-bodied men to the war, and that the penalty for cowardice was death. The Ashantees belong to that family of nations called the *Oji*, which includes the Akims, Denkeras, Wassaws, Assins, Fantees, and many other tribes. There is but a slight difference of dialect between the Ashantees and Fantees; there is no difference whatever between the Ashantees and the neighbouring bush-people—Akims, Denkeras, Assins; their language: even to its accent, is the same.

It was not the form but the spirit which distinguished the Ashantees from the other tribes of the Oji. The genius of two or three men who reigned one after the other at Coomassie had established a perfect despotism. It may be that the king was controlled by his council of chiefs; it may be that the despotism was that of an aristocracy, if one looked behind the scenes; but for the mass of the people one man commanded and had to be obeyed. It is needless to say that despotism is greedy of war and also favourable to military discipline. The Ashantees, being constantly at war, resembled trained soldiers; discipline in the field and despotism at home acted and reacted on each other. The army became as perfect as a savage army could be made; the men marched to battle singing a verse of their favourite song: 'If I go on, I shall die; if I stay behind I shall be killed; it is better to go on.' Finally, they acquired the habit of victory. The Fantees and other tribes declared it was useless to resist them, and the very name of Ashantees was almost sufficient to make them run away.

But the Ashantees could not retain the lands which they had conquered. The great feudatory chiefs of Becqua, Mampon, Kokofoo, and others, who had once been kings, dwelt so near Coomassie that they did not dare to rebel. They were required to visit the capital at certain seasons of festivity, and were strictly supervised. Besides, they enjoyed some share of power. One chief, the ruler of Duabin, still retained, at that time, the title and honours of a king. As regards the lands beyond the Prah it was a different affair. The Ashantees were not numerous; at the most they were able to put 50,000 men into the field; they could not occupy foreign territory, which, therefore, soon slipped from their hands. It was one thing to overrun a country and burn its villages, and another to rule the people of the country and draw tribute from them when the army of invasion had retired.

Much might have been done by moderation; but that is not one of the virtues which the Ashantees possess. They belong to that order of people who cut down trees to get at the fruit, and slaughter geese with golden eggs. The king ruled his conquered provinces by means of proconsuls, who extorted large sums of money, sometimes for their master, sometimes for themselves. Arrogance and injustice permeated the people to its lowest ranks. Whenever an Ashantee passed a Fantee stall by the wayside, or met a woman with a load upon her head, he helped himself to a plantain or a fish. In course of time the Fantees (a generic term for the subject tribes) forgot the horrors of war in the vexations of daily despotism, withheld the tribute, and sometimes murdered the envoys who were sent to remonstrate by the king. Then came another Ashantee invasion, and the country was conquered over again.

In 1821 the African Company was dissolved by Act of Parliament, and government took over the forts upon the Gold Coast. Sir Charles Macarthy, the governor-in-chief, resided at Sierra Leone. He was a man of superior ability, and at first gave his attention to the exploration of Inner Africa. He sent Major Laing of the 2nd West India Regiment to a kingdom called Falaba, inland from Sierra Leone. There Laing was detained, though only fifty miles from the Niger and but little farther from its source. Compelled to return without reaching that river, he was making preparations for another expedition when the state of affairs on the Gold Coast made it necessary that he should join his regiment, and that Sir Charles should proceed there himself.

It was the old story again of the Fantees being presumptuous in peace and timid in war; refusing to pay tribute and then flying like sheep from the army of vengeance and invasion. Sir Charles, it seems, did not hold himself bound by the treaty of Dupuis; he took the side of the coast natives and determined to fight the Ashantees. He had at his command the Royal African Colonial Corps, a regiment of good troops, part white and part coloured men, commanded by British officers; a detachment of the 2nd West, oddly enough the same regiment which Sir Garnet found at Cape Coast on his arrival; and the Cape Coast militia, a corps of Cape Coast natives, resembling the rifle volunteers recently raised in that town. He had also a mob of native-allies.

Instead of attacking the enemy with all the forces he could muster Sir Charles played at strategy. In the eastern districts Captain Blencarne, with Accra for his base, like Glover, had orders to operate with the view of making a diversion; and so his troops were thrown away. In the same manner Laing was sent to Assin, as Butler was sent to Akim; he was victorious in all his skirmishes; but these did not influence the issue of the war. Major Chisholm's contingent, 2,000 strong, was also separated from Sir Charles, who at the head of a puny force gave battle to the army of the Ashantees. The Denkeras were on the right and the Wassaws on the left, the regulars and militia in the centre. The Wassaws soon ran away, and carried with them in their flight the ammunition carriers whom they met upon their way. The regulars fought with success till their ammunition was exhausted, and then defended themselves to the death with their bayonets.

Sir Charles Macarthy and three other Englishmen were surrounded by the enemy. Mr. Williams, the colonial secretary, received a wound in the thigh which rendered him senseless, and on recovering he found some Ashantees attempting to cut off his head. They had already inflicted one gash on the back of his neck when an Ashantee of authority came up, and recognising Mr. Williams, from whom he had received some kindness in the African Company's time, withheld the hands of the savages. The rescued man saw at his feet the headless trunks of Sir Charles, Mr. Buckle, and Ensign Wetherell. He was taken to the Ashantee camp, and locked up every night in a hut with the heads of the white men, which, owing to some peculiar process, were in a perfect state of preservation. His daily food was as much snail soup, morning and evening, as he could hold in the hollow of his hand.

Whenever the Ashantees beheaded any of their prisoners they obliged him to sit on one side of their great war drum while they decapitated the unfortunate captive on the other. He was not taken to Coomassie, but released through the good offices of the Dutch governor at Elmina. The head of Sir Charles Macarthy was taken to Coomassie, placed in the Bantama, and, covered with a white cloth, is paraded through the streets once a year at the Festival of Yams. The natives say that the Ashantees ate his heart to inspire them with courage. They also have a legend that the last three kegs which were opened in the battle contained vermicelli instead of gunpowder, and that then Sir Charles committed suicide. The Fantees preserve a tender regard for the memory of the gallant general; they call their children after his name, they celebrate him in their songs, and their most sacred oath is 'By Wednesday and Macarthy.'

The King of Ashantee, who commanded his army in person, encamped close to Cape Coast Castle, and sent a fetish or sanctified boy to tell the governor that the walls of the castle were not high enough and should be made higher, and that all the guns from the men-of-war should be landed, as he meant to throw every stone of the castle into the sea. But soon dysentery and smallpox raged in the camp, as well as in the town, and no doubt the Ashantees feared the big guns. They deserted by hundreds under cover of the night, and at length the king, having heard that the Queen of Akim was marching against his capital, broke up his camp and returned.

Two years afterwards he invaded the eastern districts of the Gold Coast, and passed through the forest of Akim to the open plain behind Accra. A great and decisive battle was fought near the village Dodowah. The Queen of Akim commanded her troops in person, wearing a necklace of leaden bullets, and bearing a gold-enamelled sword in her hand. The Ashantees fought well. Some of the native allies as usual ran away, and the centre was beginning to be pressed, when. Lieutenant-Colonel Purdon advanced with his reserve and some rockets, which the Ashantees supposed to be real thunder and lightning. These missiles caused havoc and confusion: the enemy retreated: the Ashantee captains blew themselves up: the king was wounded in his flight: about five thousand of the enemy were killed, and twenty-four of their leading chiefs. There was no pursuit, the allies preferring to plunder the camp, and the prisoners taken were sold to slave-vessels bound for Accra. [1]

This put an end to Ashantee wars for many a long day to come; but five years passed before a treaty of peace was concluded, which was partly owing to the machinations of a certain Fantee party, who thought it to their interest that the English and the Ashantees should not be on good terms with one another. The Ashantee envoys who came down to the coast did not entirely discard their former haughtiness of gesture and tone, while the coast chiefs were exulting and prone to give provocation. However, at last a treaty was signed—the famous Tripartite Treaty of 1831. The king abandoned all claims to the kingdoms of Denkera, Assin, &c; on the other hand, it was stipulated

---

1. The authority on this war is the work of Major Ricketts, a survivor. I have closely followed an excellent summary of that work in the *Times*, October 13, 1873.

that the Ashantees should have free access to the coast.

The paths shall be perfectly open and free to all persons engaged in lawful traffic, and persons molesting them in any way whatever, or forcing them to purchase at any particular market, or influencing them by any unfair means, shall be deemed guilty of infringing this treaty, and be liable to the severest punishment.

CHAPTER 4

The Protectorate

Soon after the Battle of Dodowah, and before the signing of this treaty, the British Government, disgusted with its little war, and having defeated the Ashantees, retired from the Gold Coast. The settlements were governed by a Company, under the supervision of the Crown, and a sum of 4,000*l.* a year was granted for the expenses of the forts. The first governor appointed under the new state of affairs was a Mr. Maclean, who arranged the terms of the treaty; for which reason the Ashantees call it the 'Treaty of Maclean.'

The new governor was a man of great ability, and his rule, though stern, was so just that the natives revere his memory, and often express a wish that the queen would send them governors like Macarthy and Maclean. He exercised almost regal power over the kingdoms of the allies, now known as the Protectorate, doing much to put down wars among them and human sacrifices: if a chief refused to obey his commands, he sent a few soldiers to arrest him, lodged him within the castle, and made him pay an indemnity of gold-dust. The chiefs in return not only feared the governor, but also esteemed and even loved him for his power. Such is the nature of the Africans.

Like most men who have lived long upon the coast, Maclean looked with an indulgent eye upon the slave trade; and rumours reached the philanthropists at home that slavers made use of Cape Coast Castle as a harbour for supplies, and, perhaps, for something more. Circumstances had also occurred to make the name of Maclean detestable in England. A young poetess, L.E.L., had a manuscript lent her by a friend, describing the capture of Apollonia, a town on the Gold Coast, by Mr. Maclean. She was much impressed by his manly narrative, and, predisposed to fall in love with the author, whom she soon afterwards met. The result was that they were married, and L.E.L. took up her abode in the castle at Cape Coast.

They quarrelled, and Maclean grew tired of her: he had a passion for intrigue, which almost amounted to disease: even the natives have told me, shaking their heads, that he was a good governor, but a bad husband. In fact he spent every night at orgies in the town. Thus neglected and despised, exiled from all society, depressed by the evil nature of the climate, having always at hand a dangerous medicine for some malady to which she was subject, who can wonder that during one of those solitary nights poor L.E.L. should have released herself from life? The matter was bad enough without exaggeration, but scandal made it ten times worse. Maclean had a 'country wife' during his stay upon the coast: on sailing for England he paid her off, and she went to live at Accra.

But it was confidently declared that this woman lived in the castle, and some even went so far as to hint that she had forced the poison upon the unfortunate L.E.L. So evil was now the reputation of Maclean, that any accusation against him must have been almost welcome to the Colonial Office, and it was determined to investigate the charges made against his government A special commissioner was sent out to the coast, and in consequence of his report the settlements were resumed by the Crown, another governor was appointed, and Maclean received the subordinate post of Judicial Assessor. He sat in a court with native chiefs to try cases in which natives were concerned, according to native law, so far as it could be applied in harmony with the principles of justice.

This definition may seem vague and obscure: if so, it illustrates the character of our Gold Coast government. It has never been settled to the present day whether Cape Coast Castle is an English or a Fantee town. If it is an English town we are patrons of slavery; if it is a Fantee town we exercise illegal powers.

The government took over the Gold Coast on account of the slave trade: and one would suppose that something would have been done to abolish domestic slavery. When Lagos was ceded, all the slaves were set free. There are no slaves in Sierra Leone. Slavery is illegal in the Gambia. But on the Gold Coast it has not been touched; not even a scheme of gradual emancipation has ever been prepared. How is it that slavery is tolerated, contrary to English law? Ask this question at Downing Street and you will be informed that Cape Coast Castle is not British territory; that we only possess the castle and Government House; that the town belongs to the Fantees. But the Court of Justice is neither in the Government House nor in the fort; it is therefore out of British territory, and is not a court of justice at all. Another definition may then possibly be given: 'British territory does not extend beyond the range of the guns in the castle.' That is the strangest of all definitions, for as our artillery improves, our territory must of necessity expand. But at all events the town is within range, and is therefore British territory. Now slavery exists in the town, (as at time of first publication).

If I chose to answer a quibble by a quibble I might quote an Order of Council (in connection with the Foreign Judicature Acts) by which Cape Coast Castle was made a *colony*, and classed with Sierra Leone. But the truth is, that Cape Coast Castle has long been an English town, not indeed by purchase or cession, but by usage and sufferance. If one Fantee assaults another in the streets, he is taken up by a policeman, precisely as he would be in London, locked up in a cell, after the manner of civilised nations, brought before a magistrate in the morning, and punished with fine or imprisonment. Murderers are tried by English law before a jury, and if found guilty are sentenced to be hanged. But still slaves exist in this English town, and lawsuits in relation to that form of property are brought before the Judicial Assessor.

Since our position in Cape Coast Castle is so dubious, it may well be imagined that the duties of the government in respect to the inland provinces are even less clearly defined. At times the government has exercised sovereign powers over the Protectorate; native chiefs have been arrested and punished for treason, and at one time a poll-tax was levied. Of late years it has been the custom to instruct governors of the Gold Coast that they are not to interfere with the natives of the interior, nor to protect them from invasion. But when obligations have once been assumed, it is not easy to evade them. The treaty of 1831 having been ratified by government, it clearly became our duty to keep the road open for trade to Prahsu, and to resist all invasions of the Ashantees.

The first duty was wholly neglected, and the Ashantee traders who came to sell us their gold-dust were always troubled on the way.. On the other hand, when the Ashantees invaded Assin in 1853, the governor, Colonel Hill (now Governor of Newfoundland), marched at once towards the Prah. It is not the habit of the Ashantees to make war against an enemy that is prepared, so they retired again into their own territory. But they had not relinquished their designs: they had not forgotten that the English had once been their vassals, the Fantees their slaves. They wanted a port on the coast, as the King of Dahomey had a port at Whydah. Elmina, it was true, supplied them faithfully, but in order to reach Elmina they had to pass through the hostile Denkera. It became a policy and plan of Ashantee to reconquer the lands which had been taken from them, and to reign over the English at Cape Coast Castle and Accra; or, if the English would not submit, to drive them from the coast, and to trade only with the Dutch, whom already they regarded as subjects of the king.

CHAPTER 5

The Dutch

In 1863 two fugitives from Ashantee claimed the protection of the British flag. One of them was an old man who had kept a nugget he had found in his gold pit, and all nuggets belonged to the king. The other, a boy, was simply a runaway slave. The king sent messengers to say that if the old man and the boy were not given up he would invade the land of the Fantees. The governor, Mr. Richard Pine, refused this modest demand; the envoys withdrew, having first made arrangements for the purchase of arms and ammunition from Elmina; and shortly afterwards the Ashantees crossed the. Prah.

The governor then wrote to the Duke of Newcastle this remarkable letter:—

> It is with the deepest regret that I find myself involved, in spite of all my precautions, in a serious and I fear lingering war; but such being the case I will not conceal from Your Grace the earnest desire that I entertain that a final blow shall be struck at Ashantee power, and the question set to rest for ever as to whether an arbitrary, cruel, and sanguinary monarch shall be forever permitted to insult the British flag and outrage the laws of civilisation.
>
> This desirable object can be attained only by the possession of such a force as I fear the governor of these settlements can never hope to command, unless Your Grace should be pleased to urge upon Her Majesty's Government the policy, the economy, and even the mercy of transporting to these shores an army of such strength as would, combined with the allied native forces, enable us to march to Coomassie, and there plant the British flag.

To a stranger the course I point out may appear a visionary one; but I am convinced that, even with all the disadvantages of climate, the expedition would not be so dangerous, so fatal, or accompanied with such loss of life as have attended other expeditions in other and apparently more genial climes; and with 2,000 disciplined soldiers, followed by upwards of 50,000 native forces, who require only to be led and inspired with confidence by the presence of organised troops, I would undertake (driving the hordes of Ashantee before me) to march to Coomassie. [1]

The government, however, refused to grant Imperial troops, and Governor Pine resolved to make war against the enemy with the West India negro soldiery. As soon as they were marched into the interior the enemy retired, and a camp was formed at Prahsu. But there seems to have been no plan for the campaign; the governor and the colonel commanding were at daggers drawn; and during five months, partly in the rains, the unfortunate troops were kept idle in the bush. Dysentery and fever carried them off by scores—both officers and men—and at length it was determined to withdraw. Then, as if an enemy were in hot pursuit, the guns and stores were thrown into the river. This enterprise gave rise to a legend that 'white men cannot cross the sacred Prah;' and the Ashantees say that their priests bewitched the colonel so that he did not know what he was doing.

At home there was much indignation; the ministry were all but unseated; a commission was appointed to enquire into West African affairs; and it was resolved that no more countries should be annexed in Western Africa, and that the settlements should be delivered to the natives as soon as they were able to govern themselves. Yet no arrangements were made for the education of the natives, without which they will never be able to govern themselves; and the only practical result of the commission was one of dubious value. The Governments of Gambia, Lagos, and the Gold Coast were placed under a governor-in-chief, who resided at Sierra Leone; the lieutenant-governors were called administrators, and could only send their despatches through the governor-in-chief, who went in circuit to inspect them once a year.

No treaty of peace was concluded between the Ashantees and the English. The king still persisted in his demand for the surrender of the fugitives, and he also wanted a certain chief named Adjima, who had

---

1. Quoted in Brackenbury's *Fanti and Ashanti*.

previously wronged and insulted his father. There was, therefore, no basis for negotiations, and soon another casus belli arose.

Since 1700 the Dutch had always been firmly allied with the Ashantees, and the natives of Elmina, Chamah, Axim, and other Dutch settlements had adopted the alliance. In all wars the Elminas supplied the Ashantees with arms and ammunition, and this had given rise to war between the Elminas and Fantees. In the last century there had been such a war. In the treaty which Bowdich drew up it was stipulated that the King of Ashantee should protect the natives of Cape Coast Castle from the natives of Elmina. But now times had changed; now the Elminas implored the King of Ashantee to protect them from the people of Cape Coast. The two towns are only nine miles apart.

The immediate cause of the war between two native tribes supposed to be governed by two friendly European Powers was that transaction which is known as The Transfer. In 1850 the Danes had sold their forts to the English, and had retired from the coast; but the Dutch remained. The settlements of the two nations, originally planted not for government but trade, were confusedly mingled together. On the extreme west of the Gold Coast were Grand Bassam and Assinie, belonging to the French. Then came Apollonia, which was English, and next going eastward Axim, which was Dutch; next Dixcove, which was English; next Boutrie and Taccorady, which were Dutch; next Secondee composed of two villages, English and Dutch; next Chamah, which was Dutch; then Commenda, which was English; then Elmina, where the Dutch governor-general resided; then Cape Coast Castle and Annamaboe; then the Dutch forts, Moree and Cormantyne. Accra belonged half to the Dutch and half to the English; in one town of moderate dimensions were two distinct systems of custom-house duties, and two distinct systems of governing the natives.

The Dutch ruled the natives more severely than the English; for instance, they had a regular tariff for sheep, fowls, carriers, &c, and the market was not allowed to fluctuate. If the natives refused to sell or work, the commandant sent out soldiers from the fort, who seized provisions or men, and paid according to appointed price. On the other hand, the Dutch duties were merely nominal, and this affected the English revenue in places where the forts stood side by side. Our government proposed that these duties should be equalised; but the Dutch suggested that the English should receive all the forts to the eastward of the Sweet River (between Elmina and Cape Coast), and the Dutch all the forts to the west. In 1867 this convention was arranged and ratified. As a mere question of territorial exchange it was most convenient; but it gave rise to troubles with the natives which finally had the effect of driving the Dutch from the coast.

Let us take, for instance, the case of the Commendas. In the days of Ashantee rule they had always been turbulent subjects; they had caused that war in which Sir Charles Macarthy had been killed; they were bitter enemies of the Elminas and the Dutch. And now, without a word of explanation, they were suddenly transferred to those very enemies. Suppose that France, in cold blood and mere calculation, had bartered Alsace and Lorraine for some German province on the left of the Rhine; suppose that the Germans were not a civilised people, but savages who would ill-treat and plunder their ancient enemies. Then you will understand the position of Commenda, delivered to the power of Elmina and Chamah.

They pulled down the Dutch flag. A Dutch man-of-war bombarded the town. The Commenda canoes seized a boat passing by, captured several Dutchmen and took them to a village in the bush where they had taken up their abode. The captives were stripped and flogged; all bore it in silence, except a young lad who cried out piteously; whereupon the chief said he would take that boy as his part of the plunder, and would not have him flogged any more.

The women had at first been more cruel even than the men; but yet they were women; and after a few days, when they saw the wan faces of the captives, their hearts relented, and they brought them food.

The English administrator sent an officer to negotiate a ransom, and this officer gave me an account of the palaver. The speech of the chief was not without dignity and justice. 'The English,' he said, 'had behaved badly to the Commendas and had given them up to their foes. The Elders would be fully justified in refusing the governor's request and in giving their captives to the relatives of those whom the Dutch had killed with their cannon, and whose blood cried to them from the ruins of Commenda. But they could never forget that noble gentleman, that gallant General, Sir Charles Macarthy, who had died fighting for them against the Ashantees. For his sake, and his sake alone, they consented to receive a ransom through the English from the Dutch.'

At Dixcove there was a fort: the natives were sullen and insubordinate, but did not openly rebel. The commandant, however, feared an insurrection: he called upon them to give up their arms; they refused, and he bombarded the town.

The Fantees now determined to take the matter into their own hands. They called upon the Elminas to join them in an alliance offensive and defensive against the Ashantees; and, this proposal being rejected, marched against the town. A great battle was fought in the neighbouring plain: the Dutch artillery played upon the Fantees from an outlying fort, and the Fantees were defeated with loss. But they blockaded the town and cut off the people from their plantations. The Elminas sent word of these doings to the King of Ashantee, who called upon the Fantees to cease hostilities against Elmina. 'It is there,' he said, 'I eat my salt, it is there I drink my rum. If you do not leave it alone I will descend from my throne with my drawn sword in my hand and drive you all into the sea.'

However, the blockade continued; and an Ashantee army under the command of a chief named Atchampong marched down to the coast by the Assinie route, and then along the beach to Elmina. But he did not succeed in raising the blockade.

During all this time the Governors of Elmina and Cape Coast remained on terms of courtesy and friendship; but the Dutch declared that the English Government, while calling upon the Fantees to lay down their arms, secretly connived at the war; and on the other hand it was alleged that the Dutch governor was secretly negotiating with the King of Ashantee. Both reports were probably untrue; but the English traders began to predict with joy that the Dutch would soon be driven from the coast.

The governor-general was recalled, and Colonel Nagtglas sent out from the Hague. This officer had gained during his stay upon the coast a reputation with the natives, similar to that of Macarthy and Maclean. It was hoped that he would adjust the difficulty; but that was out of his power. The Fantees declared that the Ashantee alliance must be abandoned, and that nothing else would content them. They could never hold their own against the Ashantees, when a neighbouring people supplied the invaders with arms and ammunition. Colonel Nagtglas did not think it consistent with honour to withdraw under compulsion from an old alliance. The problem remained insoluble. It was therefore resolved that the settlements should be abandoned, and they were offered to the British Government.

Lord Kimberley refused to take Elmina except with the consent of the natives; and so it was represented to them that the Dutch in any case were going away; that they could remain independent if they pleased, but in that case no one would protect them against the hostile tribes by whom they were surrounded. If, however, they chose to accept the British flag, their lives and property would be protected by the government.

The Elminas consented to receive the flag. But now another difficulty arose. The King of Ashantee protested against the transfer, declaring Elmina belonged to him. The English Government refused to go on until that claim had been investigated. It was soon disposed of in the clearest manner. First, the Dutch disavowed it, and soon afterwards the king disavowed it himself. That, one might suppose, would be sufficient to settle the matter. But let us examine the claim for ourselves. A long time ago the Ashantees conquered Denkera, and by virtue of that conquest received the pay-note (Kostbrief) of Elmina. In 1831 Ashantee abandoned all claim to Denkera, and therefore abandoned all claim to the pay-note of Elmina, just as it lost the pay-note of Accra in losing Akim.

But it so happened that the Dutch thought fit to continue the payment of the note, stipulating in return that the king should provide so many slaves *per annum* at such and such a price. These slaves were employed in the Java Battalion and afterwards returned as pensioners to Elmina. It is therefore evident that the pay-note had changed its character; it had become a stipend similar to the stipends which are paid by the Government of Sierra Leone to native chiefs for the furtherance of commerce and preservation of peace. The British Government offered not only to continue but even to double this stipend, it being of course clearly understood that it was a payment of free will and not a payment of allegiance.

All preliminaries having been arranged, Mr. Pope Hennessy was sent out to take possession of the forts. On April 6, 1872, Mr. Jan Helenus Ferguson, Knight of the Order of the Oaken Crown, handed to him the gold and ivory baton which had been left by the famous Admiral De Ruyter as an heirloom to the castle of St. George. Handsome presents were made to the chiefs and people of the town; no disturbance took place; the two flags were hoisted together, and the Dutch quietly withdrew. The next morning the natives awoke and found themselves under the British flag. Atchampong, the Ashantee general, was conducted to the Prah with an escort; rich presents and sweet words were sent to the King of Ashantee; and so fully was Mr. Hennessy persuaded he had gained the heart of that monarch that when the Ashantees crossed the Prah he declared it was merely a border raid. To be sure, as he was at Sierra Leone, he could not know much about the matter; but he had unbounded faith in his own powers of diplomacy.

CHAPTER 6

The European Captives

In the meantime the king was keeping at Coomassie certain Europeans taken in war. The negotiations for their release, conducted by the British Government, were connected with the Ashantee invasion; their actual release was an event of the Ashantee campaign. It will therefore be proper to give some account of their capture and captivity.

At the time when the Danes still occupied the fort and town of Christiansborg, in the eastern districts of the Gold Coast, the Basle missionaries established a station in that settlement, and ever since these worthy men have been steadily working into the interior. The Church Missionary Society did great things in the early days of Sierra Leone, when shiploads of naked negroes, taken on board slave-ships, were disembarked almost every month at the Queen's Yard. But, with respect to missionary labours among independent savage tribes in Western Africa, it is certain that the Basle Mission should receive the palm. The principles on which it is conducted make it resemble those industrious communities of monks who hewed clearings in the German forest and regarded labour as a form of prayer.

As regards missionaries trading with the natives (for the benefit of the Society) a difference of opinion may prevail; but no rational man will deny that it is good for missionaries to teach their converts useful handicrafts and the discipline of industry. The agents of the Society at Basle preach, and pray, and read the Bible to their parishioners quite as much as other missionaries; they have also seminaries in which negro candidates for holy orders learn 'Dogmatik' or scientific theology, Greek and Hebrew—which language the Africans find easier than Greek, as it is difficult for them to grapple with long and involved periods. In addition to this religious education, music is taught, and

English, with the usual elements, arithmetic, history, geography, &c; and, furthermore, the lay-brethren of the mission train up carpenters, bootmakers, blacksmiths, masons, and so forth. The missionaries receive no salary, but only an allowance sufficient to feed them and clothe them; if they do not spend it all, they return the surplus to the mission chest. The Society gives them a pension when they grow old, and also educates their children.

They have pushed their stations far inland; and never in my African travels have I had so charming a sensation and surprise as when I came unexpectedly upon one of these pious settlements. In the midst of the dark and savage forest I heard the sounds of an harmonium: it was the music of Mozart. As I went on, the trees opened, and disclosed a clearing; children with bright cheerful faces, and neat blue frocks met me on the way; I saw a large stone church, and the missionary buildings arranged like a college, with a quadrangle in the midst; and then out came the honest warm-hearted Wurtemburghers,. shook me by the hand, laid the table themselves that there might not be a moment's delay, and offered me wine and bread and fruit to stay my appetite, they said, till something better could be cooked.

I spent some time in this interesting colony, and became impressed with the belief that the Basle Mission is a true civilising movement.

In the eastern districts of the Gold Coast the forest comes to an end, and its place is taken by a plain covered with high grass and stunted trees, resembling in its character the open plateau behind Ashantee. This great Plain of Guinea (as it might be termed) shoots in a mere strip or promontory behind Accra, so that if you travel straight inland you come to the forest again; but if you go east or north-east you find nothing but open land. Through this plain the Volta, the most important river of the Gold Coast, flows down into the sea. The stations of the Basle Mission are partly in the region of the forest, partly in the open plain.

The vegetation of the forest and the plain are quite of a different kind, and these two regions also represent ethnological divisions. The forest is inhabited by the Oji family of tribes, while the open country is, for the most part, occupied by tribes allied to the people of Accra, whose language, the Ga, has nothing in common with Oji. The tribes of the forest are uncircumcised even up to Cape Palmas; the tribes of the plain are circumcised, without however being Moslems. The Basle missionaries, therefore, labour among two nations of negroes, and have had to master two families of language.

Their farthest station inland was at the town of Anum in the Kree-pee country, on the other side of the Volta. The Kreepees are an in-dustrious cotton-growing people; they profess allegiance to the Gold Coast Government, and are often at war with their neighbours the Aquamoos, to whom they were formerly subject The Kreepees be-long to the Ga family, but the Aquamoos are Oji, and on friendly terms with the Ashantees. In 1868 the Aquamoos, wishing to attack Kreepree, sent to Coomassie for assistance, and the king lent them 5,000 men under the command of a famous general, Adoo Buffoo. The Kreepees collected round Domprey, a soldier of fortune, who soon made himself so famous that the king threatened to kill Adoo Buffoo if he did not kill Domprey.

In June 1869, the Ashantees approached Anum. Domprey was en-camped about twelve miles from the town; the women and children were sent away. Domprey advised the missionaries to make their es-cape, but they did not take his advice for two reasons. In the first place they believed that the Ashantees were a fine people and would not do them any harm; and, secondly, Domprey had already shown a disposi-tion to plunder, and had forced them to pay a war contribution. In the factory connected with the Mission they had 2,000*l*. worth of goods; they believed, and the belief was not unnatural, that Domprey wanted to frighten them away that he might seize upon their property. Soon the Ashantees were reported to be near Anum, and everyone left the town. The missionaries now sent their clerk and catechist and servants away, and remained alone in the house. They were three in number: Mr. Kühne, a German, with Mr. Ramseyer and his wife, who were Swiss. Mrs. Ramseyer had, also, an infant ten months old.

The Mission-house was situated at a little distance from the town on a high hill which commanded a beautiful view. Thence could be seen the blue Volta flowing through a mountain gorge; far away to the north a vast plain called the Wilderness extended; and to the north-west might dimly be descried the misty outline of the forest-covered Quow Mountains, belonging to the same range as the Adansi Hills, and marking the frontier of Ashantee. On the hill there was no water: it used to be fetched every morning from the town, and now the missionaries had to go for it themselves. Anum was quite empty; not a soul was to be seen, and all day long they could hear no sound but the buzzing and humming of insects, and the *hoo! hoo! hoo!* of the red-feathered *touraco*.

Thus they waited for the Ashantees, and on the morning of the third day they heard voices in the town. It was June 12, 1869: Mrs. Ramseyer was in the gallery spreading out clothes to dry, when she saw the barrels of muskets above the high grass. About twenty armed men appeared and pointed their guns at the house. She wished them good morning and went inside. The two missionaries went out, and asked the men if they were Ashantees, and on receiving an affirmative reply said they were friends to the Ashantees as well as to all other people, and had nothing to do with the war. They then shook hands, and the leader of the men said they must all go down to Anum and salute the general. The missionaries replied that they could not all go as they had no servants, and there would be no one to take care of the house. The Ashantees replied that they would put sentinels over the house.

The missionaries then went to their rooms and put on their coats and descended the hill, Mrs. Ramseyer carrying the child in her arms. On their way they met about 500 Ashantees who were rushing up the hill with savage yells. Anum consists of three towns separated by gardens: when the missionaries were brought to the first town they were told that the general was in the second town; when brought to the second town they were told that he was in the third; when brought to the third town they were told that he was in a village a little way off. They were made to walk all day long, and on the way they were passed by Ashantees carrying furniture and goods belonging to the Mission.

In the evening they arrived at a village where they found the King of Aquamoo. They said to him, 'You know that we are missionaries, and have nothing to do with the war; why are we treated in this way? 'He replied that they must go to the Ashantee general, who would certainly send them home. The next day they were made to march off again. Mrs. Ramseyer lost one of her shoes in a swamp, but was not allowed to wait for a moment. Mr. Kühne lagged and was threatened with the whip. Their umbrellas were taken from them. Presently they heard heavy firing; a battle was being fought between Domprey and the Ashantees. Several men passed them with blood streaming from their wounds; these threatened them and said, 'Ah! it is you who teach people to fight; but we Ashantees can eat white men up.'

They passed the rear of the Ashantee army, where policemen ran to and fro armed with whips of hippopotamus skin and flogged stragglers into action. Thousands of carriers were there in line; each of them had a small pillow or porter's knot, and each beat this in a curious manner with his hands, so that it made a noise just like the whistling of bullets, and the missionaries could not help ducking their heads. They passed a village in which were many dead bodies, and women howling with grief packing them up in baskets. It was dark before they reached the Ashantee camp, and as soon as they arrived they were taken before what they at first supposed to be a tent, but it was a huge umbrella beneath which sat a man covered with a white cloth. They were told that this was Adoo Buffoo, and the soldiers of the escort, kneeling down, presented the captives.

Some young men at once rushed up to Mrs. Ramseyer and tore off the skirt of her dress; then came other men with long knives in their hands and separated the prisoners. Mr. Kühne was taken to a hut where a chief was seated bleeding from five wounds which were being washed with hot water. He ordered Kühne to sit down, looked at him sternly, and made signs that he intended to cut off his arms. He enquired if Kühne had been fighting, and Kühne replied that he was a priest and non-combatant. The chief then made a sign, and he was put into irons. He felt sure that he was to be killed. A little way off were Mr. and Mrs. Ramseyer, also in irons, and he could hear them praying and bidding farewell to each other in heart-thrilling words.

However, their lives were spared, and though kept in irons and robbed they were not otherwise ill-treated. Adoo Buffoo called them before him and informed them with much politeness that he intended to restore them to their brethren, but first they must go to a quiet town where they could eat and rest before they proceeded on their journey. He put them under an old chief and a few soldiers and sent them off. They walked for some distance till they came to a high hill whence they could see the Volta and the direction of their route. Then they knew that the quiet town to which they were going was Coomassie.

They were taken through a part of Kreepee which was allied with the Ashantees, and then, crossing the Volta, entered the Wilderness, an uninhabited province watered by scanty streams. After five days they came to the Quow country where the forest begins, and thence to Coomassie, travelling always in the bush.

Mrs. Ramseyer had some desiccated milk in a bottle, and with this she kept the child alive for a time. When the milk was finished she made food with eggs and broiled corn obtained by charity; when the missionaries entered a village they went begging from house to house: they were not always successful, though sometimes the natives were very kind and brought them food of their own accord. But the child became thinner and paler every day, and died before the end of July. It had just been buried when they received a present from the king and a message telling them not to be afraid. They were much cheered by this, and the old chief and his soldiers treated them better; but they were still put in irons every night.

They passed through to Juabin, and on the 9th of August arrived at a village twelve miles from Coomassie, There they met a Frenchman named Bonnat, who had been captured at Ho on the east side of the Volta. When the Ashantees approached he remained in his factory for the purpose of selling them powder and guns, but they took the powder and guns for nothing and himself into the bargain.

A Wesleyan station had been established at Coomassie by Mr. Freeman, a West Indian mulatto, who was at one time the chief of the mission on the Gold Coast, and had been five times to the Ashantee capital. The Mission agent, a native named Watts, had been detained by the king seven years. The king was also keeping prisoner a number of Fantees who had been peaceably trading at Fomana, and Prince Ansah, who was himself an Ashantee, but who at Coomassie was regarded as an alien. In 1831 the king had deposited 600 ounces of gold as a security for peace, and had sent two of his sons and princes to receive an English education: one of them had died, the other was Ansah, who became half an Englishman, and had been sent to the capital as an envoy of the Gold Coast Government.

For a long time the captives were detained in Aminihia, a little village near Coomassie, where the king had a country house, and spent his *villegiatura*, and where most of the Moslems resided. They were forced to live in small shanties run up for the occasion and were far from being comfortable. At last, after great difficulty, they obtained permission to enter Coomassie and take up their quarters in the Mission-house. Prince Ansah was very kind to them, and gave them all the assistance in his power; but he and Watts and most of the Fantees were soon afterwards exchanged for Ashantee prisoners.

The captives were treated well enough according to Ashantee ideas: the king gave them a monthly allowance of gold-dust, that they might buy food, and also made them occasional presents. The administrator of the Gold Coast, Mr. Ussher, and their brethren of the Mission sent them boxes of money, provisions, and clothes, which were not interfered with. They bought slaves to wait upon them. Mr. Ussher made strenuous efforts to procure their release, and they themselves, as may be imagined, did not omit to supplicate the king. He assured them that he would soon let them go; but, as Adoo Buffoo had taken them, they must wait till he returned from the war.

When Adoo Buffoo did return, he drove in before him several thousand prisoners of war: but these were from that part of Kreepee which was in alliance with the Ashantees. The war had not been successful, and the general did not like to return empty-handed: so as he could not capture his enemies, he captured his friends. When he saw the missionaries, he said nothing about letting them go, but informed them he wanted some money.

At the beginning of 1872 the administrator send up some messengers to negotiate for their release. On February 17 the king summoned his chiefs and the missionaries to a conference. Just as they were sitting down, the alarm horn was blown, announcing a fire in the town. It is an Ashantee law that the king must attend all fires, possibly that all the young men may work all the better to put it out. When the fire was extinguished, the king returned and said to the chiefs, 'My friends, I have just received a letter from the governor, asking me to give up the white men. I have no objection to it myself; now what do you say?'

Then Adoo Buffoo rose and said that the white men had taken from them Denkera, and Assin, and Wassaw, and Akim, and now they had better keep these white men at Coomassie. The king took the votes of the chiefs, and Adoo Buffoo had the majority. However, at last he agreed to release them on a ransom. In such a case the king would demand a thousand *periguins*: he was only a chief, and would be content with 800—*i.e.* 6,840*l*.

The Basle Mission, which is not wealthy, offered a thousand pounds. In the meantime Elmina was transferred to the English, and a native of Elmina, named Plange, was sent up to Coomassie to announce the fact, and to offer a thousand pounds for the captives. At a great council the king said, 'Well, if I don't give up the white men, what will the governor do?' Plange replied he thought there would be war. Upon this there was a tumult, like that described by Bowdich on a similar occasion. All rose to their feet. The Queen Mother spoke first, and said that she with her left hand could beat the Fantees. The chief of Adansi said he was the smallest of the chiefs, but he could do the same by himself. Each chief in turn spoke to a similar effect.

Plange told them they must let their hearts cool: what he had said was only his private opinion: it was not in the letter. The tumult then ceased and a pacific answer was returned.

But there was at Coomassie a restless and ambitious chief named Amanquatia. He had learned the art of war under an old chief named Essamanquatia, and had gained some reputation as a general. He envied the fame of Adoo Buffoo, and, possessing great wealth and rank, raised and headed a strong war party. Another advocate for war was the chief Atchampong, whom Mr. Pope Hennessy had so judiciously released. Adoo Buffoo, himself, was at first for peace, as his son had been taken prisoner by the English; but Mr. Hennessy sent him also to Coomassie, and then Adoo Buffoo no longer hesitated to join the advocates of war. Coffi Calcalli (or rather Kerrikerri) seems to have been in favour of peace; but he was a young man, and had only been four years on the throne; he could not resist the united will of so many powerful chiefs.

It was, therefore, determined to renew the war which had been smouldering since 1864. Atchampong and Adoo Buffoo were ordered to march with a small army to the western districts of the Gold Coast. The main army, 40,000 strong, was placed under the command of Amanquatia; and Essamanquatia had a division. All these warlike preparations were kept secret from the missionaries (as they were at a later period when Sir Garnet invaded the country); and when everything was ready in November, 1872, the captives were called to the palace and informed that the thousand pounds would be accepted, and that they were free men. They were escorted to Fomana, on the frontier, thirty-seven miles from Coomassie, and royal envoys were sent down to Cape Coast Castle to get the money from the governor.

A certain crafty old chief had suggested in council that the missionaries should be really released and sent on across the Prah, and that the army should follow close upon them. The surrender of the prisoners would so delude the Assins that they would remain in their villages and be taken unawares. However, the chiefs did not like to forego the thousand pounds. It was resolved to obtain it, if possible, from the governor on trust, then to take back the captives to Coomassie, and pour the army into the Protectorate. However, the administrator refused to pay over the ransom until the missionaries, were brought to the Prah; and, despite Prince Ansah's assurances of the good faith of his countrymen, he would not swerve from this resolution. The envoys promised to go back and bring the missionaries to the Prah, and first purchased on credit a large quantity of goods from more than one merchant in the town. It was almost universally believed that there would be peace.

As soon as the envoys returned to Fomana the mask was taken off. Plange was flogged, the missionaries robbed, and all of them ordered back to Coomassie. On their way they met the Ashantee army in, full march for the Prah.

The captives heard little news about the war; politics were tabooed by the natives in their conversation. But in May, 1873, the king met them in the street; he was carried in a basket or cradle, lined with red cloth and leopard-skin, and wore a necklace of silver bullets, the symbol of war. He descended from his basket and danced before them like David, and brandished his sword in their faces, and said that he was at Dunquah, and that if the white men mixed themselves up in the palaver it would be the worse for them. This was the turning-point; afterwards came to Coomassie rumours of sickness and disaster, and the king did not dance any more. [1]

---

1. I obtained the materials of this chapter from Mr. Kühne at Prahsu, soon after his release.

CHAPTER 7

The Invasion

Amanquatia left Coomassie with his army under the best auspices: two men were tied at the top of trees near the outside of the town, and from their time and manner of dying from starvation the priests deduced a happy issue to the undertaking. He reached the Prah in December, 1872, and it took five days to ferry the troops across. First he ravaged the country of Assin, and sent a message to the Fantees saying he had no quarrel with them. He then marched against Fantee, and defeated the army of allies near Yancoomassie, and afterwards near Dunquah. He declared that he would bring to Coomassie the stones of the castle at Cape Coast, some sea-water in a bottle, the governor, and other curiosities. He would drive the white men into the sea and make them hide in the belly of the herring. The king sent exultant messages to Cape Coast Castle. He had heard that his forts at Cape Coast and Elmina were very dirty and out of repair, and begged to request that the Governor would have them white-washed and cleaned, as he intended to come and inspect them.

The administrator, Colonel Harley, C.B., did not follow the example of Colonel Hill who had marched in person to meet the Ashantees in the hush. He sent Dr. Rowe to Assin to find out if it was really an invasion: he afterwards despatched to the Fantee camp a detachment of Haussas (irregular troops levied at Lagos), under Lieutenant Hopkins, 2nd West India Regiment. Mr. Loggie, the acting Inspector-General of Police, also went to the front with a rocket-party, and Surgeon M'Kellar R.N., attended the troops. The administrator supplied the Fantees with ammunition: this they blazed off in the direction of the enemy, whom they outnumbered, but always refused to advance. It was said that they sometimes fought well; but the battle always ended in their running away.

Dunquah is about twenty miles from Cape Coast Castle. Amanquatia destroyed the village and cut down the great fetish tree to show that he had conquered the gods of the country. He then marched south-west in the direction of Elmina, and took Juquah, the capital of Denkera. The unfortunate natives streamed into Cape Coast Castle for protection: it was a most piteous spectacle. Many were emaciated by famine or disease: some were carrying their aged parents on their backs, or leading the blind; the wayside was littered with corpses, with the dying, with women bringing forth children. The poor wretches encamped in the streets of Cape Coast Castle, and washed themselves in the puddles and gutters. The rains had now set in, and were unusually severe; the roofs of houses were battered down, and many people perished in the ruins. Then the survivors, dreading the shelter of their houses more than the wind and rain, also made huts in the streets, or lived under the stormy sky.

The Ashantee army came close to the town and burnt a village three miles off, so that the reflection of the flames could plainly be seen from the town. The natives feared to go to the bush for wood, or to the plantations. Famine raged in the town, and two epidemics broke out—smallpox and dysentery. Night alarms were frequent: the merchants, rightly or wrongly, placed no faith in the administration, fortified their houses, and, arming their servants, established patrols. Happily the Ashantees were not acquainted with the weakness of the town, and they had a dread of artillery. Besides, Elmina was their object of attack, and there the natives of the town would assist them to take the fort and to drive the English into the sea. They therefore moved their camp to the neighbourhood of Elmina. A division marched against the turbulent Commenda, and the village was utterly destroyed; but the inhabitants escaped and were taken off in English vessels to Cape Coast.

On the other hand the Ashantees also suffered from the heavy rains; dysentery and smallpox came upon them in their unclean camps, and carried them off by hundreds. But Amanquatia did not intend to return until he had struck at Elmina: arrangements were slowly made for an attack; scaling ladders were prepared; the natives of the town were confident of success, and had a belief that if only the Dutch flag could be once more hoisted on the castle of St. George their old masters would return.

Such was the state of affairs when the vigorous measures of an English officer frustrated Amanquatia's designs, and made him relinquish all hopes of taking Elmina. On June 7, 1873, the *Barracouta*, Captain Fremantle, steamed into the roads at Cape Coast, having on board a body of marines under the command of Lieutenant-Colonel Festing, R.M.A He at once saw that something must be done with Elmina, for Ashantees were in the neighbourhood, and even, it was said, in the town. He landed his marines and garrisoned the castle; then having obtained the permission of the administrator, he arranged a scheme with Captain Fremantle for ensuring the safety of the castle and the loyal portion of the town.

A few words must now be given in description of Elmina. This our newest colony is also the oldest we possess outside the Straits of Gibraltar. It was built before America was discovered, and lost in the following manner:—In 1637, there being at that time peace between Portugal and Holland, Prince Maurice, Governor of Dutch Brazil, sent over the famous Admiral De Ruyter to take what he could find in these lawless latitudes. De Ruyter anchored off Elmina and implored the assistance of the governor. A pestilent disease was raging in the fleet, and he was anxious to establish a hospital on shore, but not too far from a settlement. Pointing to a hill at that time covered with bush, just inland of the castle, he said, 'That would answer my purpose, and being to leeward would not affect the town.'

The governor assented. The Dutch pitched tents, and carried up numbers of hammocks containing not sick men but pieces of ordnance. The Portuguese, fearing infection, did not examine them closely, and were taken completely by surprise. One fine morning there was a blast of trumpets from the hill, and the tents being struck unmasked a battery which poured such a heavy fire into the castle of St. George that the Portuguese soon capitulated. The place is still shown where the governor met De Ruyter outside the gates of the castle and delivered up the keys; and a Latin tablet on the old tower commemorates the event. Bosman mentions the taking of St. George by cannon on the hill which commanded that fort; but he did not say how the cannon came there. On that hill the Dutch built a fort which they called St. Jago.

Elmina is thus situated. The Baya, an arm of the sea, enters near the landing place and runs a little way parallel with the beach. There is a narrow strip of sand with the ocean on one side and the Baya on the other, ending in a rocky promontory. On this promontory is the castle; and the king's town beginning close under the walls was built along the sandy strip; where the town came to an end was a scrubby growth of prickly pear.

The Baya is spanned by a stone bridge, and on the other side of the water is the Garden-town, consisting chiefly of a broad street shaded with umbrella trees, and containing the houses of the merchants. Beyond it to the north-west is a cluster of native huts and the governor's garden—a grove with a summer house surrounded by a wall, and at no great distance from the sea. The fort of St. Jago is on the other side of the Baya, a little to the west of the Garden-town; beyond it is another hill and an outlying fort; beyond that hill and beyond the garden is a wide open grassy plain.

At daybreak on June 13, 1873, several man-of-war's boats entered the Baya, and lay opposite the town. At the same time a detachment of the 2nd West drew up in line behind the prickly pear scrub. Thus the king's town was surrounded by water and men. Then martial law was proclaimed, and the natives were called upon to deliver up all arms and munitions of war at the gate of the castle of St. George between the hours of seven and nine. Warning was given that if they refused, the town would be bombarded by the fort. The arms were not brought in, and another proclamation was issued giving them an hour more to obey the demand. At noon the bombardment commenced, and in twenty minutes the town was destroyed. A number of armed Elminas broke through the line of the 2nd West, and then assembling fired on the boats; at the same time some Ashantees joined them from the north. These were soon put to the rout and chased along the beach; and the troops returned to the castle at 3 p.m.

At five o'clock in the afternoon the boats were on their way back to the ship, when a Java pensioner ran breathlessly into the town and told Mr. Von Hamel, the Dutch vice-consul, that a great Ashantee army was marching over the plain in the direction of the town. Von Hamel gave the alarm; the general assembly was sounded; the Haussas, Marines, and 2nd West, under Festing, Fremantle, Loggie, and Rowe, marched on to the hill overlooking the plain. It was already black with Ashantees; some of them had entered the garden and had killed a Java pensioner, and it was evidently their intention to burn the loyal quarter of the town.

The battle began, and the Ashantees passing close to the garden were attempting to turn Festing's right flank, when all of a sudden, to the surprise of both parties engaged, a terrific fire was opened from behind the garden wall; the Ashantees fell in heaps, wavered to and fro, and then began slowly to retreat

Castle of St. George

Garden Town

Ft. Schomberg

Ft. St. Iago

Bridge

Bay a

Elrona Town

Prickly Pear Groves

This is what had occurred: Von Hamel, having alarmed the castle, ran down to the beach and hailed Lieutenant Wells, who was in command of the boats returning to the *Barracouta*. Wells landed at once with his small-arm men and some marines, and, not knowing which way to go, struck straight inland: this took him into the garden: some Ashantees ran out at the other end as he entered, and he found himself on the enemy's flank. Marching up to the wall, he poured in volleys at close range and did great execution.

The Ashantees retreated in good order across the plain, keeping in line, loading and reloading, and dropping down on one knee to fire. But, though they were 3,000 strong against a force of 300 men, they could not stand before the Snider; the bush and the dusk, alone, put an end to the pursuit. They lost about five hundred men, while the losses on our side were merely nominal.

The Ashantees remained in their former camp, but made no movement of aggression. Though only a slight engagement, this battle was decisive in its results. From that time the Ashantees abandoned all hope of taking Elmina; and so their campaign was brought to a close. On the other hand, the spirit of the Imperial Government was roused by this outrage on the British flag, and it was resolved to wage an offensive war against: the Ashantees. Captain Glover was sent to Accra with orders to raise a native army in the eastern districts of the Gold Coast, and if successful in his levies to invade Ashantee territory.

Shortly afterwards Colonel Harley was recalled, and Sir Garnet Wolseley was ordered to take the civil and military command upon the Gold Coast, to organise an army of Fantees, to drive the Ashantees out of the Protectorate, and, if he should deem it necessary, to march upon Coomassie. Two English regiments were held in readiness; but it was hoped he might be able to defeat the enemy, and establish an enduring peace, with no other forces than those of the native allies, and a small body of seamen and marines.

CHAPTER 8

The Departure

Having been an eyewitness of the principal events which ensued, I shall now write often in the first person, freely describing my own impressions and adventures. This will make my narrative seem egotistical, but may also make it more interesting. And, in the first place, I shall explain how it was I came to volunteer for the expedition to the Gold Coast.

In 1861 I happened to meet at a farmhouse in Oxfordshire a young surgeon who had just returned from his first trip on board a mail-steamer to the West Coast of Africa. His descriptions of that wonderful land so fired my foolish young head that I determined to go there forthwith; and, having bought a battery of elephant guns, sporting rifles, &c, for a country in which was no game, saddles for a country in which were no horses, a magic lantern, a tent, a cast-iron stove, and other trifles of a similar kind, I steamed down the coast to Fernando Po, and took a passage to Gaboon, which was then all the rage (in more senses than one). I spent five months in that land of controversy, ascended the river higher than anyone before me, discovered its rapids, visited the cannibal Fans, investigated the habits of the gorilla, and demonstrated to the satisfaction of all scientific men that it does not beat its breast like a drum, or scoop out negro heads like a pumpkin, but is a quiet lumbering beast, wary and shy, difficult to approach, never attacking man except when brought to bay, and even then not attacking in a very formidable manner.

Next I visited Angola, in South-Western Africa, and, sometimes riding on an ox, sometimes carried in a hammock, took a trip into the interior of that colony. Returning northwards, I indulged myself in a trip among the Cape de Verde Islands, and had some good quail-shooting in the island of St. Nicholas: after which I went over to the

mainland, ascended the Casemanche, Gambia, and Senegal, saw some-
thing of Moslem life among the negroes, and also of the wild Tawny
Moors, who, riding on their camels, came into St. Louis from the
Desert with gum, woollen cloths, and other articles of trade.

In these travels I at all events learnt my own ignorance. Often alone
in the forest, or at sea in a canoe, without books or civilised companions, I had reason to regret that I did not know the alphabet of nature.
I looked upon the trees, the water, and the earth, as many in London
look at the placards on the walls and the letters over shop-doors. Soon
after my return to England I read the *Origin of Species*, was inflamed
with a passion for science, and entered myself as student at a London
hospital. When four years had passed I longed to revisit Africa, and
to study for myself in savage life the many interesting problems with
relation to the Progress of Man which were being so actively discussed
throughout the scientific world.

I wished, also, to make a genuine exploring journey, so that I might
better deserve the title of *African explorer* which I sometimes (wrong-
fully) received. But I could not again afford to travel at my own expense in a country where a white man must always travel *en prince*;
and I should, perhaps, have never realised my hopes had it not been
for a merchant connected with the Gold Coast, Mr. Andrew Swanzy,
who desired to do something as a patron for the cause of exploration.
He suggested that I should open up the Assinie River on the western
limits of the Gold Coast; and I proposed that Coomassie should be
included in the trip. To this he assented, and finally it was arranged
that if, on account of political troubles, that journey should prove to
be impracticable, I should then select some other region which had
not been explored.

In the autumn of 1868 I landed at Assinie, which at that time was
occupied by the French. A commandant and a surgeon dwelt in a
'*Poste*' surrounded by a stockade, with a park of artillery, and a detachment of *Tirailleurs Senegalais*—troops resembling the Haussas, and levied from the warlike tribes of Senegambia. I had previously called at
Grand Bassam, which was the superior station, possessing an officers'
mess, a larger force of *tirailleurs*, and an outpost on the lagoon. These
settlements, in common with Gaboon, were governed by the admiral of the station, who used to inspect them once a year. They were
both abandoned during the war of 1870: and the '*Poste*' is let to Mr.
Swanzy; but the French still retain these settlements, and a gun-boat
visits them now, (as at time of first publication), and then to watch

over French interests.

The trade of Grand Bassam is not at ordinary times connected with Ashantee; in fact Grand Bassam, though included in the French *Cote d'Or*, does not properly belong to the Gold Coast. The trade is in palm oil with tribes who speak a language distinct from the Oji; and instead of a gold-dust currency they use copper bracelets called *manilhas*, a currency also in vogue at Bonny and other places in the Bight of Benin.

Assinie is the westernmost station on the Gold Coast, and has long been a port of Ashantee. Of the four great roads from Coomassie one leads to that settlement.[1] The king lives at Kinjabo, a town situated on the banks of the river, about thirty miles inland; and as the Assinie territory joins that of Ashantee, the traders of Coomassie can come down without being stopped on the way, which, in troublous times, more than compensates for fifty miles extra journeying. But these Ashantees are only stopped to trade under certain restrictions. They are forced to remain at Kinjabo; they may not go to the beach and traffic with the ships and factories, but must hand over their nuggets and gold-dust to Amatifoo with an order for the goods they require, and he acts as their broker through his traders on the beach.

The commandant informed me that a party of Ashantees, envoys and traders from their king, were just then staying at Kinjabo. A French trader was going there on business, and gave me a passage in his boat. We arrived after dark and invited Amatifoo to dinner. First my companion spoke of his affairs, and Amatifoo ordered 1,000 muskets for the Ashantees. These muskets were the weapons of the French army under the first Napoleon, bought from government by an enterprising merchant, and sold by him to the African trade. It is therefore not impossible that some of the guns used by the Ashantees against the Black Watch at Amoaful had been previously used by the French against that regiment at Waterloo.

This business being over, Amatifoo took a glass of tea and claret, half and half, and enquired how he could oblige me. I said that I wanted to go to Coomassie; he replied that I could do so, but must follow the usual etiquette. First, I must send up a letter (with a present) requesting permission to visit the king; and he, in reply, would send down bearers with a hammock and an escort. Such, I knew, was the usual routine; and the next day I gave the Ashantee envoys 10*l.* worth of cloth and the letter, which they said would be sent up at once. But

1. Dupuis.

no answer came down; and I am inclined to believe that Amatifoo and the Ashantees divided the present.

Having waited three months, I called at Kinjabo again, and asked Amatifoo's permission to go through his territory to the Ashantee frontier; thence I could send up a message, and there I could wait for a reply. This he refused to allow; and so, happily for me, my project broke through. Had I succeeded in reaching Coomassie, I should certainly have been detained until the British troops had crossed the Prah.

I found that nothing could be done on the Gold Coast in the way of exploration. In the interior Ashantee formed a cordon of more than 200 miles, separating the tribes of the open land from the tribes of the sea. Even the countries adjoining Ashantee would not venture to let a white man pass through them for fear of incurring the enmity of that jealous and despotic power. I therefore turned my attention to other parts of Africa: and I met at Cape Coast Castle Sir Arthur Kennedy, the Governor-in-Chief of the West African settlements, who was making his annual tour of inspection. He offered me the command of a Government Expedition to explore the Sherbro' River near Sierra Leone, provided his Council would vote the necessary funds.

I therefore went to Sierra Leone: but the council would not vote the funds; and I was about to make a reconnaissance of the Sherbro' at my own or rather Mr. Swanzy's expense, when I came across a book which showed me the route I should take. This was written by Captain Laing, of the 2nd West, who in the days of Sir Charles Macarthy fifty years before had opened a road to Falaba. He afterwards served in the Gold Coast campaign and was one of the few who escaped; on returning to England he obtained his promotion, and was sent by the African Association to discover the mouth of the Niger—at that time the enigma of geography.

Major Laing was the first European to reach Timbuctoo, where he was murdered by the Tuaricks, and, had he lived to return, would have won a reputation second only to that of Mungo Park. This gallant officer is still remembered in the three regions where he laboured. At Falaba I was lodged in the hut which he had occupied, and old men spoke of him to me with affection and esteem; Barth in the same manner heard of him at Timbuctoo; and Captain Butler in his visit to Akim was shown a place which still bears the name of *Laing's Camp*.

I took Laing's route to Falaba, and, like himself, was detained three months and not allowed to pass. Then having returned to Sierra Leone with envoys from the chief, I obtained a promise from them that I should have a free road to the Niger, and succeeded in reaching that river. The source was inaccessible on account of native wars, so I went on to the gold-mines of Bouré, a country never visited by any other European; and thus added a large region to the map.

These journeys occupied ten months, all (with a fortnight's interval) spent among savages. However, I wished before going home to ascend the Niger from its mouth in one of the trading steamers which go up that river in the season of rains. But the firms there trading wished the river kept dark, and, laying their heads together in Liverpool and London, directed their agents to refuse me a passage. However, the time I spent on the coast waiting for the rains was not entirely wasted. I made two trips into the back woods of Liberia, one from Monrovia and one from Cape Palmas; spent some weeks with the Basle missionaries; and finally witnessed a battle on the Volta which I have described elsewhere, but which gains new interest from the recent campaign.

In the spring of 1870 the army of Adoo Buffoo was still in Kreepee; and on the island of Duffo in the Volta was a town belonging to the Aquamoos. These islanders made raids upon our side of the river, and stopped all navigation by seizing canoes. An Ashantee captain with his company was residing in the town and directing these operations.

The Accras, who do business as traders on the Volta, determined to attack Duffo, and requested the aid of the administrator. The Gold Coast Government not possessing a steamer, Mr. Ussher, the administrator, applied to Captain Glover, at that time Administrator of Lagos, who placed a small river steamer, the *Echo*, and his own services at Mr. Ussher's disposal, stipulating that he (Glover) should be allowed to conduct the fighting part of the business. In 1868 Sir Arthur Kennedy had visited the Volta with Captain Glover, and had made a treaty with the Aquamoos, which treaty had now been broken. Captain Glover was therefore already acquainted with the river.

So it was arranged; and the *Echo* steamed up the Volta, having on board Captain Glover with some Haussas, Mr. Ussher with some soldiers of the 2nd West, and the colonial surgeon of the Gold Coast. The Accra army was encamped on the hostile side of the river opposite a town called Bato, a little way below Duffo; and it was arranged that on a certain day the Accras should march along the Aquamoo bank of the river, and thence storm the islands in canoes while the *Echo* covered the attack.

Having heard of this I went overland from Accra to Bato, and obtained a passage in the *Echo*. On the morning of the appointed day she weighed anchor at dawn and steamed slowly up the river. The water was unknown and the lead had to be used. We soon sighted the island with its town built on the end that was towards us. As we approached, a number of armed men came down to the bank and stood close to the water; presently they fired, and the bullets dropped into the water just under the side of the vessel. The soldiers returned the fire: Captain Glover worked the big gun and the rocket tube, Mr. Ussher the Hale's rocket trough. As the *Echo* passed the town Ussher fired a rocket which first struck the water and then making a beautiful curve alighted on the thatched roof of a house. The town was soon in a blaze.

Ahead of the island the river was black with canoes clustered together. A rocket from the tube soon sent these upstream; and as some of them paddled along their own side of the river there came puffs of smoke from the banks above; the canoes stopped, and we could see men running down the bank and jumping into them. They had fallen a prey to the vanguard of the Accras.

However, the main body did not arrive till the middle of the day, and so the attack was postponed. The *Echo* was anchored beyond the island on the upper side: and the Accras pitched their camp on the banks of the river. The Aquamoos and Ashantees dug rifle-pits in the bush at the north end of the island, and blazed away at the *Echo* all the afternoon. They hit the steamer about twenty times, but nobody on board was touched. Some of the enemy had Enfield rifles, as could be told by the sound of the bullets as they sang past our ears.

All night long the Accras fired off their muskets to show that they were on the alert, and the islanders bawled out to them, asking why they did not come across, calling them cowards, with other terms it would be improper to translate.

The next morning Captain Glover took the steamer close into the island and near the Aquamoo bank. The Accras declared themselves ready to storm; and so, to cover their attack, a heavy fire of shell and grape was poured into the bush-covered point which formed the enemy's position. But the Accra canoes, though already filled with men, did not budge from the bank. It seems they were disputing as to who should go first, as if it were a dinner party. Domprey, who was present, came on board saying he could do nothing with the Accras, and the whole affair seemed a fiasco, when suddenly the canoes, with flags waving at their bows, pushed off into the river, and were paddled towards the end of the island. The men got out in shallow water, formed a half moon, advanced steadily, under fire from the point, and on reaching land rushed up into the bush. In the meantime the canoes went back for reinforcements, and the *Echo* steaming round the north end of the island went ahead of the Accras and covered their advance. There was, however, but little resistance. The Accras forming in three lines swept the island from end to end at a double, firing into the high grass and thickets before them as they ran.

Some of the islanders jumped into small canoes and paddled across the river under fire from the *Echo*. Thus a few succeeded in making their escape. But there was one man on the island who did not wish to escape. In the midst of the fight we heard an explosion and saw a column of white smoke rising in the air. This was the Ashantee captain, who, having, first thrown his stool into the river, seated himself on a barrel of powder, and died by his own hand. So ended the Battle of Duffo, and Domprey, who was still on board, went round and shook hands with us all in turn. A few weeks afterwards he was shot in battle with the Ashantees; but I was lately informed by my old interpreter that he was really shot by the Accras out of jealousy for the favour showed him by the English governors.

Shortly afterwards I returned to England, and having accomplished the objects which I had in view, namely a study of savages-at-home, and a journey of exploration, I had no intention of visiting Africa again. However, I volunteered for the Livingstone Relief Expedition, as also did Captain Butler, already well known for his travels in North America. We were both unsuccessful candidates, though, as it afterwards turned out, the Council had more reason than we had to regret that circumstance. Captain Butler returned to America, and sledged over the region he has called 'The Wild North Land.' He had just returned to civilised quarters when he heard of the Ashantee expedition; he telegraphed across the ocean to his old commander and friend, *Remember Butler*, and at once took his. passage to England and thence to the Gold Coast.

I was equally desirous to join the expedition, but could not see how it was to be done. However, as the affair began to attract more and more attention from the public, I thought that perhaps the *Times* might send out a special correspondent Accordingly I volunteered, my offer was accepted, and I took my passage on board the *Ambriz*, a West African mail steamer which was to sail on September 12, 1873, with Sir G. Wolseley and his staff, and about forty others, chiefly special service officers. I was the first correspondent engaged, but the *Standard* also sent out a correspondent in the *Ambriz*.

When the news came of the disaster on the Prah, the *New York Herald* called Mr. Stanley from Spain and despatched him to Cape Coast Castle; and shortly afterwards the *Daily Telegraph* and the *Illustrated London News* were represented. The *Daily News* had no special correspondent, but was well supplied with news by two officers, one upon the staff, the other in a native regiment. Excellent letters also appeared in the *Scotsman*, the *Manchester Guardian*, and the *Western Morning News*. The medical papers had their correspondents; and a leading merchant at Cape Coast Castle acted as Reuters agent. Never perhaps has there been a war so fully reported for the press.

And never perhaps has there been a war of such a strange character as that in which Sir Garnet Wolseley was engaged. It scarcely belonged to the nineteenth century, but resembled the armed adventures of the Elizabethan age. It united the romance of war with the romance of exploration. Alexander had marched through Khiva; the Romans had an Abyssinian campaign; but never had a European army landed on the shores of Guinea. The forest of the Gold Coast was an unknown land: five or six travellers had passed along the main path to Coomassie: but that was all. In the rural districts, of the Protectorate, few of the natives had ever seen a white man, and some even disputed their existence.

The golden wealth of Ashantee, the enormous treasures said to be buried in the Bantama with the bodies of the kings, excited hope and curiosity: but that which especially distinguished this expedition was the danger with which it was attended; and that not of the kind which a soldier loves, not the danger of battle, but the danger of disease. The old proverb,

> *Beware and take care of the Bight of Benin,*
> *Where few come out, though many go in,*

applies to the whole West Coast of Africa. Even to accept an appointment on the Coast as an official, even to live in the settlements in a comfortable house, with a good table and all the resources of civilisation, is considered an extraordinary risk; and many statesmen have been led by their experience to doubt whether the nation is justified in sending its servants to that Land of Death. But if life upon the Coast under the best conditions was so perilous, what would it be for an army in a campaign? The dangers of the climate would be aggravated by hardships and exposure: the soldiers would be subjected to the influence of night-dews, soil-exhalations, the fatigue of forced marches, and the effects of unwholesome nourishment. Even in the healthiest countries, sickness always scourges an army: congregation is in itself a cause of disease. To all these dangers would be added those of the war itself; and though the loss in action would be but slight compared with the loss in European warfare, yet this war had certain dangers which were unaccustomed, and therefore terrible. A wound, however trifling in itself, might in that evil climate be a cause of death, and there was no quarter for the prisoners or wounded: all who were taken by the enemy would be put to death in the most horrible manner.

It is not therefore surprising that the Imperial Government should have been reluctant to cast two of its noble regiments into that dark and dismal forest out of which, perhaps, none might live to return; and it may be readily pardoned for having sent a general without an army to make experiments, and report upon them before a plan of campaign should be arranged. Sir Garnet Wolseley (with his own consent) was ordered to attempt the following scheme: he was to raise a native army, and place it under the command of special service officers (volunteers selected by himself), and to lead them against the Ashantees. It was hoped that thus he might rout and destroy the army of Amanquatia, and obtain a treaty of peace from the king, with a large indemnity of gold-dust, hostages, &c.

In private conversation and also in a published letter written before our arrival on the Gold Coast, I protested against this organising experiment as illusory and dangerous. How could it be supposed that the Fantees would ever be taught to defeat the Ashantees? What could be done with these miserable tribes who had not the head to combine or the heart to contend for their lands and homes? What reason was there for supposing that Wolseley would be more successful than Macarthy? He was a better general no doubt; but what is the use of a good general with troops who will not obey the orders they receive? It was absurd to suppose that by appointing a few subalterns here and there in the midst of a mob the nature of the people could be changed. The young officer would lead his savages, who as soon as they came into action would fire a volley, take to their heels, and leave him in the lurch, fortunate if he escaped with merely a discomfiture.

I denounced the organising movement, and declared that it would fail. This prediction has been fully verified, and it would be difficult to say whether Wolseley's or Glover's attempt to raise an army from the tribes of the Protectorate broke down most signally. Captain Glover's success was achieved by means of his disciplined negroes from Lagos and the countries of the Niger: and troops of a similar kind were also serviceable to Sir G. Wolseley's operations. But who will now venture to deny what I alone ventured to declare before the campaign was commenced, that Europeans alone could conquer Ashantee?[1] That army we met at Amoaful would have made short work of Glover's Haussas and Yorubas, and also of Wolseley's two native regiments (Wood's and Russell's), excellent troops as they were, and led by as gallant men as ever fought on battlefield.

I looked forward to the campaign with no little apprehension. Sir G. Wolseley was a good soldier and would therefore obey his orders. He would do his best to create a Fantee army; and though I knew that sooner or later he would find out that it was worthless, still by that time two or three months might have been lost, and many lives sacrificed. But what I feared most of all was diplomacy. The invasion of Fantee was at an end; the whole country had been ravaged by the enemy, and they had also been taught that all attacks against the settlements were useless.

It was therefore reasonable to suppose that the Ashantees, partly victorious and partly discomfited, would soon return across the Prah. Sir G. Wolseley's instructions were to make peace if he could without an appeal to arms. It was hoped that the threats of Great Britain would terrify the King of Ashantee; and so Sir Garnet was ordered to send him a kind of manifesto, calling upon him to withdraw his army and to make full compensation for the injuries it had caused. *After which* the general would be willing to commence negotiations with a view to making a treaty of peace.

To us who know the respective power of Ashantee and Great Britain, this manifesto appears a reasonable and moderate demand; but the King of Ashantee probably supposed that the governor was drunk when he wrote it. Not only the Ashantees, but the Fantees and other natives of the Gold Coast, were not then aware that England was a military power; they could not believe in an army of white men; for, in their eyes, all white men were born aristocrats, riding in hammocks, and ruling the blacks.

1. There is not, I venture to assert, the least prospect of the commander-in-chief being able to bring this war to an honourable termination without European troops. They need not exceed 2,000 in number, they need not be employed for more than two months; but they are essential to the success of this expedition, as Sir G. Wolseley will discover before he has been long upon the Gold Coast.—Letter to the *Times* from Sierra Leone, September 27.

While, therefore, the King of Ashantee acknowledged the superior intelligence of the white men, and even regarded them with a kind of reverence, looking upon them as 'next to God,' [2] he utterly despised them as warriors, which is not astonishing after Sir C. Macarthy's campaign. 'Do white men know how to travel to fight?' [3] said Coffee Calcalli to Plange, with a sneer. Besides, at that very time his army was in occupation of Fantee; it had failed to take a fort, and had been defeated on an open plain where it fought at disadvantage; but, on the other hand, there it was, encamped close to the settlements; and these English who called upon him to surrender had not even dared to march outside their settlements against him.

It was, therefore, quite impossible that the King of Ashantee, being in the position of a conqueror, and being unconscious of the power which the English possessed in reserve, would make any concession; but I feared that perhaps he might affect negotiation, and that so a part of the dry season would be lost. Happily the failure attending Sir Garnet's primary instructions was so palpable and complete that those instructions did not do any harm. The Fantee chiefs did not even pretend that they could muster an army to fight the Ashantees; as for the manifesto, it was never answered by the king: but the Ashantee general intercepted the letter and replied with a counter-manifesto saying the king had no quarrel with the white man, and that the white man could have peace by giving up the Kings of Denkera, Wassaw, Akim, and Assin. This letter ended with the phrase, *I send my love to you*, and was signed *Amanquatia*.

Sir G. Wolseley discovered soon after his arrival on the Gold Coast that the regiments were necessary to him, and wrote to have them sent out. Still it was not by any means certain, even then, that he would march upon Coomassie, for the Ashantees might still be in the Protectorate, and so their army might be destroyed and a treaty of peace obtained with indemnity and hostages, as after the battle of Dodowa in 1826. But even this kind of success I should have regarded as a misfortune. It seemed to me that this Ashantee war was only justified because its effect would be to secure our Protectorate from periodical invasion, to bestow on that widowed and wounded country the blessings of eternal peace. I was convinced that no victory, however signal it might be, against an Ashantee army of invasion would gain for our Protectorate more than a temporary respite.

---

2. Bowdich.
3. Blue Book

A victory more complete than the Battle of Dodowa could scarcely be expected; but of what use had it been after all? It was well enough to talk about taking from the king guarantees of peace; but what guarantee could be obtained? A treaty was no guarantee, for that was only a promise which he could break when he pleased; hostages were no guarantees, for he knew that they would not be killed; a fine was no guarantee, for by war he would hope to regain the money he had lost. History clearly showed that the Ashantees could suffer severe defeats and yet recover their former strength. In Gaman an Ashantee army had once been utterly destroyed, yet the Ashantees still make war upon Gaman. I therefore inferred that no victory on this side of the Prah would save us from future trouble with the Ashantees. That could be accomplished only by the capture of Coomassie.

Even the occupation of the town would, I believed, do the Ashantee power more harm than the slaying in battle of half the population. For the Ashantee power was based on its prestige; the surrounding tribes far outnumbered the dominant people, but remained in subjection because they believed the Ashantees to be invincible, and because they mistrusted each other. But when the white men appeared at Coomassie it would be everywhere known that the Ashantees had been conquered by a stronger race; and everywhere the tribes would throw off the yoke.

The capture of Coomassie would also. I thought, release the Ashantees themselves from a cruel and bloodthirsty despotism; the monarchy would fall with its policy of war; but the people would remain and develop the golden resources of the land. At the same time a barrier to commerce would be removed, and the Moslem tribes of the North would throng down to the seaboard with cotton and gold.

CHAPTER 9

The Arrival

Sir Garnet Wolseley appeared to be the right man for the Ashantee Expedition. 'Chinese Gordon,' who was the rival candidate, had more experience in organising the natives of another race, but even he could not have created an army of Fantees, and in the campaign which did ensue the experience of Wolseley was, perhaps, of a more valuable kind than that of his distinguished competitor, who is now confirming and continuing the conquests of Baker in Central Africa.

Wolseley was young for a major-general, but was also younger than his years. He possessed a peculiar buoyancy of mind which brightened his eyes and gave to his whole frame an appearance of vivacity. When I first saw him at the War Office I went away and said, 'That is a man who will stand the climate of the Coast.'

A friend of mine at Madeira, who merely saw him pass by, and heard him make a single remark, turned round to me and said 'Smart!'

In the same manner, those civilians who assembled on the beach at Cape Coast to see him land, were favourably impressed, and though they only judged from his face, spoke of him with enthusiasm.

Wolseley possessed in a strange degree not only the manner, but the qualities of youth. He was sanguine even to credulity, easily impressed, perhaps a little changeable, deficient in foresight, as will be seen, but vivid in imagination, full of resources and ideas, possessing a capacity for work, restless, keen, and energetic. He was most beloved and esteemed by those who knew him best; and they, perhaps, were led by personal affection to overrate his abilities. He had the talent of giving commands in such a way that they gave a pleasure to those who received them, and his manner to young subalterns was inexpressibly gracious and kind. I have been told that it was his well-known character which drew to him for the staff so many clever and distinguished men, with such a host of regimental volunteers, and this may be the case to some extent. Yet a service of great danger will never fail to attract the best men of our army, when volunteers are in request.

Already, on board the *Ambriz*, Sir G. Wolseley commenced operations. The saloon of the steamer was half a brigade office, half a reading-room, the table being covered with blue-books, despatches, and books of African travel. Captain Brackenbury, assistant military secretary, and Captain Huyshe, deputy assistant adjutant-general, were directed to prepare and give lectures on the History of the Gold Coast and its Topography, that all the special service officers might have some knowledge of the land which was to be the theatre of war. Before our arrival on the Gold Coast, some officers were despatched to other settlements for the purpose of raising labourers and fighting men.

Captain Furse, 42nd regiment, and Lieutenant Saunders, R.A., were sent to the Gambia to recruit men among the warlike Mandingo tribes. Lieutenant Gordon, 93rd regiment, remained at Sierra Leone, with orders to raise a force of negro colonists, and also to recruit among a tribe called the Kossoos. Commissary O'Connor was landed at Cape Palmas to hire as many *kroomen*, for purposes of transport, as he could obtain. A number of these men were also procured at Sierra Leone, where they have formed a colony; and Major Home, commanding the Royal Engineers, engaged at Freetown a number of skilled artisans.

At daybreak on the morning of October 2, the *Ambriz* anchored in the roads off Cape Coast Castle. The aspect of the shore was not of a kind to inspire picturesque enthusiasm, and differed much from the beautiful bay of Sierra Leone, with its towering hills, mantled in clouds, its town scattered with gardens nestling along the water's edge. Here was to be seen stretching to the right and left a bank of red clay about a hundred feet high, covered with low jungle and scrub. At its base was a strip of white beach on which the sea raged in furious surf, each wave as it broke giving a roar, and bursting into a sheet of foam which rushed up the sand, and then returned with a low hiss into the ocean. In a gorge or chasm of the bank lay the town with three hills behind it, on which were perched three small forts, one of which served also as a lighthouse and a signal station.

The great castle was built on a slope close to the water's edge, and like an old church in a rural village gave an air of dignity to the town. At its foot was a cluster of rocks on which the sea played, and from behind these rocks, which formed the landing place (such as it was), several canoes were seen coming forth. At the same time a boat pushed off from one of the men-of-war lying in the roads, and in a few minutes Lieutenant Wells, of Elmina fame, came on board for the naval mail bag, and to tell us the news. He said that, according to popular report, the Ashantees were in retreat.

The canoes that came alongside were of two kinds: first, the fish-canoes of the natives, which were merely wooden troughs hollowed, out of a tree; and secondly, strong English surf-boats of canoe build. In both, the method of propulsion was the same: the canoe-men dug the water with their paddles and spaded it away, keeping good time and singing in tune.

In the rains, the landing at Cape Coast: is often dangerous, but in the dry season it is merely attended with discomfort. Being put down on the beach, feeling very damp and with sand in my shoes, I walked up the main street towards the house of Mr. Swanzy's agent, where I hoped to get board and lodging for a time, hotels being almost un-known on the West Coast of Africa. I observed many houses which had fallen into ruins from the rains; and some tents on Connor's Hill denoted a state of war; but otherwise the town had resumed its ordi-nary aspect, the refugees from Denkera and other parts of the interior having moved off to villages along the coast.

In the afternoon, the general came on shore. He was received by a guard of honour (2nd West India regiment), a salute was fired from the Spur Battery, and the natives collected in a crowd to welcome him, according to custom, the chief or mayor of the town walking under-neath a red umbrella. There was not, however, much excitement, for at Cape Coast Castle governors are changed very often, and the natives were not yet aware that Sir Garnet differed from other governors. He then went up to Government House, where the judge, in barrister's wig and gown, swore him in, as administrator of the Gold Coast. At ordinary times the administrator is subject to the governor-in-chief at Sierra Leone, but during Sir Garnet's, tenure of the civil command, the Gold Coast was made independent.

At the time of our arrival, the situation on the Gold Coast was as follows. Since their repulse at Elmina, the Ashantees had made no aggressive movement; to use the words of a merchant, 'they had done nothing but mourn.' Yet panics were frequent in Cape Coast Castle, and more than once after Sir Garnet's arrival, natives rushed through the streets at midnight crying out that the Ashantees were upon them. The camp was at Mampon, about fifteen, miles off; but it was said that the army was on foot. I believed that already Amanquatia had received from the king that circle of *aggry* beads which is the symbol of re-call, and that the homeward movement had begun. Still, that is by no means certain, and it would be correct to say that the Ashantee army at this time (the beginning of October) was menacing Cape Coast Castle and Elmina.

The war was not confined to the environs of these two towns, for the army commanded by Atchampong and Adoo Buffoo was busy in the west. The Dutch had ceded to Great Britain not only the town and territory of Elmina, but also a tract of coast more than a hun-dred miles in length, with many settlements. Dixcove, which had been English until 1868, resisted the Ashantees, and a chief named Blay of eastern Apollonia, also fought on our side; but the other villages had the same politics as the people of Elmina, and welcomed the Ashan-tees. However, with one exception, they did not show hostility against the English, but remained neutral, so far as they were able.

That one exception was Chamah, the natives of which town, situ-ated at the mouth of the Prah, were a bitter and turbulent people. Placed between the two Ashantee armies, they supplied them both with powder and guns; for unhappily when Chamah was ceded, the fort was not garrisoned, and the natives could do as they pleased. It therefore became an Ashantee town.

Now there had been some talk of invading Ashantee by the Prah, and so to this town of Chamah, unsuspicious of evil, and rather disbe-lieving in the Ashantees, [1] came Captain Commerell, V.C. and Com-modore of the West African squadron. He had an interview with the chief and elders, and said he intended to go up the Prah. The chief and elders kindly advised him to beware of Ashantees (a very bad people), and to keep close to the right-hand bank or Chamah side of the river. He took their advice, and fell into their ambuscade. He had gone about a mile and a half up the river, when a voice was heard from the bush giving orders, and then a volley was fired into the boats, at about fifteen yards' range.

The commodore himself was wounded, and for many months his life was in danger: Captain Luxmoore, who sat by his side, was also hit and fainted away from loss of blood; and so many of the seamen were disabled, that it was a hard matter for them to get the boats back to the sea. In the meantime another disaster had taken place on the beach near the town. An attempt having been made to land some Fantee

1. See his letters published in the Blue books.

police (to garrison the fort) the natives attacked the boat, killed a sea-man, and carried off his head in triumph to the Ashantee camp. Soon afterwards, a similar event occurred at Tacorady, where the natives, lying in ambush near the beach, fired into the boats of the *Argus* with effect, and wounded the officer commanding.

However, that was the last advantage gained by the army of the west and their allies. Dixcove and King Blay continued to hold their own; Chamah, Axim and the other hostile villages were thoroughly bombarded; Atchampong himself was killed by the fragment of a shell; a steam launch ran up and down the coast catching the fishermen in their canoes, and at last not a native dared show himself either on the sea or on the beach. That the enemy might not obtain supplies, a naval blockade was proclaimed as far as Assinie, but that port being French could not be interfered with, and the Ashantees still continued to buy powder and guns through King Amatifoo.

We heard of the disaster on the Prah at Madeira, and most of us declared it was the reverse of a disaster for the expedition. Hitherto the British people had looked upon the war with languor and actual distrust: it was a war, said the world, which could bring us neither glory nor gain; it would cost money: many fine young men would perish ignobly from the climate, and victories gained over naked sav-ages could not be viewed with satisfaction. We like to hit men of our own size. Then as to the causes of the war, no one knew what they were, yet most people had their misgivings. It was a common impres-sion that somehow or other we, the strong people, were in the wrong, and that the blunders of civil officials had brought this trouble upon us. But the disaster on the Prah was a blow in the face before Europe, and it stirred the spirit of the Nation.

CHAPTER 10

Wolseley's Reconnaissance

The visit of Wolseley to the Gold Coast may fairly be termed a Reconnaissance. First he had to discover whether he was to fight the Ashantees at all; secondly he had to discover whether he was to fight them only with the natives, or with European troops as well: thirdly he had to discover what means and appliances would be required for the campaign.

He sent his manifesto to the king, but had no need to wait for an answer; it was quite certain that the Ashantees would not give in before they had been defeated.

Sir G. Wolseley then called a *durbar* of kings and chiefs of Fantee. He informed them that the Queen of England having heard with much concern of their sufferings had sent him out to assist them. At the same time Her Majesty would not assist those who did, not assist themselves. It was not an English war, but a Fantee war, and the forts were so strong that the English themselves had nothing to fear from the Ashantees, But the queen wished to help the Fantees, The only interest she had in the Gold Coast was the promotion of their welfare by spreading among them the arts and blessings of civilization (*sic*). Sir Garnet then proceeded to business, and explained that each king or chief would be required to return to his own country accompanied by a special service officer for the purpose of raising men. The chiefs would receive a bounty of 10*l*. a month for all fighting men brought into the field, and they would be supplied with food, ammunition and a small payment of money *per diem*. Dunquah was appointed as the rendezvous, and as soon as a large camp was formed Sir Garnet would go out there himself.

Sir Garnet's flowers of rhetoric were rather thrown away, for the Fantees knew very well that we keep up these settlements for purposes of trade, and they also knew it was scarcely correct to say it was not an English war. However, they replied in the same style, declaring that, 'if they had been dead the governor's speech would have made them alive,' and that it was clear to them he would walk in the footsteps of Macarthy. (Sir Garnet did not much relish this comparison, but it is the highest praise Fantees can bestow.) They reserved their reply for a second interview, but it was already evident that they had no taste for the war. They discussed the matters of bounty and pay precisely as if they were foreign mercenaries, and had nothing to do with the invasion of their country.

The truth was that the Ashantee invasion was at an end; all the mischief had been done; their villages were burnt and their plantations destroyed. Soon the Ashantees would go home, and then they would have peace for ten years or so, that being the usual period. The new governor had said in his speech, 'If you will cordially unite in fighting your hereditary foes, I will inflict upon them such a punishment that you will never be troubled by them for all time to come. I shall first drive them out of protected territory, and then, if necessary, I shall be prepared to follow them into their own country.'

Now they knew well enough that, even if they did unite under the new governor, he would not be able to do anything of the kind. For Sir Garnet did not allude to other forces which he might employ; he promised that he would defeat the Ashantees with an army of Fantees, and they, the Fantees, knew better.

A number of special service officers were sent off to the bush with the various kings and chiefs, but it was generally understood that the native levies would come to nought. There was still some hope that a large force might be brought in from the other settlements; however, this hope soon came to an end. In the Gambia not a single man could be raised; it will be some day yet an excellent recruiting-ground, but the Africans require time when asked to adopt an innovation. From Sierra Leone came some colonists, and a small but useful force of Kossoos. About a hundred Haussas were sent up from Lagos.

Lieutenant Bolton, 1st West India regiment, was sent to Winnebah, and enlisted a fine company. Captain Nicol, of the Hampshire Militia, a special service officer, went to the rivers Bonny and Opobo, and brought up two companies. From these recruits two native regiments were formed under the command of Lieutenant-Colonel Wood, V.C., 90th regiment, and Major Russell, 13th Hussars. As will hereafter be seen, these two regiments did most excellent service in the war. But they were few in number, and it was some time before they were drilled into soldiers.

Before Sir Garnet had been appointed, a few officers had already come out to the coast for the purpose of organizing native troops. Most of these had accepted civil appointments; but there was one man who, even in those early days, was always spoken of with admiration, and who went through the whole campaign to the taking of Coomassie. This was Lieutenant Gordon, 98th regiment. He was first appointed to command the Haussas *vice* Captain Hopkins, 2nd West India regiment, deceased.

Under the orders of Lieutenant-Colonel Festing he had raised two redoubts, Napoleon and Abbaye, covering Cape Coast Castle and Elmina, distant about six miles from each respectively. The use of these redoubts at once became apparent, for as soon as they were occupied the Fantees began to till the plantations lying between the earthworks and the coast. Pioneer Gordon (as he deserves to be named) then set to work with Fantee labourers, and began the road to Coomassie, widening the bush-path as far as Mansu, about halfway to the Prah. That was a most daring enterprise, for the Ashantees might at any time have cut him off from the coast; happily, as we now have ascertained, they do not indulge in cutting-out expeditions, and seldom know what is going on at any distance from their camp.

Sir Garnet at once placed Gordon on his list of special service officers, and Major Home, R.E., took up the work of road-making. This brave and talented officer pushed on to Mansu, and erected a fort, 'intrenching himself up to the eyes.' At one time his position was dangerous, and he was ordered to evacuate his post; he disobeyed orders and remained. Various officers were employed in making military surveys of the roads to Abbaye, Napoleon, Dunquah, &c.; an Intelligence Department was formed, and spies engaged, though with little success. A detachment of the 2nd West was sent to occupy Accroful, a village about fourteen miles from Cape Coast, on the road to Coomassie. The defences of Elmina and Cape Coast were improved, sanitary measures were discussed, information was gathered in a general way, and then—nothing more could be done.

It had been hoped by the government that Sir Garnet Wolseley would be able to inflict defeat upon the Ashantees soon after his arrival, and that then they would make peace, and the affair would be done with. But one slight omission had been made; the government did not give him any men. It could not be supposed that the 140 marines on board the *Simoom* and a small body of seamen would be sufficient for the purpose: no, it was hoped that he and his forty officers would be able to turn wood into iron, or, in other words, Fantees into soldiers. What was the consequence? The ludicrous spectacle was offered to the world of a major-general and his staff, without any army, and without any hope of getting an army for months to come; while the enemy lay only fifteen miles off, in such a position and at such a distance from its base that, with a sufficient force of disciplined troops, it might have been utterly destroyed.

Sir Garnet Wolseley cannot be absolved entirely from blame. He knew when he left England that the Ashantee army was close to the sea-board, and surely he might have anticipated what would be the result. He told me himself on board the *Ambriz*, when I talked (as I often did) about the necessity for regiments, that he was sure Coomassie could not be taken without them, and he was even then inclined to believe that in any case they would be required. Still I think he had a hope lurking in his breast that he would be able to organise an army of Fantees. Nor is that astonishing; for I presume, that in common with most Englishmen, he scarcely knew where the Gold Coast was before the summer of 1873.

But the great men of the Colonial Office are intimately acquainted with the history of Gold Coast affairs, and of the various wars between Fantee and Ashantee. What right had they, judging from past experience, to believe in an army of 'Fantees?' The most hopeful of men would be only justified in supposing that, if white troops were employed in sufficient numbers to defeat the Ashantees, our native allies might be useful as cavalry to harass in pursuit; or to serve as escorts to baggage; to garrison posts; and in the enemy's country to plunder plantations, and burn villages upon the flanks. The fate of Sir Charles Macarthy was alone sufficient to prove that a few Europeans, whatever their talents might be, could do nothing with a mob of native allies.

There were two ways in which the war might have been waged by the British Government against the Ashantees. If it were judged that public opinion would not support a definite campaign, such as that of Abyssinia, then the war should have been left to the Colonial Office. Festing should have been supplied with special service officers, and money, and stores, and commissioned to operate against the enemy in the central region of the Gold Coast, on the same principles as those by which Glover was guided in the district of the Volta. A war of that kind could not, with all the luck in the world, have been a genuine success, but it might have attained the appearance of success, and with good management a treaty of peace might have been concluded. On the other hand, these native expeditions might have ended in a catastrophe. In any case the war would have been conducted on consistent, though ill-judged, principles.

But if the Home Government had determined from the first to do what they afterwards did—to wage war in the Abyssinian style—then they should have employed officers of secondary rank to do the preliminary work in the way of transport, road-making, the organisation of native regiments, and so forth, and the major-general should have come out with his regiments. If the Ashantee army was close to the shore the regiments might have been landed at once: if the Ashantees had returned home, and long preparations were necessary for the march upon Coomassie, the regiments might have been sent out to sea in their troop-ships for a cruise. In no case would it have been necessary to land them until they were required.

But the government could not make up their minds as to which course should be pursued, and so compromised the matter by sending out the commander-in-chief, and leaving him to decide after his arrival on the coast whether he would like to have an army or not. Sir Garnet very soon asked for an army; but more than two months would of necessity elapse before the army could arrive. This time was spent in harassing the enemy and in making preparations for the march upon Coomassie.

While Festing was in command of Her Majesty's forces on the Gold Coast, he had planned an attack on the Ashantee camp at Mampon. The marines who had come out with him on board the *Himalaya*, and who fought at Elmina, had quite melted away? only one man remained at Elmina, and was nicknamed 'The Fossil.' But a second force of marines had been sent in the hospital ship *Simoom*; these had not been landed, and were in an efficient condition. Captain Fremantle, the senior naval officer upon the station, placed at Festing's disposal about two hundred bluejackets;[1] he had also a small force of Haussas and 2nd West.

A most distinguished officer, Deputy Surgeon-General Home, V.C., C.B., intended to accompany the troops, and had made his arrangements for medical transport. All was ready for the enterprise, when the news came that Sir G. Wolseley was on his way to the Gold

---

1. *Victoria's Blue Jackets & Marines*: the Royal Navy during Queen Victoria's reign 1839-1901 by W. H. G. Kingston and G. A. Henty also published by Leonaur.

Coast; the attack was therefore postponed until his arrival, and he judged it over-hazardous. The Ashantees were many thousand strong, and Mampon was a strong, bush-covered position. However, Sir Garnet abhorred inactivity, and he wished to do something which might gain him the faith of the native allies. So he looked round about for the means of gaining a small but certain success against the enemy; and soon he found his opportunity.

CHAPTER 11

Essaman

On October 11, about the middle of the day, I heard that the West India soldiers were being marched down from Connor's Hill, and embarked on board the *Decoy*. It was clear that something important was about to be done, for these men garrisoned the town. I ran over to Government House for permission to join the expedition, whatever it might be, and was told that Glover was in a mess, being hemmed in at Addah by a tribe called the Awoonas. The Major-General was going down there with troops to his assistance, and if I would be on the beach at 9 p.m., I could have a passage on board the *Barracouta*. No baggage allowed. Now it so happened that I knew something about the Awoonas and Addah. That town is situated near the mouth of the Volta, on the right bank.

The Awoonas, a tribe friendly to the Ashantees, lived on the other side. How then could Captain Glover, who had a strong body of Haussas, be hemmed in with a river in his front, the sea and Accra territory at his back? It also seemed to me strange that the general was not going till 9 p.m., for Addah was a long way off; and why should no baggage be allowed, since, if a battle had to be fought, we should be absent at least three days? At all events, I was not going without my cork bed and my rug, which I rolled up together, putting inside a shirt, a pair of socks, and some tins of preserved meat, chocolate, &c. It did not make a large bundle, and I thought I could smuggle it on board.

A little before nine I went down to the beach and found Festing, wrapped in a military cloak, leaning against some timber. After a little conversation I said, 'I don't understand how Glover can be in a mess.'

'Glover is not in a mess,' said he.

'Then why are we going to Addah?' asked I.

'You will find out when you get on board,' he replied. 'Don't say anything about it here; I ought not to have given you even a hint.'

This redoubled my curiosity, and I longed to get on board. At that moment we heard the song of Fantee canoe-men; then two dark objects passed through the white flashing waters, and two large surf-boats grounded on the beach. A number of sailors sprang out. Festing told me that these were to garrison the castle during the absence of the West India soldiery, and that he was left in command.

At nine o'clock to a moment the general, followed by his staff, came down to the water-side, and soon the surf-boats were filled. On arriving aboard the *Barracouta* I found all quiet; there were no preparations for departure, and so it was certain we were not going very far. Soon the truth came out; our destination was Elmina.

Lieutenant-Colonel Wood, V.C., had been appointed commandant of that town, with orders to obtain the formal submission of its chiefs. Although the king had been sent off to Sierra Leone for 'eating fetish,' or taking an oath of friendship with the Ashantees, and although the rebel quarter of the town had been destroyed, the Ashantees had still many friends in Elmina who supplied them with rum, cloth, powder, &c, which were taken by night in canoes to a village called Ampenee. It was situated on the beach, and its people were great fishermen, and supplied the Ashantees with smoked fish. They were also fishers of men, having not long before captured two Cape Coast canoes, and killed its paddlers and the passengers, dashing out children's brains against the gunwales of the canoes.

But they knew that at any moment a 'smoke-ship' might come and destroy the village with shells, and therefore another village, Essaman, was selected as the Ashantee magazine. An Ashantee captain and his company always resided in that village, which was in the midst of a dense jungle four miles away from the sea There the insurgents driven from Elmina used to speak of building a new town, where they would be secure from the white men, for white men could not fight in the bush; and there large quantities of rum, powder, dried fish, and corn were stored up.

The women of these villages went to market at Mampon, selling, for gold-dust, their fish and corn; and at times they were so numerous that the camp presented the appearance of a fair. But every evening when the sun went down the Ashantees heard the booming of the gun at Abbaye, and then they assembled and cursed.

Colonel Wood summoned the headmen of the villages to present themselves before him at the Castle. Those who lived near Elmina obeyed; those who lived a little farther off made excuses for their absence; Essaman and Ampenee refused to attend. Colonel Wood threatened to fetch them; upon which Essaman replied 'Come on!' Sir G. Wolseley determined to accept this invitation.

Cape Coast Castle and Elmina were said to be full of Ashantee spies; the expedition was therefore kept secret. Cape Coast was put on a false scent, and during the night policemen guarded every exit from Elmina. It was intended to surprise Essaman and to reach the village at dawn. But the landing of the marines in large troop-boats took more time than had been anticipated, and it was broad day before we started from Elmina, The order of march was as follows: 126 Haussas under Lieutenants Richmond, Wood, and Graves; 16 2nd West under Lieutenant Eyre (these were special service officers attached to Wood's Irregular Regiment, as yet unformed).

Next came the General, carried in a hammock, and attended by the following officers of his Staff:—Colonel McNeill, V.C., C.M.G.; Major Baker, 18th Royal Irish, Assistant-Adjutant and Quarter-Master-General; Captain Henry Brackenbury, R.A., Assistant Military Secretary; Lieutenant the Hon. A. Charteris, Coldstream Guards, A.D.C. Then 29 blue-jackets under Captain Fremantle, with Lieutenants Maxwell and Grey, R.N; a 7-pounder Abyssinian gun, carried on a bamboo by *kroomen*, the trail being run along behind; a rocket detachment with a trough and 20 men of the Royal Marine Artillery, under Lieutenant Allan, R.M.A.; 10 armed police and 30 axemen under Captain Buller of the Staff, D.-A.A. and Q.-M.-G.

Next came the main body, consisting of 129 Royal Marine Light Infantry, commanded by Captain Crease, R.M.A., with Lieutenant Moore, R.M.A. 60 labourers followed carrying ammunition-boxes and hammocks, the ambulance of the Gold Coast; they were under the direction of Assistant-Commissary Beardmore. The medical service was admirably organised by Deputy Surgeon-General Home, V.C., C.B., and represented by Surgeons-Major Jackson and Mosse, Surgeons S. Moore and Atkins, and the Royal Navy surgeons Adams and Moore. 65 West India soldiers brought up the rear, under Captains Forbes, Brett, and Fowler, and Lieutenant Devereux. Two loyal chiefs of Elmina, with 20 men, served as guides to the column, which was commanded by Colonel Wood, so that there were no less than three V.C's. in this little expedition.

It was a clear calm morning, with scarcely a cloud in the sky, and as the sun rose above the horizon birds sang sweetly from the bushes which covered the plain. We marched in single file along a footpath which was sometimes of red clay, sometimes of golden-coloured sand; at one moment we dived into a thicket deep and dark, and the next passed out into green meadows with tall tufted grass and large white flowers bathing in sunlit dew. But then came a quagmire of mud black as registration ink, and giving forth an odour compared with which the Thames at low-tide is rose-water; and never have I seen such abominable hamlets as the two we passed on our way. In the first were a few people who surveyed us with an air of innocence and virtue; the second was deserted.

The country at first was tolerably open, and we could distinguish far away the Haussas running along thickets and copses to and fro on the right of the road and on the left, like a pack of hounds, their officers in Elwood helmets and streaming white *puggerees* plainly to be seen, and always well ahead of their men. One or two shots were heard, but still it did not seem certain that we should find the enemy. We had marched three miles, and as a marine expressed it, 'we had seen no game.' I was beginning to fear that the day would be blank, when of a sudden we heard a tremendous fusillade and a strange gleeful yelling cry—the Haussas giving tongue. As we pushed on we found that the jungle was before us stretching away on both sides as far as the eye could reach. In the centre was a hill also covered with bush, except that upon its summit was a clearing or plantation.

Some men were seen crossing this open space, and Lieutenant Eyre put on his spectacles, sighted his rifle at 300 yards, and dropped his man, which probably astonished the natives. A little to the right of the clearing and also on the hill was the village. The rear was attacked, and I remained there some time. Then we saw on ahead rockets flying through the air above the trees, and soon afterwards a thick column of smoke mounted up. I followed Major Baker up the hill: a naked dead body lay across the path, and my servant told me it was a Haussa— probably an Ashantee slave. These men know one another's nationality by certain marks, upon the cheek, or by the style in which the hair is cut. We met Colonel McNeill coming down the hill, his right arm bared and covered with a bandage already reddened by his blood. This wound was very severe, precisely resembling those which are caused by fragments of shell, and the colonel was invalided home, to the general regret.

Sir Garnet Wolseley was standing up to his waist in high grass: on his right was the burning village. Brackenbury and Charteris were the first to be in at the head of some marines, while Captain Crease cleared the bush on the right. Afterwards, entering the village, that officer saved a child from the flames, and throughout the severe march which followed, the marines disputed as to who should 'carry the kid.'

The first shot of the campaign was fired at Lieutenant Graves, and the shot lodged in his gaiter. Captain Buller, who was surveying the road, had a shot in his leather compass-case. A slug passed through Captain Fremantle's right arm, but he went through the whole work of the day.

The general now gave orders that a clearing should be made. Sentries were posted. The men had their breakfast. At 7.15 the heavy firing began; at 7.50 the village was taken, and the enemy driven from the bush; at 8.30 the Assembly was sounded; and at 9.15 the march was resumed.

It is difficult to describe that human tornado which raged for half an hour over half a mile of African bush. The enemy were on all sides, and the firing incessant. The air was all flame and smoke, and filled with various sounds—the booming of guns, the whizzing of rockets, the cracking of Sniders, shouts, groans, laughter, the whistling of slugs; Haussas chanting verses from the *Koran*, English hurrahing; and then, as the village began to burn, the roaring of flames, explosions of powder, and blazing of rum.

While we were at breakfast we heard big guns in the distance: this was the *Decoy* bombarding Ampenee. We marched off again in the same order towards the seashore. Colonel McNeill and other wounded men were carried in hammocks, and our progress was slow. It was afternoon before we had reached the village Amquena, between Elmina and Ampenee. It was set in flames, and then we all threw ourselves down under a grove of cocoa-nut trees. As we looked up their winding stems, we saw nestling under the parasol-like spreading leaves great bunches of green nuts—a delicious sight for thirsty souls.

Some of these were prodded down with a pole as long as a flagstaff, kept by the villagers for that purpose. Negroes climbed up the trees and threw down the nuts, which fell with a mighty thud. Then, slashing away the green rind with a knife, and scooping out a hole, we drank from these lemonade bottles which Nature has filled and corked with such generous care. The so-called cocoa-nut milk is the colour of water, and though very sweet, delightfully cool and refreshing.

So we rested for a time on the soft grey sand, inhaling the odour of the sea. Above us the palm leaves rustled and rattled in the wind, giving forth a sound just like the pattering of rain. Before us lay the broad blue sea, and away to the left we could plainly see, like a white mountain, the castle of Elmina.

But we had to look the other way, for Ampenee had still to be disposed of. It would be a weary trudge, and the march had already been severe: so only volunteers were taken from the seamen and marines, and these passed before a doctor. The others escorted the twelve hammocks of the wounded to Elmina.

There is no harder work than walking along the beach under an African sun. The sand is soft as snow, so that you feel as if leaden weights were fixed to your boots; and the glare from the sea is not agreeable. When we drew near the village, surf-boats came off from the *Decoy* and landed a case of claret, some breakers of water, and some bottles of brandy, for which we were not ungrateful, and the following officers landed: Captain Luxmoore, having recovered from the wounds received in the Prah; Lieutenant Young, (wounded at Tacorady), with Lieutenant Hext commanding the *Decoy*; Lieutenant Burr, Sub-Lieutenant Sanderson, Surgeons Fisher and Lucas.

We found two villages before us. Akimpfoo was destroyed without resistance. We then crossed a small stream and came to Ampenee. A flag was flying in defiance, and on the beach was a naked body swollen to an enormous size by the sun, the head and right hand severed from the body. He might have been a Fantee prisoner, or perhaps a human sacrifice to avert danger from the village; for such sacrifices are not confined to Ashantee, though they have fallen into disuse on the seaboard through the influence of European opinion and law.

Ampenee was undefended, and was set in a blaze. It seemed to be filled with rats, cats, and bats, which come out in extraordinary numbers. While the village was burning, the natives crept up through the bush, at the edge of the beach, and made an attack; and here we heard rifle bullets. Only one Haussa was wounded, and the men of the *Decoy* got a fair sight at a crowd, and laid many of them low.

At 4.25 the general embarked on board the *Decoy*, and kindly offered me a passage. We arrived at Cape Coast Castle at 7 p.m. I asked my Haussa servant how he liked the fight; he replied that he liked it very much: it was just like 'shooting meat'—by which he meant to say that it resembled the pleasures of the chase.

In itself the combat of Essaman was merely a day's skirmishing, but was raised to importance by the experience it yielded, and the morale effect it produced. It proved to the natives that white men were able to fight in the bush: it showed that the new governor was not a mere bookman writing at a desk, but a man of war like Macarthy. All admired the style in which he had carried out his plan of operations. The attack on Essaman was a genuine surprise: the natives had no time to remove their powder, their corn, their sheep, and their rum: muskets and drums and powder-belts were found in the village; a mother ran away leaving her child behind.

This affair of Essaman was also conducive to peace and good-fellowship between the Elminas and the English.

Savages, when hostile, are not to be conciliated until they have been conquered. Give them presents, write them *billets-doux*, surrender captives in the Mr. Pope Hennessy style, and they, supposing that these concessions are made from fear, display more hostility, in order that the fear may increase with its consequent concessions. But put them down with a strong hand, and you gain not only their submission, but also their esteem. One might suppose that the burning of Essaman and Ampenee would have excited the undying hatred of the headmen and elders; but, on the contrary, they soon afterwards marched into Cape Coast, waving the British flag, and requesting that they might be allowed to take the oath of allegiance to Her Majesty the Queen.

CHAPTER 12

Concerted Movements

I believe that Sir Garnet after this affair did at one time think of attacking the camp at Mampon; and the Ashantees expected something of the kind, for escaped prisoners used to relate that often there would be a cry, 'The white men are coming!' and then they would all run off into the bush, and the drums would beat, and the army would form into position, the skirmishers in front, the generals in rear. There can be no doubt that the Ashantees at Mampon would have fought as they did at Amoaful. The whole army, the nation was there; and Sir Garnet could not have won a victory with three hundred seamen and marines and his negro troops. He had been taught at Essaman that the enemy were not to be despised.

He had also been taught that the Haussas, though splendid irregulars, full of dash and pluck, were quite unmanageable in battle, and fired wildly, squandering their ammunition. The West India men did not do so well at Essaman as afterwards in other skirmishes where they deserved and obtained high praise. The general, therefore, having merely a handful of men on whom he could rely, did not venture to attack the camp; but on October 25 news came that the enemy were in retreat, or, in other words, on the homeward march, and broken up into separate columns. He thought that because the army was divided he could attack it at an advantage; but strange to say, he divided his own little army, and thus copied the weakness of the enemy.

Some little time before he had sent Festing to Dunquah, the appointed rendezvous for the native allies. Festing built a stockaded fort, and cleared the bush all round. Only a few hundred natives were brought in by the officers sent to the Fantee chiefs: of these the greater part were Assins and Annamaboes. Fifty men of the 2nd West, with two seven-pounder guns and a rocket-trough, with ammunition, were

95

afterwards placed at Festing's disposal.

It having been reported by the Intelligence Department that a large force of Ashantees under Essamanquatia was moving between Dunquah and a village called Abrakrampa, the general determined to attack it, and his plan of operations was as follows. He with 200 seamen and marines would proceed on the 26th to Esseboo—a ruined village ten miles from Cape Coast—and there bivouac. On the 27th he would march through Abrakrampa into the bush towards Dunquah; and at the same time Festing was to march from Dunquah towards Abrakrampa.

But Sir Garnet's seamen and marines were so fatigued by the hot afternoon march to Esseboo, that he did not go further the next day than Abrakrampa; so Festing went out by himself, came upon the Ashantees in camp, and fought them the whole afternoon. Several officers were slightly wounded, including himself; while Captain Godwin, 103rd Bombay Fusiliers, was badly hit, and had to be invalided home. The West India men fought well, but, in Festing's memorable phrase, he had to use 'more than verbal persuasion' to make the native levies fight at all. The English claimed the victory, but a part only of the camp was destroyed, and the enemy did not abandon their position.

The next morning Sir Garnet marched out towards Dunquah, having ordered Festing the night before to meet him halfway. But the native levies would not fight two days consecutively, and refused to budge from their huts.

The Ashantee camp was about two miles from Dunquah, and seven miles from Abrakrampa. Sir Garnet marched about five miles with his seamen and marines, sat down in the shade for a couple of hours, and then marched back to Abrakrampa. The next day he returned to Cape Coast.

The simple relation of these incidents produces the impression caused by satirical writing; and, in fact, a more complete mistake than Sir Garnet's first march to Abrakrampa can scarcely be conceived. Had he joined his forces to those of Festing at Dunquah, he might have attacked the enemy with some prospect of success. But that was not sufficiently ingenious; so he planned a highly intricate movement which ended in this—that the worst half of his forces got too much fighting and the best half got none at all.

The truth is that concerted movements demanding exactitude of place and time should in African warfare never be attempted. Something is sure to go wrong. The distance is miscalculated; or the way is lost; or carriers desert; or it is 'an unlucky day' with the natives; or the white men are fatigued; or the black men are lazy. Sir Garnet Wolseley made that mistake which cost Sir Charles Macarthy his life—the playing at chessboard warfare in the African bush. Happily this time it ended in farce, not in tragedy. There is much broad comedy in the proclamation issued by Sir Garnet in the first moment of triumph after his return, and it ought to be preserved as a curiosity of military literature. To use the language of the stage, it is a Screamer:—

Garnet Joseph Wolseley, Major-General, Administrator.
To all the Kings, Headmen, Chiefs, and Tribes of the Gold Coast, allies of Her Majesty the Queen of England, greeting. I desire that you should know that immediately after the attack made upon Essaman and Ampenee, and the destruction of those places by the English troops under my command, your enemies broke up their encampment at Mampon. Finding that they were unable to contend with us either in the open or in the bush, they are now in full retreat, endeavouring to return to their own country by Prahsue. One of their retreating columns has been attacked and dispersed by my troops near Dunquah. They are trying to carry with them in their flight all the goods of which they have robbed you, all the wives and children whom they have stolen from you.
Men of the Gold Coast, will you allow this?
Will you let the hours slip by while your wives, your sons, and your daughters are being driven off to slaughter by the flying enemy?
Will you not pursue them?
Now or never is the time to show that you are men.
I for my part shall hold no man as the friend of Her Majesty or as the friend of this country who delays for one moment
You have nothing to fear. I hold the whole road from here to Mansu, so that they cannot assail it. Gather upon my strong forts of Dunquah, Abrakampa, and Mansu. No one will venture to attack these points. Thence press onwards to the Prah and oppose your enemies as they are endeavouring to recross the river. If you now act quickly and with vigour, the fall of your enemy and the peace of your country will be secured.
Given under my hand and public seal at Government House,

Cape Coast, this thirtieth day of October, in the year of our Lord one thousand eight hundred and seventy-three, and of Her Majesty's reign the thirty-seventh.

God Save the Queen.

CHAPTER 13

Abrakrampa

I lived in *Green Lettuce Lane*, a thoroughfare utterly devoid of lettuces or anything green whatever, except certain young gentlemen who sometimes called upon me to gaze with love-struck eyes on Jessie C——, the *belle* of Cape Coast. She passed the cool hours of the day in a neighbouring verandah, and sat there sewing or ironing, apparently unconscious of the admiration she excited. In Cape Coast Castle there are no white ladies, but Jessie, if not the rose or the lily, was as near to them as could be; indeed she was the rose when she blushed and the lily when fear blanched her cheek. She was engaged to a coloured gentleman, and the marriage was postponed by the war; for, first, her lover became a Rifle Volunteer, and found it easier to get into that gallant corps than to get out of it, having placed himself under military-law; secondly, when he did get permission to retire, and the cake had come out from England, and everything was ready, Sir Garnet was taking Coomassie, and in Cape Coast Castle the licence can only be signed by the governor. However, it was sent up by the post, and came down again duly signed, and the wedding party were at breakfast just as Sir Garnet returned in triumph from the war.

Like a flower in a vase, or a picture on a wall, this fair girl adorned Green Lettuce Lane, and reminded us of those who were mourning or flirting in our absence. However, to return, I had a neat little house, newly painted and whitewashed, with four rooms on the first floor and a kitchen below. Its windows, which I am proud to say were of glass, commanded a view of the light- house, where signal-flags were hoisted to acquaint the town with the approach of steamers from home, or steamers for home, men–of-war, sailing-ships, &c. At dawn, when Joseph or Lake brought me my tea, I peered out at the flagstaff to know if I had to finish my letter that morning; for as the mail-steamers came irregularly, and did not stay very long, Correspondents were always in a flutter, and I used to look at the lighthouse almost as often as I did at the verandah.

Joseph, who enjoyed the office of cook, had been with me in my journey of 1869; he was a Mendi or Kossoo. Edward Lake, who served as my footman in peace and Snider-bearer in war, called himself a Haussa, and spoke that language like a native, but was really born in the kingdom of Bornu, near the shores of Lake Tchad. I had also a Fantee interpreter, whose English name was Robert Jones, and he had engaged for me a gang of hammock-men.

It was the custom in Rome for a gentleman's clients and slaves to present themselves in a formal manner and wish him 'Good day;' the same custom exists in Africa, and is strictly kept up, for I once saw a slave being carried off to be flogged because he had not given the morning salutation. Mr. Robert Jones complied with this ancient ceremony, and also used to enquire whether I should want the hammock that day. I had always to reply in the negative, much to my discontent, for it was dull work staying at Cape Coast.

However, it was not to last. One day I was told that the Steam Sapper would perform, and that an Ashantee prisoner who was being sent with a letter to the King would be favoured with a ride. The Steam Sapper was an engine on carriage-wheels, with a steering apparatus, so that it could turn corners. The Fantees, who called it the 'Land Steamer,' collected in a vast crowd, and when it began to move uttered screams, compared with which the whistle of the engine was melodious and subdued. Several of us climbed into the truck and waited for the prisoner. We charitably hoped that the Steam Sapper would frighten him out of his wits, but he took his seat as coolly as a railway passenger with a season ticket. The fact is that when a man expects to have his head cut off every moment, he is not easily impressed by the wonders of science.

On asking the news from a staff officer, I was told that the Ashantee army was encamped close to Abrakrampa, and that an attack was hourly expected. I thought of going there, and asked Captain Butler's advice. He said the attack was imminent, and I ought not to go without an escort. I called Mr. Robert Jones, who, with the hammock-men, belonged to Abrakrampa. He said that when Amanquatia was on his way to the coast he had passed near that village, and had left it alone; but as its inhabitants (who belonged to the Arbra tribe) had troubled him much in his march, and killed many of his men, he had sworn a great oath that he would attack it on his return.

I determined to get into the village if I could, but had no right to ask for an escort: and therefore thought it best to make my attempt under cover of the night. Besides, no time was to be lost. As my men knew the village and its secret paths, I took it for granted they would get me safe in, somehow or other; and when I told them to get ready by 10 p.m. to go to Abrakrampa, they did not make any objection.

At 9.30 I went over to Government House to ask the general whether I could take anything for him to Abrakrampa, for I supposed that the regular communications were closed. The headquarters' mess were at dessert, and Charteris came out into the passage. When I told him my intention, he said, 'I wouldn't go if I were you,' and then asked me in. The dining-room presented a splendid appearance. It was always 'guest-night' at Government House.

All the officers were in full dress, and almost all wore a different uniform. There were the Guards, the Artillery, the Engineers, the Rifles, and other regiments. Then the table itself was rich in colour, with golden bananas, deep green melons, the wax-lights shining through the decanters and casting rosy reflections on the shining mahogany; for that abomination of modern desserts, the table-cloth, had been removed. I sat down for a few moments, received two bottles of champagne for Major Russell's mess at Abrakrampa, and then rose to go. As I went down the stone steps outside, I heard Charteris say, 'Well, I am sorry for Reade.' That was the last time I heard him speak. A few days afterwards he was sent on board the *Simoom* and died on the way to St. Helena. He was a handsome, noble-looking young man, and a good officer; he displayed gallantry at Essaman, and was of a most gentle and kindly disposition.

I found my hammock ready, and jumping in, was carried out of the town at a trot. Hammock-men on the Gold Coast are the substitute for horses, which will not live in that country for any length of time. Two men form a perfect animal, with four black legs, the hammock-pole serving as the spine, and the hammock itself as a saddle. If the road is wide enough, four men carry; and for long journeys, six or eight men are employed—thus giving relays. Good hammock-men will go short distances at five miles an hour, or thirty miles a day.

An excellent road had already been made as far as Dunquah, and only wanted a turnpike here and there to give it a perfectly civilised appearance. Our first stopping place was Yamolanza, where I was informed the men wanted to 'blow.' It was a wayside station, with a few shanties and a policeman's hut On a tree was a placard, announcing that 'all extravagant noises would be put a stop to by the police,' and the sergeant in command showed me a paper which I examined by the light of the lantern and found to be a time-table of the military post, containing also the announcement that henceforth a fast mail would run every day between Cape Coast Castle and Dunquah.

The moon was at her full, and the country at first low jungle and scrub. Now and then we passed through a small grove; gigantic trees, uniting their branches above, made it dark as pitch, just like going through a tunnel. Strange odours arose from the bush—odours that arise by night alone—sometimes fetid, sometimes fragrant, but always sharp and powerful.

Esseboo had been burnt by the Ashantees, but a few cottages had escaped the conflagration, and these were now inhabited. Robert woke up some people and asked them about the enemy. He was told that the bush-path from Esseboo to Abrakrampa was now in occupation, or, as they expressed it, shut, by the Ashantees; but the path from Batian was open. So we went on to the village Batian, which was a little way farther; up the main road. There I dismounted, and we struck into the forest. The moon had gone down, so Robert walked before me with the lantern.

I must confess that I did not enjoy that four-mile walk. The Ashantees, it would seem, intended to invest Abrakrampa, and they had occupied the Esseboo road; their next step would naturally be to occupy the Batian road, and who could tell whether they might not have done it that very afternoon? The idea of walking into the Ashantee camp with a lantern was not by any means attractive. My men would dash off into the bush like deer, but running is not one of my accomplishments. I should be caught to a certainty, and have my head sawed off in the morning, or perhaps be kept for exhibition at Coomassie, and starved to death on the way. Then everyone would say, 'How absurdly imprudent!' 'Ought to have known better.' 'Served him right,' &c. &c. Such were the gloomy thoughts which passed through my mind, and I gave a gasp of relief when I heard a voice cry out 'Who go dare?' and saw the dim outline of the houses in the village. We went up the street, and were challenged no less than three times, on the last occasion by a marine. The garrison was on the alert.

We arrived at 4 a.m., and at 7 a.m. shots were fired close to the village; the bugles sounded the Alarm, and I saw in all directions men running in haste, but with method, to their posts. However, it was only

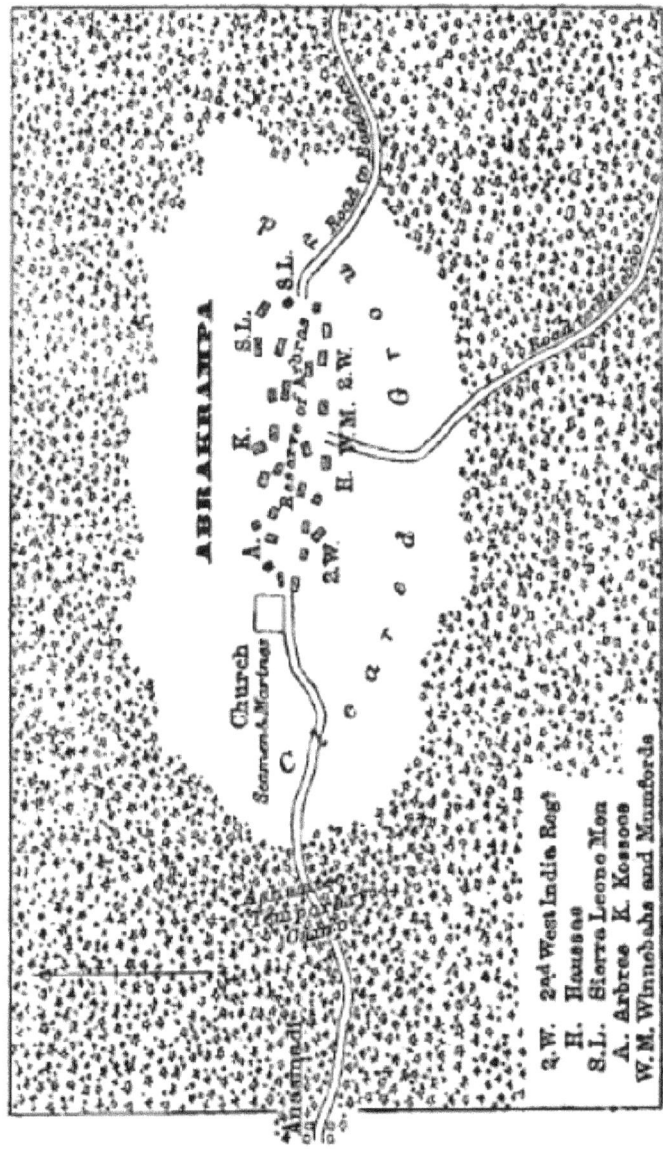

ABRAKRAMPA

Church
Seamen & Marines

Road to Bassa

Road to...

Reserve of Arbras

S.L.   K.   A.

2.W.   H.   W.M.   S.W.

C

Ansamah
The Parade Ground

2.W.   2nd West India Reg.t
H.   Houssas
S.L.   Sierra Leone Men
A.   Arbras   K. Kossos
W.M. Winnebahs and Mumfords

a few stray skirmishers.

Although Sir Garnet in his Proclamation had informed the Fantees (who knew more about it than he did) that the Ashantees would not dare to attack his fortified posts, he had prepared Abrakrampa for a siege. The garrison consisted of 50 seamen and marines under Lieutenant Wells; 100 Haussas, Lieutenant Gordon, 98th Regiment; 93 2nd West, Captain Grant; 100 Kossoos, Lieutenant Woodgate; 64 Sierra Leone Volunteers, Lieutenant Hart; 114 disciplined Fantees from Winnebah and Mumford, Lieutenant Gordon, 93rd, and Lieutenant Lord Gifford. Abrakrampa was the capital of Arbra, and the king of that province was also in the village, with nearly 500 men, who were armed with muzzle loading Enfield rifles, or, like the Ashantees, with long Dane-guns (flint locks) and blunderbusses. To these Arbras Captain Bromhead was attached.

The defences of the village were begun by Pioneer Gordon, and concluded by Captain Huyshe of the Staff and Captain Buckle, R.E. At the upper end of the village was a Wesleyan chapel, which was occupied by the blue-jackets and marines, and was a perfect fortress in itself. The thatch had been taken off, and the roof or ceiling made an upper deck, on which was placed a rocket-trough and a little Dutch gun which had the name of 'Nelly' engraved upon its back, and was an object of tender affection to the sailors. The windows and open sides of the roof were filled and padded with sacks, behind which lay the men, who: arranged port-holes or embrasures for themselves. Shelter-trenches ran down the side of the village, which was partly enclosed by a palisade, and the houses were all of them loopholed. But the chief defence of Abrakrampa was its clearing. A large space of ground had been made open so that it afforded no cover from fire, and at the same time was littered with brushwood so that it could not be crossed at a rush. Before the Ashantees could enter the village, they would have to storm this open ground under fire of the Snider, and their loss would be severe.

As regards stores there was an abundance of Snider and Enfield ammunition, but the stock of rockets was small. There was plenty of rice, biscuits, salt pork, and tinned meat, tea, sugar, and so forth. The village was commanded by Major Baker Russell, 13th Hussars.

I shall now say a few words on the native troops which formed the major's regiment, and which may, perhaps, be regarded as the elements of our African army of the future. The Haussas come from Central Africa, and are Moslem by religion; their country in former times was a great and powerful empire, but has recently been conquered by the Foulas or Fellatahs. Kano, its capital, is the Manchester of Africa, supplying vast regions with blue cotton cloths. The Haussa language is dominant over a vast area, and spoken as a common language of trade by many different nations, and the Haussa people are found far and wide as travellers or slaves. There are many in Ashantee itself, while those who served with us came from Lagos and the countries of the Niger. Captain Glover first organised these people into soldiers, and is called 'The Father of the Haussas.' They are wild and undisciplined troops, often insubordinate, but always brave and eager, loving war like wine.

Kossoo is a word meaning 'wild boar,' which was given to the Mendi, a tribe of the Sherbro river, on account of their ferocity. The Kossoos differ from all other coast Africans in this, that they do not care for the musket, but fight chiefly with the sword. They are exceedingly courageous—'keen as mustard,' for the fray, and declare they have come to the Gold Coast to die.

The Winnebahs and Mumfords are Fantees, but became good soldiers after a time by fighting always in the company of Haussas and Kossoos. The Sierra Leone Volunteers behaved very well; and the men of the 2nd West (negroes from the West Indies), though they have not all the dash of the Haussas, nor all the steadiness of regular troops, are by no means deficient in either quality, and rendered good service in the campaign.

I arrived in the village on November 2. With the exception of Essamanquatia's division (about 2,000 strong), which was still at Escaboo, near Dunquah, the whole Ashantee army was encamped in and around the village Anasmadi, about a mile from Abrakrampa.

The Kossoos used to plunge into the forest with their swords in their hands, and cut off foragers. The Arbras also under their king spent most of the day rambling about, sometimes exchanging shots with Ashantee scouts.

On November 3 the Kossoos came in and declared that they had been to Anasmadi, and that nobody was there. Major Russell had received orders not to attack, but he ordered a reconnaissance in force to find out if the enemy had taken their departure.

The advance party consisted of Winnebahs and Mumfords, supported at a little distance by the Haussas. Lord Gifford, Lieutenant Pollard, and I walked at the head of the column, a negro named Tom Dollar and a Kossoo scout keeping two or three yards ahead. These experts carefully examined the war-paths which the Ashantees had cut to the right and left of the main path; they also pointed out some half-eaten unripe papaws lying on the ground. We had gone about three quarters of a mile when we heard the jabbering of the Ashantees in their camp. Several hundred people seemed to be speaking all at once, and everyone at the top of his voice.

We ought now to have turned back, having accomplished the object of the reconnaissance; but no one made the suggestion, and so we went on. As we turned a corner, we came upon a picket. Tom Dollar fired, the Ashantees fired back, and a huge piece of iron or lead whizzed close past Lord Gifford's head with a loud musical hum. At the same time one or two shots were fired from the flank. Then there was a charming scene. The Winnebahs stampeded; the Haussas sang hymns and blazed away right and left into the bush, as 'if it were a general engagement Lord Gifford and I were knocked down and run over. The Kossoos were sent as reinforcements. On the other hand (as we heard from an escaped prisoner that evening) there was a similar movement in the Ashantee camp. The women left their cooking pots, the men snatched up their guns, and all bolted into the bush, and the drums began to beat. These panic duets are not unfrequent in African warfare.

That same afternoon, a more serious affair was taking place a few miles off. Festing again attacked the Ashantee camp at Escaboo. On the first occasion he had taken the Ashantees completely by surprise, for they are not in the habit of being attacked, but this time they were better prepared, and fought with great determination. Whenever a rocket was fired, or the seven-pounder gun, they gave a yell of derision and replied with a volley. Had it not been for the staunch behaviour of the 2nd West, there would have been a serious disaster. As it was, the Ashantees pursued the column some little way. Lieutenant Eardley Wilmot, R.A., was severely wounded early in the action, but would not go to the rear, and was afterwards shot through the heart. Colonel Festing, who was again wounded, and Surgeon-Major Gore carried the body away: it was then taken to Cape Coast and buried with military honours.

That night a Fantee woman escaped from the camp at Anasmadi, and came into Abrakrampa. She said that her name was Amba Firitumba, and that with her three children she was captured near Cape Coast Castle about six months before. Her children were allotted to three of her captors, and she herself was put into log; that is, her foot was passed through a hole in a large and heavy piece of wood, the native stocks, and there confined by an iron hoop closing over the ankle. It happened that a number of axes and hammers were within reach of her hand; so in the middle of the night she took an axe and cut the log in such a manner that she set herself free. She said that Amanquatia had really sworn to attack the village, and would do so; but the army had not much taste for the work, knowing that rockets would be used against them, and having a great dislike of those missiles.

That afternoon (November 4) Robert Jones informed me that he and the hammock-men did not want to look on while others were fighting, and hoped that they might be supplied with Enfields, to which weapons they were perfectly accustomed. Major Russell had some in store, and so I was able to gratify their wish. Mr. Jones then observed it would be necessary for them all to take medicine in order to ward off the bullets; this medicine, a red powder, he produced, and said its proper vehicle was rum. I gave him the money he wanted, merely stipulating that I should witness the taking of the medicine. In a short time they returned with a bottle of rum and a large knife: each man stirred up the medicine with the rum, and, as he drank off the mixture, pointed the knife at his own throat. I must do my men the justice to say that they did not neglect other precautions: for instance, they did not go too near the enemy.

That evening the Ashantees came down to the outskirts of the bush, and made a great noise, talking loudly and laughing. Robert told me that they often did this before attacking a town in order to frighten the inhabitants away. He acknowledged that if the Abrakrampa people were in the village by themselves at this particular juncture they would run away in the night. But it would also appear from this custom that the Ashantees prefer to take villages without fighting if they can, though they must lose much plunder by thus announcing their intention of attack.

The next day (November 5) all. was unusually quiet; in the afternoon the Kossoos bagged a chief, and brought in his hand, which was covered with rings. And now a curious thing happened. By some inexplicable confusion in heads at headquarters a letter had come on the 3rd or 4th (I forget which) ordering Major Russell to send back the fifty seamen and marines. At the same time fifty marines were ordered to Esseboo, which was in no danger of attack. Major Russell wrote to explain that the attack seemed imminent, and asked permission to retain the men a few days. To this an affirmative reply was received on the 5th, but on the 6th came a second order recalling the seamen and marines. Major Russell did not venture to disobey, and ordered Lieutenant Wells to pack up and go at four o'clock. At half-past three the church was cleared, all the carriers were ready, and the men were about to fall in when a tremendous rattle of musketry was heard. The attack had begun! In ten minutes every sailor had unpacked his kit and was again at his post.

The Ashantees, concealed by the bush, swarmed along the paths they had cut in a crescent facing the church. We heard their drums beating, and their ivory trumpets, and the voices of their chiefs; and then they began their war-song, which, chanted by thousands in unison, had a magnificent effect. The King of Arbra went out into the open near to the bush, and cried out, 'I am the king of this country; come on if you are coming!' He was answered with a fusillade.

The Ashantees kept up their fire almost without intermission through the night, ceasing only at 4 a.m. At the same time they cut paths through the bush so as to attack from other points. Lieutenant Saunders, R.A., worked the little gun, 'Nelly,' loading her with bullets, and Lieutenant Wells fired rockets which were sometimes received with a yell, sometimes in dead silence. There was a bright moon, and the enemy ventured but little beyond the margin of the bush.

The next day (November 6) at 11 a.m. they attacked the village on three sides at once, and kept it up till dusk without a moment's cessation. The sharp whistling of slugs, like that of wind through fir trees, was always in the air; but they fired at long range for such weapons as they had, and our men were chiefly under shelter. An escaped captive afterwards informed us that the Ashantees complained we shot at them through holes in the houses, and when they shot back they hit the houses instead of us. But whenever they ventured into the open a sortie was made and they were driven back. Opposite the church within the clearing was some rising ground which sloped towards the bush.

A party of Ashantee skirmishers, creeping out into the open, but covered by the hill, fired at the men in the church. Captain Grant, of the 2nd West, was stationed with thirty soldiers to the left of the church; and he had just remarked to me that he wished Major Russell would give him permission to clear the hill, when up came the major and ordered him to do so. Captain Grant took his men over the open near to the brow behind which the Ashantees were lying. Then, waving his sword in the air, he cried 'Charge!' and went at a double, followed by his men, the *Times* correspondent, and Mr. Edward Lake of Bornu. Here for the first and last time (in battle) I saw a crowd of Ashantees: they ran down the hill like mad, and, with their naked black bodies, resembled a herd of wild animals.

In the evening Sir Garnet Wolseley and his staff arrived with naval and native troops by the Batian road, just as the firing came to an end. Many jokes were made about the Relief of Lucknow; and, although Major Russell and his young officers could have held the village till doomsday against a method of attack which was feeble in everything but noise, they were not sorry to have their places taken for a time. During six-and twenty hours they had not been able to rest, and it was still necessary to be on the alert. However, the enemy did not attack during the night; and, as we afterwards discovered, the siege had really come to an end.

The next morning I went out before breakfast and found an Ashantee skirmisher under the brow of the hill exchanging shots with the sailors in the church, while another was a little behind him to the right. I stalked the man in advance till I got near enough to see him when he stood up to fire. I missed him twice, and he shot back at me, so it was quite a little duel; the third time I silenced his fire, and I think silenced him—at all events, I afterwards found a body lying close to the spot. The gallery applauded, or, in other words, I was cheered by the men in the church; and much amusement was caused by Lake, who followed me as usual, and, having picked up an Enfield somewhere, fired at the other skirmisher, holding out the gun at arm's length straight before him on a level with his nose.

Nothing was done that morning on either side except that the Ashantees made a pretended attack, a feint to cover their retreat. Lieutenant-Colonel Wood arrived at seven o'clock. He had been ordered to advance from Napoleon, and to attack the Ashantees in their rear; but, his force being chiefly composed of Cape Coast Fantees, they declined the fight, and joined Sir Garnet on his way to Abrakrampa. He now told them that they should have a last chance to redeem their character, and gave them the order to enter the bush at 2 p.m. and attack the Ashantees.

At two o'clock these miserable people advanced to the edge of the bush, and then stood still like children afraid to go into cold water. The Kossoos were ordered to drive them in at the sword's point, but nothing would induce them to go more than 200 yards. Then they squatted down.

The Ashantee army had gone, but the rearguard and the baggage were left behind. When the Ashantees did not attack the Cape Coast mob, the Arbras, suspecting the truth, ran down the Anasmadi road and took the temporary camp. Then the Haussas were ordered in and took the village Anasmadi. There was scarcely any resistance; here and there a few shots were fired, but the Ashantees dropped their loads and ran. It is said that Amanquatia, who had covered himself with mud and stupefied himself with rum, narrowly escaped capture. When the Arbras took the temporary camp a romantic incident occurred. Human sacrifices were being made for a chief that had been killed, and just as the knife touched the throat of a young Fantee woman a bullet killed the executioner. I saw her telling the story herself, and pointing to the bloody mark upon her throat. Nature, it seems, has become sensational, and imitates Captain Mayne Reid.

The path all the way to Anasmadi was littered with baskets, brass pans, stools, powder-kegs, muskets, and other Ashantee furniture. Amanquatia's sacred chickens were found in a coop with amulets tied round their necks. The carved riding-chair which he had taken from the King of Denkera was now taken from him. Yet few Ashantees were captured, and none of these were fighting-men. Many Fantee captives were released; others were found with their throats cut, lying by the wayside.

The next day Sir Garnet returned in triumph to Cape Coast. Castle, and soon afterwards was down with African fever. He was first sent up to Connor's Hill, and then taken on board the *Simoom*.

So ended the famous siege of Abrakrampa, the glory of which belongs to Major Russell and his officers. In fact, the arrival of Sir Garnet and his assumption of the command can scarcely be considered fortunate. He brought reinforcements, but would not use them against the enemy. I have been informed that Major Russell and Captain Fremantle both urged him to attack the enemy at daybreak on the 7th; and never had a general such an opportunity. The Ashantees occupied a temporary camp close to the clearing; they were disheartened and fatigued; Sir Garnet had a considerable force of seamen and marines, Haussas, Kossoos, and 2nd West.

Had he attacked at dawn he would have taken the camp by surprise, and might have cut the army into pieces. But supposing he had found them prepared, and they had fought at their best, he would have had a wonderful advantage with the village in his rear; and he could have touched and engaged the enemy with his reserve based upon the clearing. The best excuse I have ever heard made on his behalf was not a very good one, *viz.*, that his health was already affected by the fever.

Then what a pitiable business was that which, by extraordinary luck, produced a panic in the Ashantee rear! When he had good negro troops thirsting for battle, why should he have sent into the bush a timid mob of deserters whom he ought to have disarmed and turned into carriers? In fact, Sir Garnet's proceedings that day were of an enigmatical description. He posted a seven-pounder gun outside the village in the clearing; but instead of pointing it towards the enemy's position, he pointed it towards the Esseboo Road, and there he sat with his staff eagerly gazing in the opposite direction from the enemy.

In his despatch to the War Office, he wrote:—

> I have great hopes that the Ashantee army may be entirely broken up before it reaches the Prah.

The correspondent of the *Daily News*, an officer upon the staff, telegraphed his opinion that, 'except a few stragglers, none would cross the Prah alive.' The truth being exactly the reverse, that, except a few stragglers, all crossed the Prah alive. We professional correspondents were less sanguine and more sensible than the general and his staff.[1] If they could still believe in the native allies we could not; and what reason was there to suppose that the army would be broken up? Sir Garnet did not pursue the enemy; he went home again. The forces sent in pursuit were the Haussas and Kossoos without any provisions (so that they must come back the same day), the Arbras and the Fantee mob. They had not gone very far when they found Amanquatia waiting for them with his rearguard. After some little fighting there was the usual stampede. The native levies ran over the Haussas; Pioneer Gordon was knocked into a river; and more than fifty Fantees lost their heads close to Abrakrampa. As an officer who was present drily remarked, 'This was the pursuit.'

The Arbras called that day's work 'a sacrifice to Amanquatia;' *i.e.*, a sacrifice of propitiation; and it almost obliterated in their minds the triumphs of 'the siege.'

---

1. What I said was this: 'It may now be affirmed that the Ashantee invasion is over, and that soon the Protectorate will be clear. In two months the second act of the drama will commence, and in three months probably Coomassie will be taken.'—Letter to the *Times*, dated November 8. The Ashantees crossed the Prah in the first days of December; the regiments began their march in the first days of January; Coomassie was taken in the first days of February.

I shall now follow the march of the Ashantee army. We supposed that it would return by an unfrequented route; but, as if nothing had happened, it took the road by which it had come. It passed close to Mansu without being attacked, and moved with such slowness that Major Home, who was making road, continually touched it in his work. Home's party was covered by Colonel Wood's regiment, which was ordered to harass the enemy's rear, and at a place called Faisoo Colonel Wood did attack the rear-guard. But he soon discovered that the army had a sting in its tail; in fact, an attack on the Ashantee rear does not essentially differ from an attack on its front, for the rear is the position of the general, who is surrounded by the flower of his army.

Wood, with only a few hundred men against an army of at least 10,000 men, was forced to retreat, and the enemy captured a hammock, some baggage, &c. One officer lost 20*l.* worth of property; another was parted from a much beloved box of Fortnum and Mason's, containing many things precious in the wilderness. The regiment had quite enough of harassing the enemy's retreat. But now comes the extraordinary part Either the Ashantees supposed that this regiment was the advance guard of an army, or else they were seized with a mere animal panic. The night after the skirmish, they all girded up their loins, and ran to the Prah, crossed it in haste, many being drowned in the process, and did not recover their equanimity till they had reached the Adansi Hills.

They marched to Coomassie, and, Amanquatia having lost his umbrella and stool, had to wait outside till a new set of these insignia were sent out to him. He then entered the town, and was received with the firing of muskets; but less powder was burnt in his honour than for Adoo Buffoo returning from Krepee. According to Mr. Kühne's account 40,000 men had gone with him to the war, and only 20,000 returned. Seventy-nine boxes, containing the bones of chieftains who had perished in the war, were carried through the streets. Hundreds of women, the relatives of warriors, joined the procession; some of them were daubed with white clay, and wore green garlands, and sang merry songs; others were covered with red clay, and wept, and wailed, and cried to the spirits of the dead.

The army was received in the great market-place, and the king, as usual, regaled the soldiers with sheep and gin. He then summoned the chiefs in council, and proceeded to business. The king does not defray all the expenses of the war, but subscribes handsomely towards it, in virtue of which contribution, and in virtue of his royalty, he is entitled to receive so many prisoners if the war has been successful; if not, the generals or chiefs must pay him the equivalent in gold. Now the army brought but few prisoners, and therefore the king fined Amanquatia so many ounces, and the other war chiefs in proportion, and gave them a fortnight to raise the required sum. But, before that fortnight had elapsed, the king was informed that the white men were coming to Coomassie and were already at the Prah.

Let us now examine the causes and nature of the Ashantee retreat. Sir Garnet Wolseley claims to have driven them out of the Protectorate; and, at first sight, that would seem to be the case. An advocate might say that when the General arrived, the Ashantees were encamped close to Cape Coast Castle and Elmina, the inhabitants lived in continual dread, and panics were frequent. On one occasion, Lieutenant-Colonel Wood signalled to Cape Coast that he expected an attack that afternoon: more than once the cry of 'Ashantee!' was raised in the streets at Cape Coast. But Sir Garnet destroyed the villages from which the camp received its supplies, and also occupied Abrakrampa, Dunquah, and Mansu. The Ashantees were alarmed, and began to retreat; at Dunquah they were twice assailed with success; they attacked Abrakrampa and were defeated, and then got out of the Protectorate as quickly as they could. Half the army was destroyed, &c. &c.

For my own part, I believe that the true history of the retreat is as follows: The Ashantees were victorious up till the middle of May; then the rains, which were unusually heavy, produced two epidemics, smallpox and dysentery; and to these must be ascribed the frightful mortality which, if Mr. Kühne's information be correct, thinned the masses of the army.

It was the chief object of invasion to take Elmina from the English; but the repulse of June 13 proved to Amanquatia that this was not to be done. I believe that the retreat—or, to speak more correctly, the return—was then decided on, and that Amanquatia only waited to obtain the formal permission of the king, which is in such cases necessary.

The first piece of news we heard on our arrival was that the Ashantees were about to retreat; and all the natives whom I have questioned said that, 'as everybody knew,' the circle of beads was received before the arrival of the new governor.

The well-planned and well-executed attack on Essaman was a blow for the Ashantees, but its chief effect was on the people of Elmina. In respect to them its success was complete: it put down the rebellion.

But those who assert that the Ashantees were thus cut off from their supplies and forced to retreat do not understand how an Ashantee army lives. They have no commissariat: each man has to feed himself. The chiefs and their clients are able to buy with their gold-dust stores of corn and smoked fish, but the rank and file live by foraging. When the Ashantees win a victory they settle down on the neighbouring region like locusts, and when they have devoured all the plantains they proceed to another area. When I asked Amba Firitumba why the Ashantees left Mampon, she replied, 'Because they had eaten it up.' If Amanquatia had been told that he was driven by the governor out of the Protectorate, he would probably retort that he had remained a long time close to Cape Coast waiting for the governor to come; that the governor had not dared to attack him, had not even made a reconnaissance; that the white men had defeated him in the plain of Elmina from behind a stone wall and from behind houses at Abrakrampa, but they had never beaten him in the bush.

They had tried it twice at Dunquah; but had Essamanquatia been driven from his camp? They had tried the day after Abrakrampa; they had tried it again at Faisoo; and what had been the result? He did take his army home, but that was because he had ravaged and laid waste Assin, Arbra, Fantee, and Denkera. He had not won every battle: God had not given him success at Elmina and Abrakrampa; and sickness had fallen on his army. But he had passed twelve months in the governor's country, and had not once been attacked with success.

I therefore think that the reverses of the Ashantees are to be ascribed, first of all, to the accident of disease; secondly, to their presumption in dashing themselves against Elmina and Abrakrampa. Festing deserves high credit for his defence of the first, and Russell for his defence of the second; but it should also be remembered that it was Wolseley's wisdom and forethought which garrisoned the village Abrakrampa and placed it under the command of an officer whom he knew well, and on whom he felt he could rely.

CHAPTER 14

The Transport

What could have induced Sir Garnet to ask for thirty miles of railway? He says that he was misled by certain information he received; but he has often complained with justice that he could not obtain good information respecting the Gold Coast, and therefore he took that important step of asking for a railway on information which he knew to be bad. But what was that information? Did anyone who had been to Mansu assure him that the country was flat for thirty miles? If he obtained such an assurance, did he seek for other men who had been to Mansu in order to check the information? Did he, furthermore, read the works of Bowdich, Dupuis, and Hutton, who had all been by that route, and who, unless I am very much mistaken, all speak of valleys and hills? Is not Cape Coast Castle always described as a town with hills at its back? Has it not often been said that Mansu was situated on a plateau? Put this and that together, and is it not a matter of fair inference that there are hills between Cape Coast Castle and Mansu?

But supposing Sir Garnet had been correctly informed, supposing the country for thirty miles inland was quite suitable for the making of a railway, even then the project never should have been for a moment entertained. The general's time was limited, and the advantages to be gained by having a railway for thirty miles would have been more than counterbalanced by the time and toil of its construction. I even doubt whether it could have been made except by setting all else aside. The rails and rolling stock came out, but where was the skilled labour? Major Home had never enough officers and non-commissioned officers for his regular work; what would he have done had there been a railway to make as well? And it must always be remembered that, where one man is needed in England, two men are needed in Western Africa, on account of the climate. But my main objection to the railway would have been (had my opinion been asked) that the country could not produce the necessary labour. Africa is not a populous country, and the making of a railway would have drained Fantee of all its able-bodied men.

It may be said that I am writing with wisdom after the event. But I asked Sir Garnet onboard the *Ambriz* whether the railway was a fact. If it were settled I would not say anything about it, for that would be useless; but if it were a matter still to be decided, I meant to oppose it might and main. He said that he had been promised the railway. I replied that I was sorry to hear it, and I thought that he would be too. It is due to Sir Garnet to say that he countermanded the railway directly after his arrival, and so reduced the expense to its minimum.

My object in speaking of the railway is to show that Sir Garnet from the first never understood the labour difficulty; he seems always to have supposed that he could get as many men as he wanted. But men on the Gold Coast are not only men, they are trains, steamers, carts and boats, horses, elephants, and mules. In a country which has no railways, no navigable rivers, no roads, and no beasts of burden, men have to carry everything upon their heads. The one thought which should have haunted the general day and night from the hour of his landing, or rather from the hour of his appointment, should have been: 'Shall I be able to get men of labour? Shall I be able to keep them when I get them? 'I fear that, if the truth be known, Sir Garnet thought very little about the matter at all until he found that for want of men his expedition was in danger.

The war has been sometimes called an Engineers' War, and sometimes a Doctors' War; it should be called a Control War, for the greater includes the less. The science of the engineers was necessary; but they wanted men of labour to cut down trees, to build huts, and to set up the telegraph poles. It was the business of the control to supply these men. The science of the doctors was in great request; but they wanted men to carry their medical panniers and their bulky stores of medical comforts; and, above all, hammock-men were required to carry the wounded and the sick. It was the fault of the Home Government that only a few control officers were sent out at first; but they would have sent out whatever Sir Garnet applied for after his arrival on the coast; it is, therefore, his own fault that the control was undermanned and overworked. The officers were, for the most part, raw young lads, and had to do, not only their own work, but non-commissioned officers' work as well. One of them told me that while he was at Mansu he had often to work nineteen hours a day—and this on the West Coast of Africa!

The Ashantee expedition was African travelling on a grand scale, and every African traveller knows that transport is his difficulty. He endeavours to get men who do not belong to the country through which he has to pass, for they can always run away if they choose. But often the men of the country are the only carriers he can obtain. He then uses every possible precaution to keep them in his service. He treats them well, but not with indulgence; looks after their lodging and food; and, if he adopts measures of severity, takes care that they shall be of a kind which subdue, not of a kind which merely irritate or terrify.

The question of transport occupied from the first all thoughtful minds that were turned to the prospects of the Gold Coast expedition. It was suggested by members of the press, and by members of the profession, that elephants should be employed; but Sir Garnet refused to apply for elephants. Now, the Gold Coast is an elephant country, and, before they were all shot off, frequented the road between Cape Coast Castle and Coomassie. Bosman saw one walk into the governor's garden at Elmina; they are still to be found at Assinie close to the beach. Moreover we had to fight a superstitious people, and I believe that the sight of tame elephants would have had no slight effect upon the enemy.

It was also suggested at an early date, not only in the papers but also by eminent military men, that though mules and horses would not live upon the coast for any length of time, still they might live for a month, or even two months, and in that time could be turned to account. Had Sir Garnet written for mules in large numbers, his request would not have been refused. But he merely applied for a few riding-mules and pack-mules for the comfort of his staff. These animals not only were able to carry the staff to Coomassie, but even to kick some of them off; a few horses also were used, and they went through the work equally well.

It is therefore certain that mules and horses would have answered. Sir Garnet, in his speech at the Mansion House dinner, says that he could not use mules, because there were no regular roads, a strange excuse to be made by the author of the *Pocket Book*, a work which professes to teach us all about such matters! He also said something about carts; but no one ever blamed him for not taking carts. As far as mules are concerned, they can of course be used without roads being made. Horses and asses exist in great numbers all over Central Africa, and the latter are used for purposes of transport; but in those countries the art of Macadam is unknown; the roads are merely footpaths, as upon the Gold Coast.

Elephants, and mules, and draught oxen should have been employed; but still these would have been experiments, and the success of the expedition should have been made a certainty. So far as concerned fighting, success was a certainty, and it only remained to secure the well-being of the transport. I believe that labour should have been imported, and 2,000 *coolies* at least brought over to the Gold Coast. But, as this was not done, surely Sir Garnet should have used great care to enlist at an early date an adequate supply of labourers, and have taken some precautions against their desertion. He surely must have known that negroes do not love to labour day after day, and that these Fantees were not only slothful, but cowards, dreading the very name of Ashantee.

I have heard some say, 'It is not the general's business to look after the hiring of men. He cannot give his personal attention to every detail: that is the business of the Control.' But the labour question was not a detail; it was the mainspring of the whole affair. Without a supply of labour the army could not advance; and having advanced, unless the labour supply were kept up, it could not fight, could not pick up its wounded, could not retreat, could not exist for a week. The country produced no food.

Besides, the supply of labouring men was not a mere question of hiring, as in civilised countries; it was a question of diplomacy. I believe that most of the carriers were slaves. In any case the proper way to engage them was by arrangement with the chiefs, as in the case of the fighting men. Now, had the command been divided, had there been a governor and a general, the military man would have said to the civilian, 'I want so many thousand carriers; 'and the governor would have summoned the chiefs and given the necessary order. But in Sir G. Wolseley the two commands were united, and it was his duty, if not as a general, then as administrator of the Gold Coast, to have summoned the chiefs to a *durbar*.

It was evident from the first that the Fantees were useless as fighting men, and fit only to be hewers of wood and drawers of water. Indeed if they had been good soldiers, and yet not good enough to preclude the necessity for European regiments, it would have been embarrassing, for where, then, would the labourers have come from? The other settlements and regions of the coast could not supply labour. As I stated in a previous chapter, a commissary was sent to Cape Palmas to hire as many *kroos* as he could get; but his mission was a failure. The *kroos* are not numerous, and are so much in request that frequently captains of merchant vessels are unable to hire as many as they want. The Fantees, therefore, alone could be used, and, as they were useless for purposes of war, the general's path of duty was clear. After the siege of Abrakrampa he should have summoned the chiefs, told them of the regiments that were coming, and of his intention to invade Ashantee, and then called upon them to supply carriers instead of fighting men. He should have been bountiful in matters of money if the men were supplied, and remained with the army: he should have threatened measures of coercion if the chiefs disobeyed.

But, instead of doing this, he retained idly under arms several thousands of the natives for more than a month, and those fighting men that were converted into carriers were converted informally. Then these carriers were not properly organised: they were not arranged into companies, each under its own officer, who might look after them, punish them, and attend to their complaints. They were not always paid with regularity: they were not always fed when they were hungry. I believe that hundreds deserted to escape death from starvation. It is the custom on the Gold Coast to pay carriers subsistence-money, instead of giving them rations; and this answers well enough where there are markets, if the food-money be paid every day; and this was not always done. But when the carriers were taken into the country beyond Mansu, where no provisions could be bought, will it be believed that then the control fed the labourers with money? It seems to have been a prevalent idea with those who managed such matters that food could always be obtained by foraging. I shall give one instance out of many.

A special service officer who had been attached to a tribe was ordered to convert them into labourers and hand them over to the control. He did so, and after some days they came to him, crying, and said that they were hungry. He represented the case to the officer of the control at the station, who replied, 'Oh, that be damned! They can get plenty of plantains in the bush.' This evil was afterwards remedied by order of the general, but not before many had deserted for that cause alone.

It was early in December, a few days before the arrival of the regi-

119

ments, that the general's eyes were first opened to the danger he was in. He had been up country himself and seen how things were going on, or rather not going on. As he returned he met a number of chiefs at Dunquah and told them the regiments were coming (the announcement was rather late) and that he wanted 5,000 men (the demand was also rather late). And what was the threat he used in case the 5,000 men were not produced? Did he say he would punish the chiefs, fine them, imprison them, or burn their villages for disloyalty and base ingratitude? No: he said that if the 5,000 men were not forthcoming, he would send the regiments home again and go away himself.

Now I venture to say that the chiefs would have liked nothing better. Their country was clear; they were safe from invasion for the next ten years; they wanted to sow their crops and to build their villages; and they did not relish the idea of an Ashantee campaign, for they did not believe that it would have any effect except that of giving the enemy fresh provocation from which they would be the sufferers. Sir Garnet was mistaken in supposing that his presence on the coast was necessary to their happiness; while some, no doubt, were shrewd enough to see it was only an empty threat which he dared not, for his own sake, carry out. But, whether they believed or disbelieved it, the threat was impotent against them.

Sir Garnet's final measures were as successful as any measures could be when employed so late in the day. He took the transport virtually out of the hands of the control and placed it under Lieutenant-Colonel Colley and military officers. Colley was an extraordinary man; he dashed about all over the country, sometimes using persuasive words, sometimes burning a village. In a marvellously short space of time he had carriers in hundreds on the road. When the march to Coomassie commenced, he travelled backwards and forwards, bringing up convoys himself, now and then taking part in a battle or a skirmish—his only kind of holiday. Much of this travelling was through parts of Ashantee infested by parties of the enemy. He had many narrow escapes; his servant was shot: as one of his officers said, 'he seemed to bear a charmed life.'

More than once I have heard the remark, 'What should we have done without Colley?' To use Sir Garnet's own words, 'he restored order to chaos:'but, strange as it may appear, Sir Garnet did not seem to think, when he made that observation, that he himself was partly to blame for the chaos.

To Colley it is due that Coomassie was taken when it was. Had it not been for him there would have been more delay; and delay in Africa is death. I do not think that in any case Wolseley would have left the country without going to Coomassie. If he lacks forethought, he does not lack dash and determination. If the worst had come to the worst, if the carriers had not been forthcoming (and this contingency was at one time often discussed in the camp), he would have done permanently what he did for a time. He would have converted the 1st and 2nd West India regiments with Wood's and Russell's regiments into carriers, and then taken on as many white soldiers as those men could supply with food and ammunition, marched to Coomassie with a flying column, and back again, without attempting to provision and garrison posts upon the way.

But this would have been a flashy kind of success at the best, and might have been attended with serious disaster. As it was, we shall see that, in spite of Colley's noble exertions, the question of supplies never ceased to retard the advance, and finally hastened the return of the army. Had that one 'detail 'received the general's attention at the first, the success of the expedition would have been as dramatic and complete as that of Magdala. The troops, instead of being delayed upon the road, could have stayed a week or ten days in Coomassie. There Wolseley and Glover would have met—and what a meeting that would have been! There the treaty would have been signed, and the gold paid over by the king.

CHAPTER 15

The Prah

For a fortnight nothing was heard of the Ashantee army; to use the military phrase, we had 'lost the touch.' However, it crossed the main road near Mansu, and the touch was regained in the following manner:—Surgeon-Major Gore was travelling from Mansu to Dunquah with a guard of Fantee police and a postman carrying the mailbag. They saw several unarmed Ashantee foragers who ran off into the bush; next they came upon a man carrying a musket. He was seized, disarmed, and tied to the postman with a cord. Mr. Gore went on, and next came upon a party of armed men; they fired, wounded him slightly, and killed a policeman dead. The Ashantee prisoner tried to pull the postman into the bush, so the latter untied the cord and let him go. The police returned the fire, the Ashantees ran off, and Mr. Gore returned to Mansu—a promenade of two miles which he did not much enjoy, expecting every moment to be fired into from the bush. However, he arrived safely with the body of the policeman. Lieutenant-Colonel Webber, 2nd West India regiment, who commanded at Mansu, sent two messengers to Dunquah by a circuitous route, and informed Festing that he was surrounded. Festing sent him reinforcements under Captain Huyshe, but they marched from Dunquah to Mansu without seeing any signs of the enemy.

When the news of this incident came to Cape Coast, I at once ordered my hammock and proceeded to Mansu. I was told that the *Head of the Sap*, the farthest advanced point of the Royal Engineers, was at Akrofum, seven miles farther on, and that the Ashantee camp was somewhere in its neighbourhood. Lieutenant Gordon, 93rd, was going there with some Haussas, so Captain Huyshe and I followed in his rear, picking up an Ashantee straggler (a slave) on the way.

We found at Akrofum a large camp of Denkeras, who lay idle in their huts day after day, refusing to scout, and refusing to skirmish, though the Ashantees were close by, though they were hired to fight the Ashantees, though the Ashantees had ravaged their country, burnt their villages, killed their relations, and captured their children and wives.

We found also a couple of tents in which resided Major Home and his two subalterns, Lieutenant Bell, R.E., and Lieutenant Hearle, R.M.L.I., a most industrious young man, who was attached to the Denkera tribe, but had volunteered to serve as assistant engineer. Major Home informed us that the enemy's camp was close by; that the night before he had heard Ashantees jabbering close to the clearing with which Akrofum was fortified; and that a few hours ago they fired a few shots, probably by way of bravado, to cover their departure. This afterwards proved to be the case. Home said he intended to go on with his road, and not to attack the Ashantees unless they came in his way. However, as Huyshe and I were on our way back to Mansu, we met a body of Kossoos and 2nd West sent to reinforce Akrofum with a 7-pounder gun strapped on a bamboo; and that same afternoon Home went out on a reconnaissance and heard the noise of the Ashantee camp. Lieutenant-Colonel Wood had been ordered up to the front to cover Major Home's road-making operations, and had arrived at Mansu. He received a note that evening from his friend to the following effect: 'I attack the Ashantee camp at daybreak, and expect you to breakfast at nine.'

Wood gave orders to his men to be ready to march at 3 a.m. that he might be in time to act as a support. But I knew that a march at such an hour would be attended with delay, and determined to go back that same night to Akrofum. I afterwards found that Huyshe had the same intention, and that Captain Butler was going too, although he had just come from Western Akim, and had travelled thirty miles that day.

At nine o'clock we lighted three lanterns, for the night was pitch dark, and journeyed along the forest path. We had to go very slowly, and it was past midnight before we arrived. We then made beds of our hammocks, and enjoyed a short but comfortable sleep.

The next morning at daybreak Home gave us a breakfast of tea, oatmeal-porridge, and regulation pork, and we then started for the bush. The Kossoos under Lieutenant Woodgate formed the advanced guard, six Denkeras serving as guides. Huyshe, Butler, and I walked at the head of the column.

When we came to the place where Major Home had heard the loud talking of the camp all was perfectly silent; then we knew that either the Ashantees had gone, or that they were waiting for us.

I have found nothing so trying to the nerves as to walk along in the dense bush at the head of a column, or, rather, at the head of a line, knowing that at any moment one may pass an ambuscade, that the enemy's fire will be delivered at ten yards' range, and that the white men will be singled out. However, in bush warfare, the man who is in search of incidents must be quite at the front, or content himself with hearsay.

We now crossed the Oki River on a native bridge, the trunk of a tree. The banks were high and the stream was swift. Presently we came to three or four lean-tos or shanties, and a fire still smoking. This had, no doubt, been a picket. A little while afterwards we heard voices and the chopping of wood. The Denkeras now became highly excited, gasped under their breath '*Shanti fo! Shanti fo!*' (Ashantee people), and, plucking green leaves, laid them by the way-side to show that the enemy was found. We then told them to go on; but they seemed aghast at such an idea, walked a few yards, then stopped and listened, were then kicked by Woodgate, and then went a little way farther, till I suggested to Huyshe we should go on without them. Woodgate gave the word to his Kossoos, and they at once dashed ahead, spreading out to the right and left just like a set of spaniels hied into cover.

Then of a sudden they threw themselves together and knelt in a close group, their swords pointing upwards, while two or three of them went on ahead. The leader of the group turned round to the others, made grimaces expressive of delight, writhed and twisted his body as if he were dancing, and made movements with his sword. At that moment we heard an Ashantee bawling out at the top of his voice, and the interpreter told us he was calling to his chum, and saying, 'Come away, come away, there are people in the bush!' The Kossoos now dashed on ahead at a pace with which I could not keep up: I heard two or three shots, and the sounding of a horn, and thought we had touched the rearguard and were in for a fight. But it was a Kossoo horn, and the voices we had heard were only stragglers. The Kossoos, some of whom had guns, killed a few of these wretches before their hands could be stayed.

A boy was taken alive: he was about fourteen years old, and a wound on his foot showed why he was not with the main body of the army. Huyshe at once gave him a biscuit, and spoke to him in his gentle voice, while the lad, who was as pretty as a girl, looked up in his face with his great black lustrous eyes in wonder and awe: it was the first white man he had ever seen.

The boy told us that Amanquatia had marched the morning before, and that the sick camp with the rearguard had followed in the afternoon. They were most likely on the move when Home made his reconnaissance. He also told us that we had gone round the camp, and showed us the way. Here we saw the Ashantee trail: apparently they marched in three columns through the bush. In the centre was a broad track, with a smaller track on each side.

As we passed through the camp Gore overtook me. He was in a tremble of delight, having had an object-lesson in anatomy. An Ashantee had been cut down by a Kossoo, and the sword had laid bare the great muscle which is called the diaphragm. The man was unconscious, but not dead; and so the diaphragm was ascending and descending with the respiratory movements. As human vivisection is not yet allowed even in the Paris schools, this spectacle was quite unique in its way, and reminded one of the American soldier who had a hole in his side through which his doctor used to put in pieces of beef, mutton, vegetables, &c, to find out which were most easily digested.

Just at that moment I saw a skull lying by the side of a brook, and, showing it to Gore, was about to say I would take it home to Mr. Huxley, when the enthusiast cried out, 'Hurrah, I have got the lower jaw-bone!' and rushed down the bank. The skull was as white and polished as any specimen in the Museum of the College of Surgeons, and Gore, who had picked up a lower jaw-bone just before, found that it dove-tailed in. The Ashantees had probably been aware of Home's approach the day before, for they seemed to have departed in haste and had left many things behind, among others a small package of gold-dust.

We returned to Akrofum disappointed of our fight; but, perhaps, it was just as well. The Major had a compact little force of good fighting men, Haussas, Kossoos, and 2nd West, with a rocket-trough; but we could not have done much against the Ashantee army; and behind us was the Oki, with only its trunk of a tree for a bridge, which, in case of retreat, would not have been agreeable.

I returned to Cape Coast, for, as a gatherer of news, I could not stop too long away from headquarters; but in the first week of December I again paid a visit to the Head of the Sap.

It was now much farther on, being at Yancoomassie Assin, about fifteen miles from the Prah. The Assin scouts had reported, a few days before, that the Ashantees had crossed over, and two West India soldiers volunteered to go on to the river. They came back and reported all clear to the Prah, and said they had written their names on a piece of paper and posted it up. Major Home and Captain Buller went on with some 2nd West soldiers, intending to be the first to arrive; but Captain Butler, who was in Akim, pushed in before them. I went to Akumfudi, a temporary post, with the advance guard of Wood's regiment.

First Butler, and then Home and Buller, came in from the Prah. Lieutenant Grant, 6th Regiment, had command of the Assin scouts, and we agreed to go the next morning and have a look at the river. But in the morning the scouts mutinied; they said they were starved, and could not bear the fatigue of the journey; they observed also that their pay was in arrear. Grant, who had neither silver nor food at his disposal, told them that he was going to take them through a land flowing with milk and honey. But it was their land, and they knew all about it. I then produced a box of Huntley and Palmer's mixed biscuits, and said if they would take us to the Prah I would divide it amongst them. They at once agreed to this, and we started.

The Ashantees had marched along the main road, and vestiges of them were plainly to be seen. In some places the grass at the side of the path had been trampled down, as if by a herd of deer; this showed they had been running. Many dead bodies were scattered about, and the forest smelt of death; this showed they had left their sick to perish on the way. When we came to our destination (about eleven miles' march) dead bodies lay around, and vultures swarming on the opposite bank showed that corpses also were there. Through the dark forest rushed the Prah, a dark and troubled stream. A sombre silence prevailed.

On the site of Prahsu, the deserted village, were a number of camp huts thatched with withered leaves; and, the scouts setting fire to these, red 'flames gleaming through clouds of smoke heightened the sense of destruction and death already imparted to the mind. However, I saw with pleasure that the banks of the river were high, and that it would be a healthy site for the encampment of the regiments. Robert divided the box of biscuits among the Assins: each man had a cracknel and two or three macaroons, with which light repast they were quite satisfied. We saw the paper posted up by the two brave men of the 2nd West India regiment.

During this trip to the Prah (seventy-four miles from the coast)

126

I had been troubled with dysentery, and had kept it within bounds by means of opiates. On returning to Cape Coast Castle the disease became violent, and I began almost to fear that the Prah would be my Pisgah, and that I should not enter the Threatened Land. But I had recourse to *ipecacuanha*, given in full doses, and this pulled me through. The Jesuit missionaries who discovered Peruvian bark (from which quinine is obtained) also discovered *ipecacuanha*, which they named the *radix dysenterica*. It is strange that we owe to the 'Society' our two specifics for the two great tropical diseases. But between these two maladies there is no comparison. Fever is to dysentery what the slug is to the Snider-bullet. I have had dozens of fevers, and dread them little more than a cold; but as for dysentery, that is another affair.

I had scarcely recovered when (December 24) Lieutenant Rolfe of the *Active* kindly invited me on board for a day's trip to Chamah. The people of that town, after the bombardment by the *Rattlesnake*, had gone to live in a bush-village about three miles off. On the other hand the people of Commenda, whose town had been destroyed by the Ashantees, and who had been taken off to Cape Coast Castle in ships, had now returned home. Behind Chamah is the land of the Wassaws, our allies; and Sir Garnet Wolseley had ordered the Wassaws and the Commendas to carry war against the Chamahs, after which they were to unite and invade Ashantee *via* Wassaw.

But the Wassaws asked for guns and ammunition, and then would not do anything; they would not even attack Chamah; and the Commendas made but a poor business of it, as will be seen. It would have been much better if the Wassaws and Commendas and Akims had been made to serve as carriers. But the humble business of transport was neglected for the art of strategy.

The general and his staff were also on board the *Active*, and Commodore Hewett kindly made me his guest. We steamed to Chamah; but it was found that the Commendas would not be ready to fight till the following day, so the Commodore gave his friends a trip of half a mile up the Prah in a steam launch and took them back to Cape Coast. The *Encounter*, Captain Bradshaw, and the *Merlin*, Commander Day, remained at the mouth of the river, and it was arranged with a Mr. Hughes of Cape Coast, sergeant in the Rifle Volunteers, who commanded the Commendas, that they should be on the banks of the river at 8 a.m., and that then the boats of the two men-of-war should ferry them across. The Commenda camp was a mile or so down the beach.

The next morning about 700 Commendas made their appearance, some of them armed with Enfields, others with flint-locks, and the boats, manned by *kroos*, soon put them across. They then marched towards Chamah, which was a quarter of a mile from the mouth of the river. In the meantime Captain Bradshaw determined to make a little voyage up the Prah. The steam pinnace was armoured with mantlets or plates of iron which rose above the sides, and she also had a round shield of iron in her bow. Every man was armed with a Snider, and was ready; so there was not much fear of another disaster on the Prah, even had the natives prepared an ambuscade; which was quite possible. We rattled along at a swift pace in a narrow lane of water, with green walls and towers of vegetation on either side.

Sometimes we saw a crocodile lying on a log, or a family of monkeys which went off into the bush chattering, gambolling, and looking back at us over their shoulders. We passed the place where Commerell was shot, and had gone about four miles, when Lieutenant Evans, of the *Encounter*, quietly remarked 'A narrow escape!' and, looking behind us, we saw the brown surface of a rock which was almost covered by the water. Had we touched it there would have been a hole knocked in the bottom of the pinnace; and, as rocks in African rivers are seldom alone, Captain Bradshaw thought it best to return. As we reached the mouth of the river, we saw smoke rising above the trees; the Commendas had set fire to Chamah, and so added the finishing touch to the bombardment

It was low water when we crossed the bar, and the pinnace bumped on the sand. This was not pleasant in the midst of the breakers, and it happened again and again; but the little craft was beautifully handled. When she struck the sand, Bradshaw gave the word, and the engineer, with a movement of his hand, turned off the steam. Then would come a big wave and float her off; and, as soon as the water passed underneath, the steam was turned on, and she dashed ahead till at last she got out into the sea. Decidedly the Prah, though picturesque, is of no avail for navigation.

We had a naval artist on board, so steamed near the town to give him a subject for a sketch, and then returned to the *Encounter*. Captain Bradshaw, wishing 'to save his daylight,' weighed anchor at 2 p.m., to rerun to Cape Coast, and we were watching the Commendas driving a herd of Chamah cattle: along the beach, when we heard shots and saw puffs of smoke. A skirmish took place, and the Commendas were apparently victorious; but next day Mr. Hughes petitioned to be once more ferried over to the safe side of the Prah, declaring that his men had eaten their food, and shot away their ammunition.

Let us now return to the main stream of events. In the beginning of December, the *Sarmatian*, *Himalaya*, and *Tamar* came with the 42nd, the Rifles, and the 23rd regiment; and the *Thames*, a small transport, brought out a battalion of marines under Colonel de Courcy. The 1st West India regiment also arrived.

At that time little had been done in the way of preparation, and so the troopers were sent out to sea, and the first days of the New Year appointed for the landing of the regiments. On December 27, Sir Garnet Wolseley and his staff, with the Naval Brigade under Captain Blake, R.N., started for the Prah. The commodore went up afterwards. Fifty seamen and marines had been already some weeks at the front with the 2nd West and the native regiments of Russell and Wood. Two hundred marched with Sir Garnet, all picked men from the *Active*, *Amethyst*, *Argus*, *Druid*, and *Encounter*. The men of Abrakrampa had been for the most part invalided, and Lieutenant Wells had died of yellow fever on his way home to take command of the Queen's Yacht. Consul Livingstone (Dr. Livingstone's brother) also fell a victim to this disease, which was raging in the Bights. All homeward-bound steamers were put in quarantine, and the Gold Coast escaped infection.

After much honourable but bitter dispute, it was arranged that the Rifles should march first, the Black Watch second, and the Fusiliers last. Each regiment would land half a battalion at a time, so that on January 6 all the troops would be on the road. They would march to Prahsu in eight days, there concentrating; on January 15 they would cross that river, and the Invasion would begin. On the same day three other columns were to enter Ashantee territory. Captain Glover would cross the Prah with his disciplined Yorubas and Haussas, his Eastern Akims, Croboes, Kreepees, Accras, &c, at some point to the east of Prahsu; Captain Butler would cross with the Western Akims at a place called Akim Prahsu, about thirty miles to the east of the main road; Captain Dalrymple and Moore, both of the 80th regiment, would cross the Ashantee frontier with the Wassaws.

These arrangements were perfect. On paper; but concerted movements in Africa do not usually succeed. Sir Garnet could not cross on the 15th because the transport broke down. Glover crossed, but with only his Yorubas and Haussas. Butler crossed with Brabazon, Macgregor, and Surgeon Low, but without any Akims. Dalrymple did not cross the frontier at all, being unable to move the Wassaws, who seem the worst of our native allies.

I must now attempt to give some description of what had been done upon the road from Cape Coast Castle to Prahsu. My description of the country will also apply in a general way to the country between Prahsu and Coomassie. It is all the same forest, and all the same race.

The primeval forest is composed of tall and massive trees, with creepers extending like cordage from one to another, and so mat- ting the foliage together overhead that a green roof is formed, almost impenetrable to the sun. Here and there are chinks and skylights, through which the sun shoots in and falls upon the tree-trunks and ground in gleams and splashes of crystal light. There is not much undergrowth, for that kind of vegetation cannot exist without sunshine, and in the virgin forest is always a kind of twilight or Dim. There is no danger of sunstroke in the forest, but the heat is often suffocating—a moist dank sunless heat, an atmosphere of Kew. There are many hills and dales; the hills are composed of primary rock which sometimes lines the hollows at their feet, and then bright streams sparkle along over quartz beds glittering with mica like rivers of gold. But more often the valleys are marshes and beds of black mud, where grows the bamboo with its drooping branches and pale green leaves.

Through the forest runs a red or yellow path, winding as a river, and joining village to village. These are usually perched on hills, are always near water, and are embosomed in broad-leaved plantain groves. But the plantations of the village are at some little distance, and are frequently changed.

The natives make a plantation by cutting down trees and letting them lie, but burning the branches. They sow their crops in the ashes, and in three years' time the soil is exhausted, and they have to cut a clearing again. Now, on the site of the abandoned plantation, which is freely exposed to sun and rain, springs up a thick scrubby vegetation, which I shall term jungle; it is all thick undergrowth, almost impenetrable, except to the axe and the knife, but rises to a considerable height.

The seaboard region, having been the most thickly populated since the advent of the European trade, has been almost entirely turned into jungle, and few large trees are there to be seen; but in the interior the forest chiefly' prevails. From a military point of view the forest is to be preferred, because it is comparatively open; but in the neighbourhood of villages (just where the fighting is sure to be) there is always an area of jungle.

In the beginning of 1873, the Ashantees marched down the main road and destroyed all its villages—Prahsu, Yancoomassie, Seuta, Mansu, Dunquah, and so forth. We found on the sites of these villages a clearing overgrown with shrubs and high grass, with here and there a gable end or a piece of a wall. As we advanced into the country, some of these clearings were converted into camps for the engineers at work upon the road, and for the troops by which they were covered. Others, as Dunquah and Mansu, were made store *depôts* and fortified posts. Finally, when it was decided that the regiments were to march upon Coomassie, seven clearings were selected in addition to Prahsu, the terminus, and these were specially prepared as camps for the accommodation of the troops. The natives were not allowed to encamp in these clearings for sanitary reasons.

The preparations made were as follows:—Large huts of bamboo were built, with a raised bedstead or couch running along each side, leaving a gangway in the centre. These gave sleeping accommodation to half a battalion; and huts with separated couches (of split bamboo) were built for the officers. A stream was always in the neighbourhood, and here a washing-house was built, with a trough and plugs. But this water the men might not drink. A Crease's filter, with a tin mug beside it, answered that purpose. Two latrines (on the dry-earth principle) were dug, one for the officers, One for the men. A hut was set aside as hospital; another as guard-room (seldom or never required); another as control store, from which were issued the salt pork and Australian meat, biscuits, rice, preserved potatoes, salt and pepper, tea and sugar, which formed the excellent rations served out to the troops.

In the larger stations, such as Mansu and Prahsu, were post-office huts and telegraph stations. In each camp were, at the least, two officers: one a control, the other a medical man. In no campaign has the British soldier ever had such comforts and luxuries on the march. Each camp was like an hotel, and some were almost elegant, with neatly swept roads, and boards fixed up pointing the way to the water, the latrine, &c. The men also had fresh beef every day up to the Prah. Sir G. Wolseley organised much that was remarkable in the Ashantee campaign; but I think the arrangement of the camps must be regarded as his best piece of work.

I left Cape Coast Castle on January 1, and for the fifth time passed over the Iron Hill, which lies behind the town. At Dunquah I found Festing still in command; and my gallant friend was in very low spirits, it having been decided that he was not to go to Coomassie, but to take charge of Prahsu. I said that it was impossible for him to better his position, and that nothing he could do would really add to the fame he had gained already by his exploit at Elmina of June 13, and his two wounds received in action near Dunquah. But he did not look at the matter from that point of view; what he wanted was not reward, but the realisation of an idea.

Before Sir Garnet came out, or perhaps before he was appointed, Festing had taken up the question of a march upon Coomassie: he had collected much information, and corresponded with the War Office on the subject. It was a bitter disappointment to him, that having had so much to do with the Find, he was to be taken out of the saddle with no chance of being in at the death. It is true that there was no command to which he could have been appointed; for he was not of sufficient seniority to be made brigadier to the native regiments, as was afterwards done with Colonel McLeod; but he might have been taken as a handy man upon the staff, and his knowledge of the natives acquired during long residence at Dunquah would have been of service to the general. In that kind of knowledge the staff was undoubtedly deficient, and in that kind of knowledge alone. Every other kind of ability was possessed at headquarters; but Sir Garnet and his officers never learnt to understand the Africans.

It was a quarter past 6 a.m., on January 3, and I was just about to start, when Festing came to me and said, 'Did you not hear a bugle just now?' As he spoke it sounded again. Presently we heard a low, deep, solemn tramp, and some men came round the corner dressed in Norfolk grey, with pith helmets on their heads, rifles on their shoulders, pocket filters round them, and tin mugs at their belts. Then came others with axes and spades in leather cases; and then an officer on horseback, another with his face covered by a brown veil, to keep out malaria; and then the main body marching by fours. It was the first half-battalion of the Rifle Brigade. I felt a thrill as I saw for the first time British soldiers on African soil. My hammock-men looked at them with astonishment. Robert asked me what the sappers were for, and when I answered his question he shook his head and thought I must be mistaken. Their use was clearly emblematical. The axes they carried were to show that Ashantee would be cut down, and the spades indicated that Ashantee would be rooted up.

When I came near to Mansu I heard rifle-shots and tumultuous cries, and Robert told me that there was 'a beast up in a tree.' I alighted and found a crowd of about three hundred natives, all looking up at a brown animal, about the size of a rabbit, which was lying along a bough at the top of a gigantic tree. The creature must have lost its way, for it had come into or rather over the native camp. One man had an Enfield rifle, with which he was shooting at the animal; he got right underneath it and held out his gun at arm's length. He fired six shots or so, and then I took the Enfield, for I had no Snider ammunition with me at the time. The first shot made it move, and the second brought it down, much to the delight of the crowd, who laughed, and yelled, and shook hands with me, and patted my back, and seemed as grateful as if I had killed a goat-eating leopard or venomous snake.

The animal was a species of hyrax, and will be known to all who have travelled on the Gold Coast as the beast which makes an extraordinary screeching at night, not unlike the hyena, or a negro being flogged. A story is told of a sentry in one of the regiments being found with his bayonet fixed ready to resist the onslaught of this ferocious creature. The natives say that when it is on the ground it is modest and well behaved, but as soon as it gets safe on the top of a tree, 'it begins cursing everyone's father and mother.' This, I believe, was the only quadruped bagged in the Ashantee Expedition. The forest is not a game country on account of the absence of pasture; a few antelopes and boars exist, with here and there a leopard and hyena, but these are rare and difficult to find.

It was pleasant travelling to the Prah; the road was broad and firm, so that my men could trot along in good style, and every night I came to a station where an officer's hut was placed at my disposal, and where I drew my rations at the store. Sir Garnet Wolseley, who was most kind and liberal to correspondents throughout the campaign, had placed us on the footing of Staff officers; we could draw for ourselves and four men. I had a gang of bearers carrying provisions for myself—soups, tinned meats, claret, Swiss milk, sardines, biscuits, and pots of jam, which sweet food for some physiological reason was much relished in the bush. Other bearers had barrels of rice for my men. These bearers were chiefly women, who carried fifty or even sixty pounds, in addition to a bustle, and sometimes a child. Many hundreds of women were employed in the transport of the expedition.

On arriving at Prahsu (January 5) I found it transformed. The forest had been converted into a plain. A city of huts had sprung up with various wards, or quarters, or lines, assigned to the Naval Brigade, the 2nd West regiment, Wood's regiment, Russell's regiment, the Haussa

Artillery, and the Engineers. In the midst was a vast square, and at one side, along the banks of the river, a line of huts, the dwellings of the Staff, and Sir Garnet's own abode with the Union Jack floating overhead. On the opposite side of the square was the post-office, and the huts of the correspondents. Large buildings were being erected for the accommodation of the regiments; and there was a hospital, over which was painted on a board 'The Forlorn Hope.' Major Home's bridge, built on American cribs, spanned the river, and on the other side an earthwork (a redan) was being thrown up, and a large clearing being made. Every morning and evening the seamen and marines were marched over and set to work. Then axes were heard ringing in the forest, then trees were set on fire, their foliage dried to tinder by the *harmattan* or desert wind. At night the sailors built up an enormous bonfire, and, seated around it, made the camp merry with their songs.

Here I remained till the 19th, a day marked by a melancholy incident. Captain Huyshe, since his arrival with Sir Garnet on the coast, had been almost always in the bush. He had made a military survey of the road from Cape Coast Castle to the Prah, pacing the whole distance; he had been sent on missions to many native chiefs; and here at Prashu his last work had been to make a plan of the Camp, which he did with his usual neatness and precision. During all this time he had escaped illness; but now dysentery came upon him, and in a few days he was in a dangerous condition. I went to see him on the 18th. He was in bed reading a letter. I said a few words, and then, as I saw he was very weak, rose up to go. 'Goodbye,' said he in a voice faint as a whisper; 'we shall meet at the front.' These words of hope and courage were almost the last that he uttered; that night he was seized with fever, and the next day this brave and amiable man was no more.

CHAPTER 16

Negotiations

We had all of us supposed that if the Ashantees fought at all they would begin to resist our advance as soon as we crossed the Prah. But though the Prah is in one sense certainly the frontier, Ashantee Proper begins on the other side of the Adansi Hills. The intervening country formerly belonged to Assin; it was conquered by the Ashantees, and in the days of Bowdich was well populated, and subject to the king. On our side of the Prah was also an Assin country, extending to Mansu; and the Ashantee Assins being oppressed by their lords migrated into the Protectorate. So the land was left desolate, and is at the present time but thinly inhabited, whether by a remnant of the Assins, or by Ashantees, or by a mixed race, I could not ascertain.

Thus the Ashantees scarcely felt themselves invaded until we had climbed the Adansi Hills; and our forces were able to take this first thirty miles of forest almost without opposition. That brought us nearly halfway from the Prah to Coomassie. Had there been no delay in respect to supplies, the Imperial troops might have marched right on to Fomana (preceded by the native regiments), Coomassie would have been taken a fortnight earlier, and the march upon that town would have been a masterpiece. As it was, the native regiments, instead of advancing, were detained at Prahsu some days to serve as carriers; and the 23rd regiment was re-embarked.

At this time the fate of the expedition was precarious; the control officers at Mansu (the halfway depot) declared that the game was up, and that the troops in advance would have to return by forced march-es; there was a dead lock along the road, each half-battalion being de-tained in the camp which it then occupied. Brief as was this detention it had evil effects, for an army in Western Africa is like water; while it moves it has sparkle and life, but putrefies as soon as it stagnates. 'That stoppage in Mansu,' said an officer of the 42nd, 'did more harm to our men than all the hard work in Ashantee.'

At this critical time Sir G. Wolseley, I am told, had always high spirits and an air of confidence, not only in public (as was evident to all), but also in the private circle of his staff. Brightness of mind in adversity, and a sanguine spirit when things seem at their worst, is a fine faculty to possess; but the man of the *cœur léger* is often somewhat improvident; a less light-hearted commander- in-chief would have been more anxious, and therefore more careful of the future.

Russell's regiment carried its own provisions, and was thus enabled to cross the Prah at an early date. A corps of scouts was organised, consisting of Assins who knew the enemy's country, with picked men from the Bonnys, Opoboes, Haussas, Kossoos, and 2nd West. These were now placed under the command of Lieutenant Lord Gifford. He marched in advance of the regiment, and took the villages which lay upon the route. At Essiaman he met with some resistance, and one of his men was wounded. A villager was killed and two women captured. These he afterwards released, and they went off to Coomassie.

The Ashantees were astounded at this proceeding and said, as Mr. Kühne informed us, 'What a curious people these white men are to send the women away! *Why this is money*' (A woman in Ashantee is always worth at least four or five pounds; and a young marriageable lady who has just come out will sometimes fetch seven or eight.) Lord Gifford went on and on, till at last he came to the Adansi Hills. The road leads over a forest-covered mountain about fifteen hundred feet above the level of the sea and exceedingly precipitous.

As Gifford climbed the hill voices called out to him and ordered him to go back; an old woman cursed him, and said there was a thousand men at the top; a priest dressed in white held up his arms, and warned him not to enter Ashantee. But on went the gallant lad, and the enemy retreated before him, beating their drums. On the summit of the mountain is a flat space of ground where a small post was afterwards established. Through openings in the forest a beautiful prospect was afforded. Below lay an ocean of trees, their topmost branches like green water moving in the wind, and other hills rising in the midst.

Russell's regiment followed the scouts, and made fortified clearings at Essiaman, Akrofum, and a place called Moinsey, at the foot of the hills. Wood's regiment followed on the 15th, and garrisoned these stations; and the 2nd West encamped in *tentes d'abri* on the Parakome River, about half-way to the hills. Home's engineers made a rough marching road, cutting the bush on either side, bridging the streams, and 'corduroying' the marshes, that is, laying down logs of wood. They also made a zigzag road up the mountain.

On the other side was a descent, but not equal to the ascent, so that Ashantee may be considered a plateau. Certain new species of trees were detected, even by our unscientific eyes; but still it was all forest to Coomassie, and (so it is said) more than fifty miles beyond.

About two miles from the top of the hill was Quisah, the first village of Ashantee Proper; and a quarter of a mile farther on was the spacious town of Fomana, capital of the province Adansi, and the residence of its powerful chief. Both Quisah and Fomana were deserted by their inhabitants, and occupied by Russell's regiment. Lord Gifford scouted every day in the neighbourhood, and almost every day he met Ashantees, or, rather, the provincials called the Adansis. He had orders not to fire first. They used to call out and say, having first presented the butts of their guns as a sign of parleying and peace, 'What are you white men come here for? Do you mean to fight?' Gifford replied that we did. 'Very well,' said they, 'we will go and ask our chief to let us fight with you.'

A white thread was drawn along the road from Quisah to Fomana as a fetish. Kids and other animals were staked into the ground by the wayside. A wooden apparatus was found—a model of knives and gun with points and muzzle turned towards the south. A man, also, had been impaled and mutilated in a manner too horrible to be described, then laid by the roadside to propitiate the savage gods of the country, and to strike terror into the hearts of the invaders.

Sir Garnet Wolseley arrived at Fomana (January 24, 1874) with the Naval Brigade and the first half-battalion of the Rifles. He took up his abode in the palace of the chief, and remained in this town to concentrate his troops. He was also detained four or five days waiting for supplies.

Meanwhile, let us pay a visit to Coomassie. The captives were all well, though obliged to live like the natives on a meagre allowance of snail-soup and plantains. Two children had been born to the Ramseyers, the youngest being only two months old. There were also about seventy Fantees detained in the town, and a certain Mr. Dawson, a coloured man, Fantee, with English blood in his veins, at one time a missionary agent, but sent up to Coomassie as government envoy. Many of his letters addressed to the Gold Coast Government will be found in the Blue books, and he wrote the letters which Sir Garnet received from the king.

The army had dispersed; Amanquatia and the war chiefs were raising gold-dust to pay the fine imposed upon them; and the king wrote a letter to the governor. This letter has not yet been published, but it is said to have been a complaint in respect to the skirmish at Fesoo. The envoys expected to find the governor at Cape Coast, but they found him at the Prah. Sir Garnet Wolseley refused to see them, saying he would treat only in person with the king; but he kept them some days. The Gatling was exhibited before them and made to play upon the river. At midnight of that same day a shot was heard, and it was found that one of the envoys, or an attendant of the envoys, had blown out his brains, lying down on his couch, putting the gun to his head, and pushing the trigger with his foot. Some say it was pure fright at the Gatling; others, that he had said something treasonable which his companions intended to report against him to the king. They put his body in a wicker coffin, and buried it on the other side of the Prah. Each Ashantee threw a handful of earth upon the grave.

The envoys were sent back over the bridge which had been built while they were at Prahsu; and the Naval Brigade was marched over before them as a feint, and then marched back again. Before the messengers arrived at Coomassie rumours were already in the air. The missionaries heard that the white men were coming; that the king was going to make war; that they the captives would be taken with the army, employed to intercede in case of defeat, and killed if the Ashantees were victorious. There was a certain chief to whom they had been as- signed, whose business it was to protect them and receive their complaints. They went to him for information, but could obtain no definite reply.

When the envoys returned they were summoned to the palace; the king and chiefs assembled in council, and Dawson was ordered to read the governor's letter. It was received in profound silence. No one rose, no one uttered a word; at last the captives were dismissed. They heard that the king said after their departure that since Coomassie had been built it had never been invaded; to which the chiefs replied that ancient times were not now. The Queen Mother said that when the Ashantees were in the right God had always given them the victory; but they had done wrong in not giving up the white men after they had promised to accept a ransom.

Kühne saw gold-plated envoys leaving the town in every direction, to gather an army as he supposed. Messengers also came and informed him that he was to go that night, and must get ready at once. They brought him as presents a *periguin* of gold-dust, and a royal robe, such as only the king's relatives may wear. This was intended to remove any unfavourable impression which four years and a half of captivity may have made upon his mind. So forgiving is the nature of the African, that presents and kind words will often remove all rancour caused by prolonged ill-treatment; but Europeans do not so easily forgive.

After sunset Kühne was called to the palace, and passing from courtyard to courtyard was brought at last to an inner apartment, where on a low stool, and wearing a white cloth, the king was seated playing with his cats. Only three or four persons were present. The king told Kühne that he must plead for him with the governor, and must say that he could not fight with the white men, no, not even if they came into the market-place at Coomassie, for his ancestors had never fought with the white men. This was a strong statement, even for an Ashantee, when the scull of Sir Charles Macarthy was at that moment adorning the Bantama. Kühne was sent out at night, lest the people should notice his departure, and say 'Ha! see; the king is afraid.' At night no one may go out of Coomassie, except with the sanction of the king, and policemen patrol their streets, their heads half shaved, long hair falling over their foreheads, and lances in their hands.

When the troops ascended the Adansi Hills the king also liberated Bonnat and the Ramseyers, and sent them with a letter to Fomana, where they met the General. The Ramseyers journeyed on to Cape Coast, but Bonnat remained with the expedition, messed with the Naval Brigade, accompanied them in all their engagements, and went with them to Coomassie.

With the released captives came a letter, in which the king said he would make Amanquatia pay the indemnity. I believe that this promise was coupled with a proviso that we should remain at Fomana. In that case it was not a promise at all, for we were going on to Coomassie. But in any case, what was a promise from the King of Ashantee? Had the letter been made public I should have thought twice before I went to the expense of telegraphing such a promise to the *Times*.

Very different was the effect produced on the mind of Sir Garnet Wolseley. His instructions had been at first not to invade Ashantee if he could help it; to make peace if possible without crossing the Prah. When the regiments were sent out he was still instructed to avoid war, not to provoke the Ashantees more than could be helped, not to destroy villages, and so forth.

Such at least I presume from Sir Garnet's acts to have been his instructions; and his friends always made his instructions serve as an excuse for his many unsoldier-like proceedings. But I have since learnt from a reliable source that Sir Garnet's instructions were quite in accordance with his own personal wishes and views. *He did not want to fight.* He had made his reputation as a soldier, and now aspired to be a diplomatist. But he was matched against men compared with whom he was merely a child. It is a mistake to suppose that the Africans are a stupid people because they have no books, and do not wear many clothes. The children do not go to school, but they sit round the fire at night or beneath the town-tree in the day, and listen to their elders, who discuss politics, and matters relating to law and religion.

Every man in a tribe, and every slave belonging to a tribe, has learnt at an early age the constitution by which he is governed, and the policy pursued towards foreign tribes. In such a land as Ashantee the king and chiefs are profoundly skilled in the arts of diplomacy. Their weapon of offence is treachery, their weapon of defence suspicion. They have no scruples and no illusions. They never hesitate to betray, and always hesitate to believe. Opposed to them was a man who could practise some trifling little devices, but who felt himself bound by the laws of honour, and who, so far from being distrustful and suspicious, possessed a 'fatal facility' for believing whatever he wished.

As a soldier he did wrong in exhibiting the Gatling to the Ashantee envoys: these surprises should be reserved for the battlefield. And why did he detain the envoys till he had finished the bridge and sent Russell's regiment over in advance? And why did he send the Naval Brigade on a make-believe march along the road? Was it to warn the king that he had no time to spare, that he must make haste and collect his troops if he did not wish to be taken by surprise? Evidently it was the proper policy to make these dilatory people suppose that we were not ready to invade. But Sir Garnet thought that the Gatling and the advance of the white men would frighten the king into peace.

In the same manner it is not customary for a general to write to the enemy and tell him where he is going to be attacked, and where he had better send his troops. But this kind office was performed for the king by Sir Garnet Wolseley, who informed him he intended to invade Ashantee from four points at once. This announcement was also made with a view to avert war, and to obtain the peaceful submission of the king.

On the other hand, the King of Ashantee was also desirous for peace, having nothing to gain and everything to lose by a war in his own territory. He thought that the war was being made on account of the captives, to whom he had always attached a high diplomatic value; to avert war he gave them up, and would perhaps have been willing to pay an indemnity.

As for a treaty, he would have signed anything and everything with the greatest pleasure in the world. But he could not tamely consent to the march upon Coomassie. That would have been a sign to all the surrounding people that his power had been broken. He might keep it a secret from the Gamans and other tribes to the north, about white men marching to Fomana, and having been paid with a treaty and gold-dust to retire; or if the story did get about, he might even circulate a version of his own, and cause it to be believed that the white men had been defeated in battle and repulsed.

But the occupation of Coomassie, in which town were always many foreigners and traders, would soon be known all over the African world: He was therefore disposed to make concessions; but the white men must not advance beyond a certain point. Sir Garnet was disposed to be moderate in his demands; a treaty of peace signed by the king would alone have done much to content him; but on one point public opinion forced him to insist He could not stop short of Coomassie.

The King of Ashantee displayed much wisdom in the negotiations. He was right in making sacrifices to avert a war of invasion, even supposing that the chances of victory seemed to be on his side. He was right to resist the advance upon Coomassie, even supposing that there seemed little hope in resistance. But Sir Garnet Wolseley in wishing premature peace did not know what was best for the country or what was best for himself.

So far as his own reputation was concerned he would have won and deserved few laurels by an unopposed march to Coomassie, His military achievements in the Protectorate had not been of a brilliant kind. The attack on Essaman was perfect in its way, but that was only a small affair. His attempt to shoot the Ashantees flying, to attack their divided columns in retreat; had been a ludicrous fiasco. At Abrakrampa he had shown himself deficient; and, when the merest luck gave him a showy success, he turned from a flying enemy and returned to Cape Coast. He did not attack the Ashantees as they were crossing the Prah. Then, as to organisation, he had bungled his transport, his published arrangements had been altered and postponed; one of his regiments boiling with rage had been re-embarked on account of the break-down in the Control. Nothing in fact could save his reputation except a great victory. Had he returned to England with a treaty of peace, and a few thousand pounds' worth of golden curiosities, and a long list of deaths from inglorious disease, he might have pleased Lord Kimberley, but he would not have satisfied the Nation.

To Lord Kimberley [1] must, I presume, be chiefly ascribed the weak and faltering instructions which Sir G. Wolseley appears to have received. The object which that statesman had in view was wise and laudable; but he adopted precisely the worst method to attain it. He desired to establish a lasting peace between Great Britain and Ashantee, and he feared that if the war was waged with too much severity we should provoke their undying enmity.

So Sir Garnet was to conduct the invasion of Ashantee with all possible politeness and humanity; he was not to destroy the poor people's villages; he was not to burn Coomassie if he could possibly help it. I venture to doubt whether such half-and-half measures are of much use in European warfare; but in a contest with a savage people they defeat their own object; they prolong and germinate war. Already we had excited the bitter enmity of Ashantee; what we had now to do was to render that enmity innocuous. They hated us because we had aided the tribes of the Protectorate to regain their independence; they hated us because we refused to be, as once we had been, their vassals and tributaries. They yearned to win back what they had lost. Nothing would quench this hatred, nothing would stifle this ambition, except the conviction that it was folly to cherish it any longer in their hearts.

Once prove to them that we were a strong military people, and that they could never hope to beat us in battle, and they would submit to destiny. They would fear us, admire us, and finally love us. Lord Kimberley has been Viceroy of Ireland, and ought to know something about savages. They are not like civilised men. A hostile savage is like an ill-tempered dog: try to pat him and he bites you; give him a cut with your whip and he attacks you furiously; take him by the collar, thrash him within an inch of his life, and he will never try to bite you anymore. Then feed him and treat him kindly and he becomes affectionate and faithful.

---

1. I must add that Lord Kimberley is a sincere friend of Africa, and intimately acquainted with the history, politics, and geography, not only of the Gold Coast, but also of the other West African settlements, especially Sierra Leone.

Now the patting process had been tried with the King of Ashantee; this bandit chief kept white men in captivity, and sent insolent demands to Cape Coast; in return he received handsome presents, prisoners *gratis*, and polite words. He then in the most treacherous manner invaded our Protectorate. Lord Kimberley ordered the beast to be flogged; but Sir Garnet must not flog him too hard. Sir Garnet faithfully tried to carry out these instructions, and did even more. He patted the king with one hand and flogged him with the other. He invaded the Ashantee country, drove the people out of their villages along the main route, and at the same time indited peaceful and soothing letters to the king.

Sir Garnet's advocates may assert that by means of these soothing letters the release of the European captives was effected, and that had the general refused to open negotiations until he arrived at Coomassie, their lives would have been endangered. But our invasion had nothing to do with the captives, and they had no claim upon the British Government. Of Mr. Bonnat it is needless to speak. As for the missionaries, they were not captured within the Protectorate, and had only themselves to blame for being captured at all. Sir Garnet would not have been justified in allowing his military movements to be checked and retarded on their account. He did not stop his army because Mr. Dawson wrote to say that he and the Fantee captives would be killed if the army came on; yet, despite the difference of colour, Mr. Dawson and the Fantees had more right to be considered English prisoners than the missionaries.

However, the truth is that it was not the letters but the advance of Sir G. Wolseley which procured the liberation of the captives. Mr. Ussher and Mr. Hennessy had written letters enough to the king. Had the General marched to Fomana rejecting all negotiations the captives would have been released all the same. When he did fight his way to Coomassie, Dawson and the Fantees were not killed or taken from the town. The defeat of the English alone would have been dangerous to them.

When the captives made their appearance at Fomana with a letter from the king, stating that he would make Amanquatia pay the indemnity, Sir Garnet Wolseley seems to have taken for granted that there would not be any more fighting. That was what he wished, and that was what he believed. Although in a few days he would certainly know whether the king was acting in good faith, he, on this mere promise of a savage noted for his treachery, composed a telegram in cipher and sent it to the coast, with an order to the senior naval officer to despatch it by the fast steam-ship *Sarmatian* to Gibraltar.

Not a moment was to be lost The telegram arrived in England, and shed a brief and delusive gleam over the last days of Mr. Gladstone's Ministry. The Ashantee War was at an end, and no blood had been shed. But when the news came of the five days' fighting, and the great battle Amoaful, the effect on the mind of the public must have resembled that which is produced by a practical joke.

The voyage of the *Sarmatian*, which carried no freight but an Ashantee lie, cost several thousand pounds; and the style in which the telegram was sent, the employment of cipher, the air of mystery with which the matter was surrounded, makes the after process of disillusion all the more entertaining. For why should there have been any secrecy at all? Then again, if Sir Garnet thought it advisable to send a special steamer to Gibraltar, he should have allowed it to be utilised in other ways. The *Sarmatian* might have taken a number of invalids; but the orders were peremptory, and she got up steam without delay.

Sir G. Wolseley showed himself a little too much the child of nature, in believing the promise of the king, and should not have employed a special steamer at all until he had facts, not promises, to send. Secondly, he should not have sent such a vessel as the *Sarmatian*, but one of an inferior class, for the *Sarmatian* brought out the 42nd regiment. When they arrived on the coast, she had not returned, and in order to accommodate the regiment, a hospital ship for sailors and marines, the *Nebraska*, had to be cleared out of its patients, who were sent back to their ships, not to the improvement of their health.

Though I blame Sir Garnet Wolseley for having sent, at great cost, the news of peace to England, before peace had been secured, I do not blame him for having supposed that the king would submit. At Fomana the probabilities appeared to be in favour of peace. The released captives declared that the king had no powder, and that he did not wish to fight, that he could not fight if he wished. They had not the least idea that a great army was being assembled in the field. On the other hand, they mentioned one fact which seemed at variance with their opinion, and which alone should have deterred Sir Garnet from sending home the telegram. They said that in every house in Coomassie slaves were busy breaking up iron-stones into slugs. It was difficult to suppose that the whole labouring population of a city could thus be employed, if all intention to resist invasion had been abandoned by the leaders of the people.

CHAPTER 17

Amoaful

While Sir Garnet remained at Fomana waiting supplies, Russell's regiment and the engineers went ahead. Lord Gifford scouted in every direction, and discovered that on the flanks of the road were villages in which were armed men, and from which the women and children had been sent away. These villagers received warning to quit, and, as they did not go in peace, Major Russell was ordered to dislodge them. He destroyed a village, killing two men, and taking five prisoners, one of whom was the head scout of the chief of Adansi. Sir Garnet was much distressed at the village being burnt; he sent off one of the prisoners with a letter to the king, containing an apology, I suppose; and orders were issued not to burn any more villages, there with the Chief of Adansi, and a considerable body of men.

Lord Gifford, from whom all this intelligence was obtained, intercepted a convoy of powder on its way to that village from Coomassie. Colonel McLeod, 42nd regiment, who had been appointed Brigadier to the native regiments, was ordered to visit Borborassie; to parley first of all, not to attack it except in case of resistance, and even in case of resistance not to destroy it. More ridiculous orders could not have been given. Either the village should have been left alone until Sir Garnet had thought fit to finish his amiable correspondence with the king, or it should have been attacked in a military manner. Had this been done, Essamanquatia might have been captured; at all events the village would have been surprised and taken without resistance.

As it was, we were the chief losers. Captain Nicol was in advance with the Amanaboes; he stopped to parley according to orders; the alarm was given; the villagers streamed out into the street, and Captain Nicol was shot through the heart—a human sacrifice offered up by Sir Garnet Wolseley to Exeter Hall. Colonel McLeod took the village, but, according to orders, did not destroy it. This emboldened the Ashantees, who attacked the troops on their way back, severely wounded a seaman, and killed a Fantee. Altogether, it was not considered a success by many of the officers engaged, though it read well enough in despatches.

Sir Garnet Wolseley often made the vulgar mistake of applying to warfare in Africa axioms derived from warfare in Europe. An outcry had been raised against the destruction of villages in Europe: he therefore gave orders that villages should not be destroyed in Ashantee. But there is no analogy between the two cases; the sound only is the same, the sense is opposite. In Gold Coast warfare villages are equivalent to fortified posts; there the warriors store up their powder, and assemble in order to attack. It was no use to take Borborassie and not to destroy it, for that same afternoon the Ashantees were back there again. Had it been burnt they would have gone to some other village; and had all the villages near to the road been destroyed, these small parties of marauders, who could give more trouble than an army, would have joined the general camp.

On that same day Colonel Wood received orders to ambuscade the road which led from Borborassie to Coomassie, as the Ashantees might be expected to retreat that way. The idea was Lord Gifford's, and a good one; but in what a style it was carried out! Colonel Wood received orders not to fire first. Imagine an ambuscade with orders not to fire first! Happily the Ashantees did not retreat so far, or perhaps another officer's life would have been sacrificed.

Again, on that same day, January 28, Ashantee messengers came in. They speedily returned, and it was proclaimed to the army that all negotiations were over, and that there was going to be war.

The king had promised that Amanquatia should pay the indemnity; but Amanquatia, instead of collecting gold-dust, collected a large army, and took up his position at a town called Amoaful, about twenty miles from Coomassie.

On the morning of the 30th, Wood's and Russell's regiments occupied the village Quarman. Half a mile further on was the village Egginassie, the outpost of the enemy. The English army was concentrated at or near Insarfu, four miles behind Quarman. The Ashantee army was encamped about half-a-mile behind Egginassie, and extended up to Amoaful.

On the afternoon of the 30th, Major Home made a road close up to Egginassie, working his way in silence, and cutting through trunks of trees with an oiled saw. He heard voices in the village. In the night Gifford scouted and reported the position of the army. Then we all knew that a great battle would be fought on the morrow.

Sir Garnet's little army consisted of:

1. The 42nd regiment or Black Watch, commanded by Major Macpherson, Colonel McLeod being Brigadier to the native troops.

2. The 2nd battalion of the Rifle Brigade (the old 95th), Lieut.-Colonel Warren.

3. A hundred men of the 23rd, Lieut.-Colonel the Hon. Savage Mostyn. Sir Archibald Alison commanded the White Brigade.

4. The Naval Brigade (seamen and marines), Captain Grubbe, R.N.

5. Wood's and Russell's regiments, now reduced to but a few companies, the rest being employed to garrison posts along the road.

6. A small company of the 2nd West India regiment, Lieutenant Jones.

7. Rait's Artillery, consisting of Haussas working seven-pounder mountain guns and rocket-troughs.

The order of battle was as follows. The 42nd regiment would advance along the main road and take Amoaful. It would be accompanied by Lord Gifford and the scouts; by Major Home and a party of engineer labourers; by Captain Rait and Lieutenant Saunders with two guns. Its flanks were to be protected by two columns, one upon the right and the other on the left. The left column would be commanded by Colonel McLeod, with a part of the Naval Brigade in advance; Russell's regiment; engineer labourers, Captain Buckle, R.E.; and a rocket party, Rait's Artillery. The right column would be commanded by Lieut-Colonel Wood, V.C., with the rest of the Naval Brigade in advance; Wood's regiment; engineer labourers, Lieutenant Bell, R.E.; and a rocket party, Rait's Artillery.

In rear of the front column would be the general and his staff, with Commodore Hewett and the company of the 23rd. The Rifle Brigade would be behind them in reserve. Lieutenant Jones with the 2nd West would garrison Quarman. The baggage of the native regiments was parked at that village; the baggage of the main body with a quantity of stores at Insarfu.

Having studied the plan of battle the night before, I determined to go with the front column, and to be in the advance. It was no idle motive which induced me to thrust myself into 'the forefront of the hottest battle.' In a bush battle no bird's-eye views are to be had, and a war correspondent who wishes to see anything of war must go very near the enemy. Besides, I wished to study an important and interesting problem. I had often heard it said by military men that British soldiers are poor bush-fighters, and that in the New Zealand and Cape wars they never much distinguished themselves against the Maoris and Caffres—that is, they did not display such a superiority, and achieve so decisive a success as they usually gain in contests against an inferior race.

Now hitherto we had never beaten the Ashantees in the bush. The battle of Dodowa was fought in a plain. At Elmina the Ashantees were defeated by Festing, but that was in the open. At Essaman Sir Garnet won a bush-fight, but there were few Ashantees present. At Abrakrampa Russell repulsed a great army, but he held a fortified post. On the other hand, the experiment of Europeans *versus* Ashantees in the bush had never been fairly tried. When Sir Charles Macarthy was defeated and surrounded and killed with nearly all his officers in a great bush-battle fifty years ago, he had merely a handful of inferior European troops and a mob of Fantee allies. When Festing fought twice in the bush near Dunquah, when certain British officers fought near Abrakrampa, when Wood fought at Fesoo, they commanded disciplined negro troops or attempted to command undisciplined native allies.

Never had a regular regiment engaged the Ashantees, and now at length the great question was about to be put to the test. I wished to observe for myself the procedure and issue of the combat. I knew that the Ashantees on their own ground, never invaded before, would be at their best; and every Englishman knows that the British Army is well represented by the 42nd regiment. Its history is glorious; on its banners are inscribed proud and imperishable names. Raised from loyal clans in 1739, it was at first composed of independent companies under their own officers, and employed to watch the borders of the Highlands. The uniform consisted of dark-green coats, kilts, and hose: hence the regiment was called the *Freacadan Dubh*, or 'Black Watch,' to distinguish it from the red-coated soldiers of the king. On the Gold Coast they wore a grey uniform in common with the other troops, but their pith helmets were adorned with the red hackle which was given to the regiment in honour of its having retaken in Flanders some British guns captured from another regiment by the French.

About half-past seven on the morning of the 31st I was at breakfast at Quarman when Lake, who was on the lookout, rushed in and said, 'White soldier come!' I gave him a knapsack and water-bottle, and snatched up my Snider. The 42nd did not halt in the village, but marched along at a pace which, after four months of West Africa, and an attack of dysentery, made me pant and perspire. Presently we heard a few shots—the scouts clearing Egginassie. The faces of the men brightened, and one of them said 'That's good.' Two Assins ran past us towards the rear, blood streaming down their bodies. We marched through the village, then for half a mile through the forest, and as we were descending a hill the battle began.

The soldiers extended to the right and the left of the path in line, and we found that we were in the Ashantee camp. On all sides were little huts with low sloping roofs, thatched with the green broad leaves of the plantain. Each hut or lean-to had a couple of bamboo bedsteads raised on posts. Among these huts were fires with cooking pots upon them, and inside the pots boiled plantains, or messes of Indian corn. They had also taken the pains to make comfortable settees with backs. A vast number of carriers' bundles containing provisions and other property lay scattered about.

A hundred yards ahead the forest was filled with smoke, and seemed to roar: tongues of flame shot forth, and these alone served as a mark, for not a man was to be seen. The slugs hummed and danced in among us, rattling against the trees, and against the pots on the fires. I was hit three times in about five minutes; but these hits were so innocuous that I thought it was all going to be mere child's play. However I was soon undeceived. In that part the forest was tolerably open; but as the Highlanders slowly advanced, moving from tree to tree as directed by their officers, and lying down to shoot, we came to a thicker part of the bush, and the enemy fired at close range.

Finally we came to a swampy bit at the bottom of the hill, with a dark sluggish stream flowing through its midst; beyond this was another hill, covered, not with forest, but jungle. Then the business began to be severe. The air was filled with that music which Charles XII. said he preferred to every other. I am not exaggerating when I say that for more than an hour the leaves fell just as they do on an English autumn day when there is a strong wind. At one time, whichever way I looked I saw wounded men. One poor fellow ran past me with a strange staggering gait, his eyes fixed and his hand upon his heart, and then suddenly fell and rolled over stone dead.

This went on for some time: the Highlanders advanced but very slowly; the bagpipes were playing, but even when close to could scarcely be heard for the din. Presently a big ,gun boomed on the right; I went in that direction and found Captain Rait and Lieutenant Saunders proceeding along the main road or path with their Haussas and a seven-pounder gun, and a train of naked Fantees bearing ammunition. The Haussas had been indefatigably drilled by these two officers, and the pains bestowed upon them had not been in vain. We were now at the foot of the jungle-covered hill on the summit of which was Amoaful. Up went the gun; every five minutes there was a halt; the gun was fired two or three times; the Highlanders crept into the bush on the right and on the left.

Then I heard a clear cheery voice cry out 'Advance!' and then the 42nd gave a cheer, and the Haussas cheered, and the Fantees cheered, and the gun was wheeled along for fifteen or twenty yards. The jungle was now so thick that the men were formed again in column; it was too thick even for the Ashantees, who had not cut war-paths, and so were obliged to occupy the road, where they suffered severely. Soon we had to lie down among dead bodies marked with great red wounds: yet still the slugs sang over us, and savagely slashed the boughs above our heads. 'Rough work this for a civilian!' said one of the soldiers; and I saw them all eyeing me with an air of puzzled curiosity.

I now observed that the officer who always cried out 'Advance!' was limping in evident pain. It was Major Macpherson. He had been shot through the leg, and had tied it round with a handkerchief, but still bright-faced and smiling urged on the men. And they, when the order was given to advance, looked at one another and smiled. Just at this time another officer came up to the extreme front He had only one arm, so I knew that it was Brigadier-General Sir Archibald Alison, the son of the historian.

Light! light! light! I saw clear sky on ahead and knew that it was the town. The gloomy forest was behind us; soon we saw houses and an open street. The fire of the enemy' slackened. Rait fired a shell down the street, and it killed a group of men running out at the farther end of the town. This was the *finale*; the day's work was done so far as the 42nd was concerned. 105 men were wounded and 2 killed; 9 officers were wounded, and one of them, Major Baird, afterwards died.

We sat down under the shade of the trees in the middle of the town. Clouds covered the sky and a sweet wind was blowing; it was deliciously cool. Under another cluster of trees a field-hospital was established. The doctors probed and bandaged the wounds; then the men were laid gently down, and their chums sat by them holding their hands and gave them comforting words.

Lake soon made up a fire, and then, opening my knapsack, we lunched together on chocolate, biscuit, and sardines. After which I despatched him to 'loot' curiosities; for when the town had been occupied, and all precautions taken against a surprise, the men off duty had been told they might 'go and hunt;' in such cases a harmless recreation, which it is mere pedantry to forbid. Lake found some stone implements (now in Sir John Lubbock's collection), and also a small metal box, with a portrait of Mrs. Beecher Stowe embossed on the lid. Lake had behaved with his usual steadiness and courage, and had picked up some curiosities under fire on the battlefield. Several canopies, or umbrellas, were found in the town; these are equivalent to colours; and their loss is eternal disgrace for the chieftains to whom they belong.

Our fight began at 8, and the town was taken at 11.45. We passed some quiet hours; a few Ashantees hovered round the town like birds of prey driven from their nest, and fired harmless shots out of the adjacent bush. But in the distance we could hear, on the right and left, the rolling sound of musketry.

The general took up his position in the village Egginassie; there he received the reports of Sir A. Alison, Colonel McLeod, and Colonel Wood. Now and then he gave an order; Colonel Greaves, the chief of the staff, wrote it down on a scrap of paper, carried it himself, or sent it by another staff officer to the columns engaged. The wounded men were brought into the village, and then despatched with an escort to Quarman. Early in the day Captain Buckle, R.E., was killed on the left, and Colonel Wood was brought in wounded from the right column, which had to be supported by a part of the Rifles. Egginassie itself was attacked. In the afternoon an onslaught was made upon Quarman; the handful of 2nd West behaved gallantly, and the village was relieved by a detachment of the Rifles. It is needless to say that the Naval Brigade, which headed the two flank columns, was hotly engaged. Several officers were wounded, and Sub-Lieutenant Mundy afterwards died.

Sir Garnet went on to Amoaful; the Rifles and the 23rd kept the road open; an attempt was made to bring up some of the baggage from Insarfu, but the convoy was attacked, and a few loads were taken. Some of the staff officers lost their campaigning kit, and in fact everything but what they had on.

The soldiers were quartered in the houses; two kegs of rum, brought on by Captain Baker of the Fantee armed police, were served out, much to the contentment of the army; and soon after dark sleep fell upon the town. But about 3 a.m. I happened to wake up and heard the sound of shots far away. It was a night attack upon Quarman.

CHAPTER 18

Becqua

It is needless to say that the problem was now solved; Ashantees could not beat British soldiers, even in the bush. They could bear the fire of the Sniders, for they are marvellously dexterous in taking cover, but they could not stand the advance. They load so slowly that they must retire before an advancing army armed with the breech-loader, and those who continually retire must eventually retreat. The 42nd owed much of its success to the fact that it kept moving on. 'Thank God!' said one young officer, 'our men don't know how to skirmish.' It must not be supposed that the soldiers of this gallant regiment were indifferent to cover; they lay down to fire, and got well behind trees, but Macpherson never let them stay long in one place; and as soon as he cried out 'Advance!' the evident joy of the men, their smiles, their words to one another, the sparkling of their eyes showed that charging was their speciality.

It had been frequently discussed whether buck-shot or bullets were the best for this kind of warfare. Upon that point I speak without hesitation after Amoaful. If I had to travel through the Ashantee country with a small escort, running the risk of an ambuscade, and perhaps a personal encounter, I would choose a double-barrel breech-loader with buck-shot cartridges, because I might have to take a snap-shot. A certain officer in one of the posts along the road went down to the outskirts of the clearing into the bush, and suddenly met an Ashantee who howled with fright. The officer had a Snider, fired a snap-shot, and missed! The Ashantee gave him a charge of slugs from his flint-lock and bolted. But as for the weapon with which the troops should be armed, that no longer admits of dispute.

At Amoaful it was all shooting in the dark; we did not see the Ashantees; all that we could do was to fire towards the flashes and

153

smoke which marked their lurking-place. Now a storm of rifle-bullets rushing through the air is far more deadly than a shower of buck-shot. The Snider, aimed low, sends its projectile skimming along about three feet high a considerable distance; nothing can stop it but the trunk of a tree, and perhaps it kills a chief seated on his stool, beneath his umbrella, far away in the rear. Then the wounds caused by the Snider are terrific, and must tend to demoralise the enemy.

We all thought, before the experiment was tried, that the three columns (parallel) formation was the best for a great battle in the bush. But though with that formation Sir Garnet won a great victory, I do not think he would adopt it again. The right and left columns did no doubt protect the flanks of the 42nd regiment, but lines of skirmishers thrown out, keeping touch of the main column, would have answered that purpose. The disadvantages of parallel columns in bush-fighting are these. They cannot see one another, and cannot keep measure in distance and time. One column finds the bush tolerably open, and therefore advances freely; the other is retarded by a patch of impenetrable jungle, by the enemy's fire, or by the caution of its commander.

One flank column will diverge, another will perhaps converge upon the main column. One gets ahead of the others, loses its way, and crosses the line of fire. As guns in cover shooting are connected by beaters, so perhaps the three columns might be connected by a line of skirmishers; but if they happened to meet a thick bit of undergrowth which they could not penetrate (and that sooner or later is tolerably certain), the skirmishers would fall into the columns on the right or the left. Thus between the parallel columns is a strip of dark bush, and let us suppose that into this strip glide a party of Ashantee skirmishers. Lying close to the ground, they fire with deadly effect to the right and left. In both columns men fall. But if they return the fire, they shoot over the heads of the enemy into each other. Then the bugles sound, the officers cry out, 'Don't fire, don't fire, our own men are there!' the soldiers find that slugs and rifle-bullets are coming from the same quarter; fear and confusion fall upon them.

At the hottest part of the fight of Amoaful I heard a Snider bullet come over my head from behind to the left. I must own that I felt for a moment a little bit afraid, and earnestly wished to be saved from my friends. I got in front of a tree, taking my chance of the slugs so long as I could be covered from the rear. For a long time we saw guns flashing away on our left, and feared to shoot in that direction; yet it was never, I believe, ascertained whether they were friends or foes. If this was the case in the main column, what confusion there must have been in the flanks! One officer was wounded by a Snider, for the bullet was extracted. One officer made his men fire by compass. There was much doubt and mystery as to the position of the other troops.

The best formation is a single column, strong and continuous as a chain. With its head should be a mountain gun throwing shell, and the rear-guard should be not less powerful. The ammunition and medical hammocks and baggage (if any) should be distributed throughout the central part, a soldier between each couple of bearers. The column should never cease to advance except for five minutes or so at a time; it should advance by leaps, so to speak, the men moving quickly and then lying down to fire. Thus always moving on, keeping up a continuous fire on the right and on the left, lining itself with sheets of flame and clothing itself in smoke, the column passes through the enemy's position, takes the village, if there be one behind the position, as is usually the case, and at all events leaves the enemy with its war-paths and ambuscades behind it in the rear. All parts of the column are brought under fire; but every segment is in a fighting condition. There are no gaps or weak parts in the chain.

At an early hour in the forenoon the baggage was brought in from Insarfu and Quarman. I saw, not without emotion, the familiar faces of Robert and Joseph; but the sight of my black bullock trunk, and my brown leather bag, touched me to the heart. I now recognised their value. Joseph told me that when Quarman was attacked two of my Fantee hammock-men, following their instinct, ran out of the village into the bush—the enemy's bush. The others seemed inclined to follow their example, but Joseph was a Kossoo, and snatching up a cutlass he threatened to 'chop' any man who moved out of the yard. I shuddered when I thought of what would have been my fate if the baggage had been lost. Imagine a special correspondent with long letters to write and all his stationery stolen by the Ashantees. The next time I was separated from my baggage I put in my pocket some pens and a patent ink-bottle, with some foolscap and large envelopes.

A mile to the left of Amoaful was Becqua, the capital of a province, and the residence of a great chief who ranks with the chiefs of Juabin or Duabin, Adansi, and Mampon. It was known that he had furnished a considerable force to the army, and it was dangerous to leave a great town upon the flank. Lord Gifford, scouting early in the morning, reported its position, and also that the enemy were there in force. At 12.30 the Naval Brigade and Russell's regiment, with the 42nd in reserve, marched against the town. The brigadier commanded. Gifford dashed into the town in advance with his scouts, the Haussas did not support him, and he was in no little danger. Two of his best men were wounded. It was for this plucky lead that he received the Victoria Cross, which is only bestowed for single exploits; but he was really recommended for the distinction by Sir Garnet on account of the perilous nature of the service in which he had so long been engaged. For weeks he carried his life in his hand; and Sir Garnet once said to me, 'Every day I expected to get a letter saying that Gifford had been shot.'

The men at Becqua were taken by surprise. There was a street fight, and then, taking to cover, they kept up for some little while a hot fire on the town. One seaman was killed.

Becqua was nearly as large as Coomassie, and the palace was a house of two storeys. When the enemy were silenced we had little time to look for curiosities; the town was set on fire, and there being a brisk wind was soon all over in a blaze. There were several explosions of powder. It was curious to see the hawks. In West Africa there is a species resembling a kestrel in plumage, but much larger in size, which frequent towns and are almost as numerous as vultures. They now darted and swooped round the burning houses, almost touching the flames with their wings, as if attracted by fire like the moths. By some strange instinct (perhaps inherited experience) they knew that the fire would drive out the rats. So in South Africa, when the plains are on fire, birds of prey accompany the conflagration, and feed on the lizards and other small animals which run out of the thick high grass.

We were told that next morning (February 2) the army would march, and though (as then arranged) it would not be post-time for two or three days, we thought it best to write our letters while we were in comfortable quarters.

The afternoon before, I had taken a stroll through the town, looking for a house. I discovered a detached building surrounded by a high palisade. Forcing my way inside, for it was completely enclosed, I found myself in what appeared to be a fetish house or temple. There was a yard in which were two ancient and majestic trees. All round were earthen pots daubed over with white clay and many kinds of filth. The building itself consisted of an alcove or portico, raised two or three feet above the ground. Its doorway, or rather the open side looking out on the yard, was in the form of a Moorish arch. The floor and basement were crimson in colour, being painted with a kind of red ochre which takes a beautiful polish. The walls inside were washed with the white clay of the Gold Coast, which the natives frequently chew, or drink in solution, the young people taking it as a sweetmeat, the old people as a medicine for heart disease and other complaints. The walls were also adorned with arabesques. Overhead was a thatched roof.

The night was clear and still. The moon was in the heavens, all the stars were alight, from the distance could be heard the sounds of the forest, mingled with the camp fire songs. When all else was silenced in sleep, there rose from time to time the sentries' cry, like the baying of some faithful watchdog, and the half-hourly chimes of a large bell taken at Fomana, and suspended in the middle of the town.

It was the 2nd February, 3 a.m. I had been writing all night. Placing two little Ashantee tables one above the other, laying on the top my writing materials with a lantern, and seated on a barrel, I had scribbled away to my heart's content. In two hours the march would begin.

It is usually supposed that the signs and portents which ancient writers record as having preceded the ruin of a kingdom, a city, or a man, were either entirely fictitious, Or were only called to mind after the event. In the case of Coomassie, however, various prophecies and omens were current with the natives, and were even mentioned by correspondents in the papers, before Coomassie was taken, and at a time when no one supposed that it would be destroyed.

For instance, as early as October I was told this legend while visiting Elmina. There was in Coomassie a famous doctor of the Moslems; he wrote certain words upon paper, sewed them up in leather cases, and sold them as charms against wounds in the war. He fumigated the nostrils of the sick with the smoke of mysterious herbs set on fire: he wrote texts of the *Koran* on a wooden board, washed off the ink into water, and gave it to patients as a draught: he cupped for fever, inoculated for smallpox, applied the hot iron; he also divined future events from a book filled with diagrams, or from figures drawn in the sand. The king called him and said he wished to know the future of Coomassie. The priest made auguries and replied that the fall of Elmina would be also the fall of Coomassie. The king, who did not expect such an answer, went to an old Ashantee sorceress. But she, having consulted the gods of the country, delivered the same oracle. 'The fall of Elmina would be also the fall of Coomassie.'

'Well,' said the king, 'what does it matter? Elmina has been from the creation of the world, and so has Coomassie. It is impossible that either can fall.'

Now Coomassie was destroyed a few months after the destruction of Elmina.

Before we had crossed the Prah a story came from Akim that certain omens had alarmed the people of Coomassie; stones fell from heaven; a child was born which spoke from its birth; suddenly it disappeared, and the room was instantly filled with bush. One evil omen did actually occur. Mr. Kühne relates that just before he left Coomassie the old fetish tree from which the town takes its name fell down and was shattered to splinters. No one ventured to touch them, and they were left lying in the street.

In two hours the march would begin: the Time was approaching; the Hour was at hand; soon the guilty city, which for nearly two hundred years had devoured human flesh, and made itself drunk with blood and tears, deceiving and destroying the nations, spreading solitude, pouring forth human hurricanes, withering corn-fields and plantations, kidnapping tribes, dealing out famine and pestilence and death—soon Coomassie would be fallen and covered with shame.

CHAPTER 19

Ordahsu

The defeat of the Ashantees had been perfect. Amanquatia and many chiefs had been killed; yet still it was probable that another pitched battle would be fought before we could enter Coomassie. The king had not been present in the fight at Amoaful, and for him it would be accounted a disgrace to surrender the capital without having once appeared on the field.

On February 2 we marched about six miles to a village called Ingimmamu. Russell's regiment led the advance, and had a skirmish or two on the way. At Ingimmamu an important decision was taken. The transport again embarrassed our progress, and the general had two evils offered for his choice. Either he must halt, as at Fomana and the Prah, till supplies were brought up, or else be content merely to make a raid upon Coomassie. Instead of staying there a week, opening up communications with Glover, and deliberately concluding a treaty with the king, all that he could do, owing to his early neglect of the transport, was to run into the town, and run out again back to Ingimmamu. He determined to do this rather than delay, and no doubt his decision was a wise one; for even when the next convoy arrived he would have been in the same position: it would have brought him only a few days' supplies.

His position was this. He had four days' rations for his men, and the dash to Coomassie and back would probably occupy five days. Colley promised him that on his return he should find food at Ingimmamu. He would go back for the convoy and fetch it up himself. Thus then it was arranged, and the captains of companies were ordered to ask their men if they would consent to take four days' rations for five days' work. To this they one and all agreed. Hence it will be seen that Sir G. Wolseley left Coomassie on the 6th by previous arrangement, and that the rain had nothing to do with his departure) Had the weather been perfectly fine he must have brought back his troops to Ingimmamu on the 7th; for the British soldier in the best of weather cannot live on moonshine and air.

Preparations were made at once to put Ingimmamu in a position of defence, for this little village had now become the base of operations. It was strongly entrenched and garrisoned; the heavy baggage and weakly men were left there, and so a flying column was prepared, consisting, besides the soldiers, of Fantees who carried ammunition, medical hammocks, and the four days' rations of the army and their own; a herd of cattle was also driven with the column, which, though reduced to the smallest possible dimensions, extended over a third of a mile.

The next day early in the morning the march began, and the Ashantees gave much trouble on the road. Russell's regiment had to shoot its way through ambuscade after ambuscade; and in one place where a hill faced a valley swamp—a position resembling that of Amoaful—the enemy mustered in considerable numbers and stood some time. Two companies of the Rifles supported Major Russell, and skirmished in good style through the bush. Lieutenant Saunders was to the front with his gun throwing round shot and shell. Lieutenant Bell, R.E., also distinguished himself, taking his engineer labourers right into the enemy's position when he found they had built a kind of stockade. In the afternoon the troops arrived at the Ordah (incorrectly named by Bowdich the Dah), and here Sir Garnet, pushing up to the front and surveying the position, resolved to bivouac.

The sappers at once set to work on a bridge under Major Home's supervision; it was nearly ready before dark and complete before the dawn. Russell's regiment forded the river, and encamped on the other side. In the rainy season this tributary of the Prah is a deep and swift flowing stream. It is regarded by the Ashantees as a sacred river, and the king bathes in it with religious ceremonies once a year.

About the middle of the day, just after an ambuscade skirmish, those in the front heard a loud musical voice crying out 'Mercy O! Mercy O!' and then saw two men running down the path towards them. One carried a white flag in his right hand and a large letter in his left; the other wore a golden plate upon his breast—the badge of a royal messenger. According to the usual routine they were detained in the front, while the letter was passed down the column to Sir Garnet Just as they seated themselves by the roadside the Ashantees again opened fire, and we could see by the envoys' expression of face that they were apprehensive for their heads. The letter requested the general to stop a few days; to which he replied that he intended to sleep at the Ordah, and that if the king wanted peace he must send as hostages the Queen Mother, and Prince Mensah, the heir to the throne.

Some of the staff, it is said, were sanguine enough to believe that these distinguished persons would come in that night; and much amusement was caused by an order issued to the pickets that they were on no account to fire if they saw an old woman coming down the road. Lord Gifford's scouts ascertained the existence of a large army in and around the village Ordahsu, about a mile from the Ordah. It is needless to say that all military precautions were taken against a night attack. When it became dark the camp and picket fires extending right and left a considerable distance presented the appearance of a large town by night, and the murmur of voices was like the roaring of the sea.

It was the dry season, but soon after sunset the sky became overcast, a cold gust of wind poured through the camp, dashing up the dry leaves into the air, and thunder could be heard in the distance, prolonged and continuous round the horizon, with sharp isolated denoting cracks precisely resembling an Ashantee fusillade. I thought a tornado was coming, but soon the thunder ceased, there was no longer any wind, and down came a regular steady English kind of rain, which lasted almost throughout the night. It was very uncomfortable, and the soldiers' *tentes d'abri* were left behind at Ingimmamu; but I heard some light-hearted officers say it was not much worse than the autumn manoeuvres. At all events it kept off the Ashantees, which was some consolation for those who like myself slept on the further side of the river.

About eight o'clock the postman arrived! Among my letters was one in an unknown hand, and contained in an envelope of enormous size. It was addressed to the Special Correspondent of the *London Times*. This seemed American, and I took it for granted that some enterprising publisher had written to offer me a handsome sum for the advance sheets of my book. Tearing it open I found that it was an essay on the virtues of chloride of sodium or common salt in cases of fever, and the author implored me to lose no time in diffusing a specific by which hundreds of lives might be saved. I regret that the moderate size of this work prevents me from quoting at length the many ingenious arguments and facts by which the writer supported his theory; but I

161

think it right to publish this astonishing discovery for the benefit of suffering mankind; and I sincerely trust that it will have (by means of this book) a world-wide circulation.

I received a letter from my kind masters, in which I was told that 'a correspondent is bound to take the same precautions for his personal safety as a general,' and I could not but confess to myself that the statement was true. I therefore determined not to go *quite* in the front the next day.

When I crawled out of my hammock from under a thick Inverness cape (like all tropical travellers I carried warm things) I saw Colonel Wood with Furse and Eyre and Mosse, who had been left behind, but had come on by a forced march with a company of Bonny men. They were to have the advance. Wood seemed to have recovered from the slug received at Amoaful, though it had not been extracted. As I shook hands with Eyre he told me what a terrible march they had gone through, not having arrived till midnight. 'Never mind,' said I, 'it is worth the walk; for today I suppose we shall be into Coomassie.' There is something very touching in the thought of this poor boy, who had suffered much from sickness, toiling and toiling along, to cause his own death, and secure his own execution.

That morning an order was issued that the troops in advance were not to fire first. This excited much indignation, after what had happened to Nicol, and one hot-tongued subaltern said—'Reade, we look to men like you to save us from being murdered in this way.' If publicity can prevent generals in future from giving such orders they have it here. There were times when Sir Garnet seemed diplomacy-mad. The worst of such an order is that it seems humane while it really is most inhuman and cruel: it exposes a general's own soldiers to considerable danger.

The Bonny men led the advance up the hill, followed by the Rifles, and the battle speedily began. Russell's regiment came next and I remained with them for a time, but when the firing continued I could not stand it any longer. I forgot all about my instructions; something inside like a spring seemed to push me on despite of myself, and I went right on to the front. The advance companies of the Rifles were lying on the ground, Some facing to the right, others to the left, firing low and slow. The air was filled with a sulphurous stench, and was thick with smoke, through which dark forms could be seen moving slowly: These were the officers, who walked backwards and forwards giving orders to their men. I saw poor Eyre lying by the path: his face, pillowed on a comrade's arm, already bore the ghastly impress of death. A little while before Colonel Wood had bade him farewell. Stooping down he kissed his cheek, and Eyre drawing a ring from his finger said, 'Give this to my mother.'

I sat down by the path-side, taking the best cover I could find. On the other side, a young surgeon was attending to the wounded. Lieutenant Wauchope, who was severely wounded in the shoulder, came up just after a Haussa, but would not be probed and bandaged before his humble companion in arms. 'No,' said he, 'it is his turn first.' These are the little incidents that a special correspondent picks up in the front; they not only give him items for his letters, but also give him a higher opinion of human nature than he had before. As the doctor dressed Wauchope's wound, I saw the slugs chipping off the twigs just over his head.

The army ought to be grateful to its surgeons. They incur their full share of danger, and do not always receive their full measure of reward. To my mind there is nothing so impressive, even amid the varied and startling scenes of the battlefield, as the group which encircles a wounded combatant. There lingers the friend, forgetful for a moment of glory, and there, with the bullets whistling around him, kneels an unarmed man examining and dressing the wound with clear head and steady hand, as if he were in the peaceful hospital.

At Ordahsu the order of battle was in single column; but the head remained too long without moving on. At last the word was given, and the Rifles rushed into the village. I was just behind the first section, and saw one man rolled over like a rabbit; it was not a serious wound, the slug having grazed his head, but it stunned him at the time. Among the last to clear out of the houses was a warrior aged fourteen, armed with a gun considerably taller than himself. A man was caught in the bush close by, who said that he was a deserter. If we would please not kill him he would show us just where the king was; he would show us Coomassie; he would show us plenty of things. This gentleman was conducted to a hut, bawling, gesticulating, and assuring us he would do anything in preference to being killed. .

The 42nd lined the road from the river to the village; the ammunition baggage and stores were passed up; then followed Sir Garnet and his staff; the Naval Brigade, like an iron shield, closed up the rear. This movement was justly admired.

The Ashantees attempted to retake the village, coming between it and Coomassie, and poured in a furious fire. They also attacked it from other points. When this had gone on for some time, Colonel McLeod asked for the command of his regiment, instead of the native Brigade, and volunteered to take it right on to Coomassie. His offer was accepted, and Sir Archibald Alison accompanied the advance. The Black Watch marched down the hill and dispersed the enemy. Coomassie was more than six miles off; but no one then knew exactly how far we had to go, or what opposition there might be upon the way.

Chapter 20

Coomassie

The Highlanders marched along at a rattling pace. At intervals of a mile or so, the foremost company came upon parties of Ashantees. Then we heard shots, and cheers 'for Old Scotland,' and the bagpipes played, and the whole regiment broke out into a double. By the side of the road we saw kegs of powder which had been emptied in battle, and camp huts with fires still smoking; and then we saw in the road itself state-chairs and umbrellas belonging to chiefs, mingled with dead bodies, some of them laid on stretchers and thrown down in haste. At one village the regiment was halted to get water, but none was to be had. Several officers had in their hands an Itinerary or road-book, drawn up by Major Wilson, R.E., of the War Office; and when we came to Quarsi, the last village before Coomassie, we all became highly excited.

Presently there was a halt which gave me time to get to the front. The treacherous white flag had again made its appearance, accompanied by three or four miserable slaves, who were offered as hostages if only the advance might be delayed. They also brought a letter from Dawson to the general, imploring him to stop and arrange a treaty outside the town, or else he, the poor Dawson, and the Fantees would be killed, and then, as he very justly observed, 'the destruction of the whole blessed kingdom would not bring us back again.' The messenger with the flag and the letter was sent on to the general; but the brigadier and Colonel McLeod continued the march. Two of the hostages, one of them a woman, were detained and made to walk in the front; not wishing to be shot by their friends they cried out, in a loud and dismal voice, '*Shanti fo! Shanti fo!*' (Ashantee people). This showed that armed men were before us on the road.

A sergeant marched a few paces ahead of the column. As he turned a corner he encountered an armed Ashantee who raised his gun, whereupon the sergeant fired. The women cried out '*Dabbi Oh!*' (No, oh !) to the Ashantees, signifying that they should not return the fire. Presently we came to the dead body of a fine young man, whose head had just been cut off, and was lying by the body. This was a human sacrifice to prevent us from entering Coomassie.

The forest had now dwindled into jungle; the path became wide, and was joined by other paths from the right and left, like tributary rivers. This showed we were approaching a large town, and many earthen pots like those in the fetish-house at Amoaful stood by the wayside. As we came to some cross-roads, we found a number of men with large knives in their hands on the point of killing a man who was tied up for the sacrifice. He was at once liberated, and the Ashantees, with their knives still in their hands, saluted us with a friendly air, saying, 'Thank you, thank you,' which they suppose is our 'How do you do?' or 'Good day.' Several others came up with guns in their hands and presented the butts towards us, One man fell down on his knees, with hands raised and clasped in the attitude of prayer, and a face of woe and supplication.

A king's servant was there, wearing some ornament covered with leopard skin; he begged the brigadier-general to wait, and said that not having sent back the white flag, and not having halted, we had taken them quite by surprise. He hinted, in fact, that we had played them a trick to escape opposition. As the men required a rest, Sir Archibald agreed to wait half-an-hour. Down a path to the right were a dozen or twenty armed men who surveyed us with looks of hatred and fear, contrasting strongly with the politeness of the gentlemen with knives, who belonged, no doubt, to the best families in Coomassie. These saw that the men on the right meant mischief; it was evident enough by their looks; so they cried out, again and again, 'Do not shoot! do not shoot!' But there stood the warriors with the same savage expression of face, restlessly moving their guns in their hands. At last the leopard-skin man walked down the path and spoke to them for a little while. Then they shouldered their muskets with an air of disgust, and walked away, looking back at us with an evil eye.

Sir Archibald's orders were to take up a position by the water outside the town, and there wait further instructions; but soon after we had started (the half hour having elapsed) Captain Buller came up and said, 'The general thinks you had better press on.' We passed through the filthy marsh which insulates Coomassie, and then came to the town. The first street was a broad road of rising ground, with here and there a detached house on either side. At the top of the hill we turned to the left, and passing the execution grove, which perfumed the air far and wide, marched down a spacious street. Numbers of men came up to the soldiers and shook hands. One man, either drunk or a professional buffoon, performed a dance, and seemed desirous to bestow caresses on the Highlanders.

The demeanour of the mob was simply that of the Africans when they see something in the way of a show: they laughed and opened their eyes and mouths, and uttered cries of amazement and delight, just as I have seen them do when I have entered a large town where no white man had been seen before. They seemed to have no feeling but that of wonder and pleasure. I imagine that most of them were slaves. But far away at the end of the street was a dense black crowd, above which floated a huge red canopy. I could see men with whips in their hands flogging the people to make them get out of the way, and the umbrella turned round a corner.

It was certainly some great chief, and I have often thought it might have been the king. But all the released captives said that the king did not return to Coomassie after the Battle of Ordahsu. Two Haussa slaves, who deserted on the field to our side, said that the king took up his position in the rear to the left of the village. He sat on a golden stool beneath a silk and velvet canopy, and declared that he would cut off the head of any chief who tried to run away. But when, as our troops advanced, the bullets whizzed past his royal head, he ran away himself, and passed on to Aminihia, where he has a country seat.

Coomassie was taken; and now we saw something extraordinary. Up to the crowd which was gazing on the soldiers, or giving them water to drink, came men powder-stained and naked, shot-belts round their bodies, and guns upon their shoulders. Not only their appearance, but the affectionate manner in which they were embraced by their friends, showed where they had been spending the day. At the same time there was a constant stream going by of people with guns and with boxes on their heads. This sight must have been distasteful to those two true soldiers, Sir Archibald Alison and Colonel McLeod: but what could they do without orders? and they knew it was not a regular war, but a diplomatic war. So the men were not disarmed, and the people were allowed to carry their property away.

Coomassie was taken by the brigadier-general and the 42nd regiment at 5.30. The major-general arrived at 6, riding on a mule, and followed by his staff and the special correspondents, whom I had distanced in the race. Sir Garnet made the troops present arms and give three cheers for the queen, which sadly scared the, Ashantees.

The citizens were still streaming past with their goods. 'Now, at all events,' thought I, 'a stop will be put to this sort of thing.' But Sir Garnet did not interfere with the innocent people. He gave strict orders there should be no plundering, and hanged a policeman who stole a cloth; but he gave the people of Coomassie free regress and egress, and so before the next morning they had taken away most of their belongings.

Much gin was found in the town, and having been carefully tasted by the medical men, was pronounced to be excellent Hollands, and was served out as rations to the troops. So the town gin was seized, and some powder, but that was all.

Sir G. Wolseley knew what was before him. He had only one day. In that day he would have to obtain the submission of the king and the signing of a treaty, or burn the town and the Bantama, and go back to Ingimmamu. Under such circumstances he should surely have prevented the people from taking their property away; above all he should have placed a strong guard over the palace. The more he had in his possession, the better security there was that the king would give in.

The great mistake which Sir Garnet made throughout his negotiations, and especially at the last, was in showing the king that he was anxious for peace. This too evident anxiety the king of course attributed to weakness and fear. Sir Garnet also showed no little vacillation. He said at the Prah that he would see no one in person excepting the king: at Coomassie he did receive messengers himself. He demanded the mother and brother of the king as hostages: at Coomassie he said that he would take any hostages of rank. He demanded a certain indemnity, and a certain sum of money down: at Coomassie he said that he would not require so much money down as he had demanded at first. When the king found that in return for his false promises, and his armies gathered on the sly, such important concessions were obtained, it is not remarkable that he should go on as he had begun.

As soon as we entered the town I saw a man coming down the street dressed in European clothes, and carrying a large gingham umbrella. On either side were Ashantees, who, by their gestures, were evidently urging him to do them a favour, while he, placidly waving his hand, was evidently saying, 'Do not be uneasy; I will do all you wish.' This, I knew, must be Mr. Dawson, and it was no less clear that the Ashantees were begging him to intercede on their behalf. The Ashantees, although savages, have the power of keeping their passions under control, when it suits their interest to do so, in a manner which would do credit to civilised diplomatists. They did not love Dawson, but they utilised him all the same.

That night Dawson brought to the general some people from the king. Sir Garnet wrote a letter, which has been published with his despatches, and also spoke to the following effect:

> The king had deceived him, but he had kept his word to the king: he had come to Coomassie. He earnestly wished to be friends, and to make a lasting peace with Ashantee. He invited the king to come back: his palace had not been occupied: and there he might sign the treaty... But if the king refused to make peace, he would then show through the length and breadth of Africa how great was the power of Great Britain. There was no occasion for delay and there must be no delay. The affair must be settled by eight o'clock the next morning.'

I was told of this speech the same night, and went to bed in a happy frame of mind. That, I thought, was the way to negotiate. But unhappily Sir Garnet did not adhere firmly to his words.

The king promised to come in. But eight o'clock passed. Sir Garnet waited and waited all day long.

He had often been told by those who were well acquainted with the Africans that the King of Ashantee would use every possible means to delay him on the march. He declared that no message from the king should detain him a day on the road; and he kept his word. He promised the king to wait a few days at Fomana, but that delay was necessitated by the transport.

Yet it would have been better that he should have waited some days on the road than lost that one priceless day at Coomassie. He squandered away his brief and valuable time— the few hours he had to act—in looking like Sister Anne up the street. He then said he would be content if the king signed the treaty without coming in; but that also failed. In the evening he saw that all was over, and indeed, he had received a convincing proof of Ashantee treachery in the course of the day. Two of the envoys who had told him the king was just coming in were discovered taking off powder from the town. They were made prisoners.

169

Sir Garnet ordered Colonel McLeod to destroy the Bantama, and an hour afterwards, for reasons best known to himself, revoked the order he had given. As a last resource he circulated a report that the next morning he intended to advance, hoping that this shallow device would frighten the king into submission. Had he at half-past eight on the morning of the 5th marched out his troops to the Bantama the king might have submitted; at all events Sir Garnet would have done all that was in his power, since owing to the state of his transport he could not remain more than a day and two nights in the town. As it was the Bantama escaped.

'Why was it of so much importance,' the reader may ask, 'that the Bantama should be destroyed?' In the first place I reply that the work of destruction if done at all should have been complete. But there were special reasons why the Bantama should have been destroyed. It was the mausoleum of the Kings of Ashantee, a place of human sacrifices, the great spiritual stronghold of the priests. It was also the royal treasure-house, and a kind of religious and political museum; there the skull of Sir Charles Macarthy was preserved. No stranger was allowed to enter its sacred precincts; it was placed under the care of a powerful chief, and a guard watched over it day and night. According to some accounts it was a mile and a half, according to others only half a mile from Coomassie, with which it was connected by a wide road.

There can be no doubt that men were sacrificed and much fetish worked by the priests to avert the destruction of this sacred place, and the fact that it did escape will always be a kind of consolation for the Ashantees. 'The Braffoos,' they will say, 'took Coomassie, but they could not take the Bantama.' Then the rites and sacrifices practised on that occasion will be noted down as efficacious against the power of the white man; and no doubt the priests say, 'In the next war we will do so and so, and we shall conquer.' Indeed, I look on the sparing of the Bantama as an actual calamity; and the article of the treaty in which Sir G. Wolseley requests that the king will abolish human sacrifices is a poor substitute for the destruction of their sanctuary.

That night fires broke out all over the town, lighted as some suppose by our native allies. Home's sappers worked hard to extinguish the flames.

The next morning I went out for a walk round the town. One street alone was occupied by our troops, and the Ashantees had all gone away. I walked through several streets without seeing a man. It was like a City of the Dead. I passed a flock of sheep wandering uneasily along, baaing plaintively, as if distressed by this unwonted condition of affairs. Vultures of course were plentiful, and also a kind of black and white crow, common on the Gold Coast.

Presently I saw a strange and melancholy object. It was a man whose feet were manacled together so that he could just shuffle along at the pace of a snail; his right hand, secured by an iron loop, was passed through a hole in an enormous log of wood which he had to carry in his arms. He was a Fantee prisoner; the others had been released the night before; but he had been imprisoned a long way off, and had managed to creep thus far travelling all night. His ankles were bleeding and covered with flies. Lake and I worked for some time to set him free, and I saw in the distance a Haussa soldier whom I called and who also joined in our efforts. But we could not break or unloose the diabolical contrivance.

At last there came three Fantees, released prisoners and friends of the captive; they understood the iron and the log, which are used also in Fantee, and setting to work with a knife and a stone soon set the man free. There is not much one can like in the Fantees; but it was very pleasing to observe how tenderly they handled their friend, how they brushed the flies from his wounds, how; sweetly and soothingly they spoke, and with what joy they welcomed him back to liberty as the fetters and wood fell with a thud and clatter on the ground.

These prisoners had been captured while trading at Fomana in an interval of peace. One of them was a nephew of Dawson's and could speak English well enough. He served me as 'valet-de-place,' and showed me the sights of Coomassie. First we went to the king's palace, which consists of many courtyards, each surrounded with alcoves and verandahs, and having two gates or doors, so that each yard was a thoroughfare. These doors were secured by padlocks. An ordinary house has one courtyard; a large house three or four; the king's palace had ten or twelve. But the part of the palace fronting the street was a stone house, Moorish in its style, such as those that are built at Cape Coast, with a flat roof and a parapet, and suites of apartments on the first floor. It was built by Fantee masons many years ago.

The rooms upstairs reminded me of Wardour Street. Each was a perfect Old Curiosity Shop. Books in many languages, Bohemian glass, clocks, silver plate, old furniture, Persian rugs, Kidderminster carpets, pictures and engravings, numberless chests and coffers. A sword bearing the inscription 'From Queen Victoria to the King of Ashantee' A copy of the *Times* October 17, 1843. With these were many specimens of

Moorish and Ashantee handicraft, gold-studded sandals such as only the king and a few great chiefs may wear, with, strange to say, Arabic writing on the soles; leopard-skin caps lined with yellow velvet and adorned outside with beaten gold like that of Cashmere, and a plume of the same precious metal; saddles of red leather, magnificent canopies or state umbrellas of velvet and satin, baskets or cradles in which Ashantee chiefs are accustomed to be carried on the heads of slaves, with other curious and tasteful things too numerous for me to describe or even catalogue.

It was now eight o'clock in the morning. There were no sentries in the palace. Anyone might enter, and anyone whose conscience allowed him could take whatever he pleased. As I passed through the courtyard at the foot of the stairs I met some natives passing in. I supposed them to be Fantees, and told them they must not go up to the private apartments. But it turned out that they were Ashantees, people of the king, and they said with a charming candour that they had come to fetch things away. I presume that this sort of thing had been going on all the night. Some golden treasure was still left in the palace; how much then must have been taken away?

My friend and servant Mr. Edward Lake was not much impressed by the palace. I regret to say he applied the word 'rubbishy' to the contents of the private apartments and said he thought that Kerrikerri (Calcalli is a misnomer) was more of a king than that. If I went into the palace at Kukawa (in Bornu), ah, there I should see what a king was like. No doubt Lake was right; the kings of the Niger region can display the cultivated wealth and splendour of the East.

We passed the Garden Golgotha—the carrion bower where the bodies of sacrificed victims are deposited; it gave the whole town an odour of death. I must now explain the philosophy of human sacrifices. Among most savage nations it is believed that the body contains a ghost or spirit or soul which lives after death. Some believe that this ghost or soul inhabits the grave and flits around its neighbourhood, and comes to its old home and frequents the company of those whom it formerly loved. With savages of a higher type it is believed that the souls live in a special world, usually supposed to be under the ground, though some place it above the sky. One step more and we have the belief of the Persians, and some other ancient nations, that there are two worlds outside the earth, one of torture for the wicked, one of pleasure for the good.

Now it is the belief of savages that not only human bodies have souls, but also animals; and not only animals, but also rivers and trees and all things having movement or life: and not only all things having movement or life, but also inanimate objects—such as food and palm-wine, weapons, beads, articles of clothing, Willow-pattern plates, and so forth. So in Western Africa when a man dies food is placed by his grave, and they say that the spirit of the man eats the spirit or essence of the food. On the Gold Coast the natives believe in a world below the ground, a *Hades* or *Scheol* where the soul of the dead dwells in a life that shall have no end.

They also believe that all the garments he has worn out will then come to life again—a resurrection of old clothes; but besides this, his relations display their affection by giving him an outfit of weapons, ornaments, new cloth, crockery ware, &c, so that he may descend into Hell like' a gentleman. But who is to carry these things? and who is to look after them? Evidently his wives and his slaves. So a number of these are killed to keep him company; and often a slave is killed some time after his death to take him a message, or as an addition to his household. In Dahomey this custom of sending messengers is or-ganised into a system.

Thus originated human sacrifice, which is, granting the truth of the theory on which it is based, a most rational custom. Death is disa-greeable to us because we do not know where we are going; but to the widow of a chieftain it is merely a surgical operation and a change of existence. That explains why the Africans submit to death so quietly. A woman at Akropong selected for the sacrifice was stripped accord-ing to custom but only stunned not killed. She recovered her senses and found herself lying on the ground surrounded by dead bodies. She rose, went into the town where the elders were seated in council, and told them she had been to the Land of the Dead and had been sent back because she was naked. The elders must dress her finely and kill her over again. This accordingly was done.[1]

But there is another kind of human sacrifice—the slaying of men and women as gifts to the gods. In Ashantee the first form of sacrifice is practised; when one of the royal family dies, slaves are killed by the hundred. But I presume the bodies we found by the way-side, killed to avert the invasion, were gifts or bribes to the gods of the country. Be that as it may, one thing is certain: human sacrifices have become in Ashantee, as in Dahomey, public entertainments. The sight of an ex-

---

1. This was told me by a German missionary who was living at Akropong when the circumstance took place.

ecutioner in shaggy cap of black monkey-skin—the kind used for ladies' muffs—chopping off the head of a slave is to the Ashantees what
the sports of the amphitheatre were to the Romans, or bull-fights to
the Spaniards of the present day. Public executions in all countries
draw large crowds of admiring spectators, and in Ashantee this pen-
chant of the multitude has been cultivated and developed into an
artistic feeling. Decapitation has become with them an art as various
as music. There are two movements in vogue—the *allegro*, in which
a head is twirled away by a sharp knife with a dexterous turn of the
wrist; and the *adagio*, in which the head is sawn off in slow time.

According to Bowdich only persons of rank are allowed to have
portico verandahs or alcoves fronting the street, and the first thing I
noticed in Coomassie was the number of houses so built. This town
was the court, and the residence of the nobles, each of whom had a
vast crowd of clients and slaves. The people of the provinces belong
to an inferior class and are not considered pure Ashantees. 'You talk
of Ashantees,' said an interpreter at an early period of the campaign,
'but you have not seen any yet. The Ashantees are all noblemen and
gentlemen like the English; these people you have been fighting are
like the Irish and the Scotch.'

In such a verandah-alcove I took up my abode in a house that
fronted the market-place. Soon after securing these quarters I heard a
great noise and found it was the master of the house who complained
that someone had stolen his cloth. I said it was wartime and that such
accidents could not be helped. He laughed and said it was so. I then
told him I wanted to buy some fowls and plantains; if he would bring
me some the next morning he should be paid: 'See,' said I, 'here is
some money I brought with me on purpose;' and I jingled a bag of
threepenny bits, and gave him one as a proof of what I would do. In
half an hour he returned with some plantains and said it was a gift. He
did not come back again, but did not like to take off the threepenny
bit without making a return. Such is Ashantee honour. Such in fact is
the African character. I gave him the money on purpose to make sure
of seeing him again.

The first was a night of fire: the second a night of water. It rained
heavily for many hours, an unusual event at that time of year. In the
morning (February 6) we had to turn our backs upon Coomassie.
The palace was blown up and the town set in a blaze. The regiments
bivouacked again on the Ordah, and again it was a rainy night. The
General and his Staff went on to Ingimmamu. The rear-guard de-

stroyed all villages.

I pushed on down to the coast. Amoaful I found levelled to the ground with a stockaded fort in its midst. So it was with Fomana, which had been attacked by the Adansis. They had got right into the town and set some of the houses on fire, hoping to burn the garrison out The hospital was in some danger; the sick were armed and maintained its defence; some of them fell back fainting after they had fired. But the repulse was complete.

Parties of marauders had also infested certain parts of the road, and had shot carriers, engineer labourers, a soldier of the 2nd West, and others. This was because the villages on the flanks had not been destroyed. The 1st West Indian regiment and 250 of the 23rd regiment had been ordered up and were useful in keeping the road open and safe. It is much to be lamented that these regiments did not accompany the invading force, as at one time there were not enough troops to serve as escort to convoys and to garrison efficiently the posts along the road. Convoys were delayed and Fomana had a narrow escape. I found that the telegraph had been brought as far as Akrofum, twenty miles on the Ashantee side of the Prah. It was of great service in the Expedition.

Captain Butler and Captain Dalrymple both passed me on their way to the General. Captain Dalrymple had been unable to move the Wassaws across the frontier, and when he travelled with the king and a few warriors through the country, the rural Wassaws fearing 'requisitions,' drove off their sheep and concealed their fowls, plantains, &c. Captain Butler had been many weeks in Western Akim. Little by little he had succeeded in persuading the king and 2,000 men to follow him into Ashantee territory. They took some villages, and on the day of Amoaful were near enough to the battlefield to hear the sound of the firing like distant thunder in the air. Butler intended to join the main body next day; but now an extraordinary panic seized the Akims. They insisted on going back across the Prah. Butler made an eloquent speech, but even as he was speaking the men were going off.

To have attempted forcible measures, such as I have heard recommended, to have arrested the king and pointed a revolver at his head, would have been useless. The officers had not a single man on whom they could rely. They were therefore obliged to go back. The party consisted of Captains Butler, Brabazon, and Paget, Lieutenant Macgregor, and Surgeon Low. For several days not one of them smiled, or made a good-natured remark of any kind; and it certainly was most

175

mortifying to be so near success, and then to be thrown back into failure by these useless savages.

In point of strategy it appears to me that these native columns were a mistake. In the first place, the Wassaws and Western Akims would have been more useful as Carriers than as fighting-men; but placing that aside, of what use could be two native mobs marching, from different points into Ashantee? No doubt there is something captivating in the idea of several simultaneous invasions; but after all it is mere clap-trap, and will not bear examination. A weak auxiliary force may be of use if added to the main body, but can be of no: use if separated from it. One of two things must happen. Either it will not draw a large body from the enemy, in which case it might as well be at home; or it will draw a large body, and in that case would be destroyed. Sir Garnet Wolseley in his despatches has asserted that the Wassaws drew off the people of Becqua, and the Western Akims the people of Kokofo. There is no evidence whatever to support such an assertion. The Akims were within ten miles of Amoaful and did not encounter any large force. The Wassaws did not invade. Such statements are very ingenious, but will not do for an old African.

Had the army been accompanied by a force of Wassaws and Akims, they might have been useful in destroying villages upon the flanks, and plundering plantations. That is the only way to utilise native allies. They should not be officered by Europeans, but allowed to fight in their own fashion. They should not be fed, and therefore would be forced to scour the country. They would run away whenever they met anything resembling opposition, but that would not do any harm. Sir Garnet's method was the worst that could be conceived. His main body was quite strong enough to fight all the Ashantees in the kingdom; and by dangling a weak body of men as a bait to draw off a part of the Ashantee army, he imperilled the lives of the officers employed. It is pleasant to read the praise he accords not only to Butler, his friend, but also to Captain Dalrymple; but there is nothing else pleasant in the affair.

Lieutenant the Hon. H. Wood, A.D.C., was sent home as special messenger with despatches announcing the Fall of Coomassie. He travelled day and night, relays being provided at all the posts along the route, and was of course the first to arrive at Cape Coast; I was the second, reaching that town before daybreak on the 12th, having made the trip from Coomassie in less than six days. Mr. Stanley, who raced me hard, was a good third, arriving that same afternoon. Next came the commodore and Major Baker of the staff, to make arrangements for the re-embarkation of the troops.

Well, it was all over, and the expedition might, on the whole, be considered a success. The Ashantees had been defeated in two pitched battles; the king was a fugitive, his capital destroyed. Yet still the success was incomplete. Every officer with whom I conversed expressed a sense of disappointment. The king had not capitulated, and had not paid an ounce of gold. Thousands of armed men were still in the field, and it must be owned that, if they had attacked us on the way home, it would have unpleasantly resembled a retreat.

What indeed is a retreat, but a compulsory return? and on account of his supplies Sir Garnet Wolseley was compelled to return in haste, to the prejudice of the expedition. He had won the victory, but could not stay to gather its results. He was like a boy who spends the afternoon in thrashing down walnuts, and then has not time to pick them up. I comforted myself with the reflection that the Ashantees at all events had been thoroughly thrashed, and that Coomassie had been burnt. These were facts that they would not forget in our generation.

As I was out walking in the street, the day of my arrival, I met Mrs. H———, who belonged to the party of Elmina, and was suspected of Ashantee proclivities. She swept along, dressed in all the colours of the rainbow, and followed by a slave girl dressed entirely in black—a becoming kind of apparel, which washed very well, but could never be changed; so I leave my readers to guess the material. 'Well,' said Mrs. H———, 'what news?'

'We have burnt Coomassie,' said I, with a radiant face.

'Have you caught the king?'

'No, your fine king ran off into the bush.'

'Have you made him pay any money?'

'No, but we cleared out his palace.'

'Ha! ha!' said she, shrugging her shoulders, 'that is no good; the Ashantees will come down again; what does the king care about some men being killed;' then she gave a shrill laugh, drew her shawl over shoulders, and went off highly delighted.

I did not agree with my friend Mrs. H———. The king, of course, did not care about some of his men being killed; but the men themselves did not like it. After all, the army was based on the voluntary system, and the king could not make his subjects undertake a war unless the war was popular. Now the Ashantees, though a brave people, are not like European soldiers; they do not love fighting for fighting's sake. They receive no pay, and fight in the hope of plunder. They had now been taught that on this side of the Prah were a people who could always defeat them in battle, and who, if they chose to garrison a village, could make it impregnable. I believed that Sir Garnet had attained the main object of the expedition—namely, the securing of the Protectorate from periodical invasion. Yet still I wished his success had been more definite and more complete.

Suddenly news arrived that the king had sent after Sir Garnet, asked for the treaty to sign, and paid a thousand ounces of gold, chiefly in ornaments, showing that the treasury was bare. What could have induced Calcalli to make such a sacrifice when Sir Garnet had already done his worst, and would in a few days have been out of Ashantee? That shall be explained in the following chapter.

CHAPTER 21

Captain Glover

When the hero of this chapter was a lieutenant in the navy he distinguished himself by surveying the Niger, and took part in more than one expedition up that important and interesting river. He had to encounter the well-known hostility of the natives, was several times in action, and received a wound. Having lost his steamer on a rock near the Confluence, he spent much time in the interior, and became friends with the celebrated Massaba, a warrior king of the Felatahs. Accompanied by Haussa slaves and others, he travelled overland from the Confluence to Lagos; other Haussas from Lagos joined his followers (I suppose they were runaway slaves), and with Glover's assistance founded a town. Hence he was called 'The Father of the Haussas.' Being afterwards appointed Governor of Lagos, he enlisted, with Massaba's assistance, a number of Haussas, formed them into a body of armed police, and was soon able to assure the Secretary of State for the Colonies that he no longer required West Indian troops.

This service alone entitles Captain Glover to a high reward. He greatly improved, and indeed transformed the town of Lagos, and gained long ago a high reputation on the Coast for his energy and zeal. But Lagos is not without its troubles, and Glover, it is said, adopted the wrong policy. It was at all events the wrong policy for him, as he was recalled; and Lord Kimberley promised Captain Glover's opponents that he should never visit Lagos again. I have already explained how it was that he came into contact with the Gold Coast. That government having no steamer, Sir Arthur Kennedy borrowed Glover's services and colonial steamer when he went up the Volta in 1868, and made a treaty with the Awoonas and the Aquamoos.

In 1870 Captain Glover and his steamer were again borrowed—this time by the administrator of the Gold Coast—to punish a violation of the treaty. Thus it will be seen that Captain Glover's African experience had been acquired in the countries adjoining Lagos and the Niger. He knew nothing of the Gold Coast, excepting the Volta, and there he had spent but a short time. With the Haussas and Yorubas (the people who live behind Lagos) his name was 'strong,' his power unbounded; but he had no special influence among the tribes in the eastern districts of the Gold Coast.

However, the Africans are much alike, and the man who has succeeded with one set of tribes is likely to succeed with another. At all events Glover was not unknown; he had commanded the 'smoke-ship' at the Battle of Duffo. When the Ashantee War was beginning to engage the serious attention of the government, Captain Glover proposed to raise the eastern tribes of the" Gold Coast, and with a nucleus of Yorubas and Haussas to invade Ashantee. Lord Kimberley accepted his offer, gave him the appointment of Special Commissioner, furnished him with stores, money, and arms, and by arrangement with the War Office and the Admiralty allowed him to select certain officers, *viz.*, Mr. Goldsworthy, Colonial Secretary on the Gold Coast, now made Deputy Commissioner, and second in command; Captain Sartorius, 6th Bengal Cavalry; Lieutenant Larcom, R.N.; Lieutenants Cameron and Barnard, 19th regiment; Lieutenant Moore, R.N.; Surgeon-major Rowe, P.M.O., Gold Coast; Drs; Bale and Parke, R.N.; Assistant-Commissary Blissett; Sub-Lieutenant Ponsonby, R.N.

It was, I believe, Captain Glover's original scheme to invade Ashantee by the Volta. That river was known to be navigable by small steamers as far only as the rapids of Kpong; but he hoped to navigate it above that point with steam launches. There is a great town called Salgha on the upper waters of the river; the people were said to be enemies of Ashantee, and he had some idea of inducing them also to join the invasion. He relied on the Akims, Kreepees, Croboes, Aquapims, and Accras; but he also thought it possible to wean the Aquamoos from the Ashantee alliance.

This, in the first place, seemed to me quite impracticable; it had first to be proved to the Aquamoos that the English were a stronger people than the Ashantees. The scheme of Salgha and the Upper Volta appeared to me wild and fanciful; few, if any African rivers are more than mere torrents above the first rapids, and no one knew anything about Salgha and its people. I had no doubt that Glover would leave the Volta at Kpong, in which case, what was the use of the Volta at all? Kpong was not much nearer to Coomassie than Accra, and Accra was a true base, an English settlement; while Kpong would be merely a secondary base, in fact, a wayside *depôt*, which would have to be supplied with all things from Addah.

There were many fallacies involved in Glover's expedition. One was that the eastern route to Coomassie, though longer than that from Cape Coast Castle and other points, . was the best, because it passed through an open country. This I always denied. It is true that Accra is situated in a plain, and that the Volta in its lower course flows through an open country; but from whichever side Coomassie is approached, a vast forest has to be traversed. I always maintained that the best road to Coomassie was the shortest and the most frequented. That was the Cape Coast Castle route; but there was a trading road from Coomassie to Accra, leading through Aquapim and Akim, and this I thought was the best for an eastern expedition. Striking out a new route is interesting for a geographical explorer, but too experimental for the leader of an army.

As for the scheme itself—the project of invading Ashantee with an army composed of various tribes commanded by a few Europeans—the opinions I have already expressed with regard to a Fantee army, apply with equal force to the tribes of the eastern districts. Glover's experience at Duffo seems to have made him believe he could do great things with the natives. Such was not the impression made upon me. The attack upon Duffo was a trifling operation, resembling that of Essaman; yet it had not been accomplished without much dispute and delay. The natives fought well enough when the fighting actually began, but it was plainly to be seen that the chiefs were jealous of one another, and not always inclined to accept English arbitration; that their men were a wild herd; that a victory was followed by frantic anarchy, I believed that whatever a white man could do with such materials would be done by Captain Glover, who has much tact, -and whose energy is not to be surpassed; but I did not believe that he or anyone else could conquer an Ashantee army with such a confused and various mob. However, he had a regiment of disciplined Haussas and Yorubas on whom he could rely.

It was not till after Glover's appointment that Her Majesty's Government decided to make it a national war. Accordingly Sir G. Wolseley was appointed commander-in-chief, and Captain Glover was placed under his orders. At the same time it was understood that Glover would retain to some extent an independent command. For instance, Sir Garnet could not very well have superseded Glover, or meddled with minor details. Glover would make reports to Sir Garnet; but he was really the servant of the Colonial Office, while Sir G. Wolseley, though sending despatches as administrator to Lord Kimberley, was the servant of the War Office. It must be confessed that this was a curious arrangement, and the two expeditions were actually rivals.

Captain Glover has indignantly denied that there was any want of cordiality between Sir Garnet and himself. I do not say there was any want of cordiality; but I am certain of this—that they both wished each other at the devil. They did not entertain these kindly sentiments as man to man, but as commander to commander; and it could not well be otherwise. For Glover began his work as commander-in-chief with no one to give him orders excepting Lord Kimberley. All of a sudden he finds another man placed over his head. This was not agreeable.

On the other hand, Sir G. Wolseley was appointed to the supreme military command and conduct of the Ashantee War; but he finds another commander operating against the enemy, and his relations to that commander are undefined and obscure. He was appointed Governor of the Gold Coast; but a vast region of the Gold Coast is 'taboo;' he cannot enlist fighting-men or carriers without poaching on Glover's preserves. And supposing that Glover made a dash at. Coomassie while Sir Garnet was waiting for the regiments and the Ashantee army was in the Protectorate! If the movement was successful, people would say, 'Sir G. Wolseley, the famous general, did not dare to invade Ashantee without European troops; but Glover took Coomassie with an army of natives and a few officers.' If Glover were repulsed, the Ashantees would have been encouraged, and Sir Garnet's difficulties mightily increased.

It is quite certain that the cordial Glover and his officers intended to be first into Coomassie if they could. I have heard that one of them drew up a plan of the town with various quarters assigned to the 20,000 Akims, the 10,000 Accras, &c, &c.; while up in one corner was a small group of houses with an inscription underneath, 'For the Cape Coast contingent *when they arrive!* However, they did not find it such easy marching as they supposed, and could never have reached Coomassie at all had it not been for the European regiments, any more than Sir Garnet could have reached it with only his native regiments and native allies.

Captain Glover commenced operations by dealing out with a liberal hand, money, muskets, and rum. He soon collected a considerable army. But now he was informed by the Accras and friendly tribes upon the Volta that they could not think of invading Ashantee until they had crushed the Awoonas and Aquamoos, who, if they were left untouched, would cross over the Volta and ravage the country.

It cannot be denied that Glover was placed in a difficult position. He had somewhat incautiously expended large sums of money in advance, and the natives had the game in their hands. If he declined the Trans-Volta campaign, the Accras, Croboes, and Kreepees might not join him at all. He therefore agreed to their request. He did not bear in mind that an African war is like a suit in Chancery; no one can tell how long it will last, but it may be safely inferred it will last a long time. Now he knew that his time was short, and so should have left the Awoonas alone. Or he might have adopted a middle course. I heard from a native source, as early as October, that the Accras had no intention of invading Ashantee. They said that it was too far; besides, they lived in an open plain, and did not understand fighting in the bush.

It would have been better if Glover had given up the Accras, as far as Ashantee was concerned, and employed them to garrison the banks of the Volta. Some have attempted to justify the Trans-Volta campaign. Aquamoo and Awoonah, it was said, were Ashantee provinces, their armies commanded by Ashantee captains, their ports, Quitta and Jella Coffee, supplying Ashantee with powder and arms. The same might be said of the districts Chamah, Axim, and other western settlements; but that would not have justified Sir Garnet in frittering away his time in petty operations against those allies of Ashantee. The way to make war is to strike at the heart and the head; when once Coomassie was destroyed, all opposition at a distance would cease. There can be but one apology for Glover's Trans-Volta movements, namely, that they were forced upon him by the natives; but he should have showed more firmness, and not turned from the Ashantee campaign even for a moment.

He thought no doubt that in a few weeks with a sweep of his hand, so to speak, he could crush the Awoonas and Aquamoos, and then push on to Ashantee. But he had to deal with Africans. He went to Addah and there formed a camp. Week followed week and nothing was done. The Accras were not ready. At last they took the field, and the Trans-Volta campaign *commenced* just after Christmas Day. When Captain Glover intended to march upon Coomassie it is difficult to say. He seems to have been surprised when a despatch came from Sir Garnet ordering him to give up the Awoonas as a matter of secondary importance, to march at once to the Prah, and to cross it on January 15 with whatever forces he could muster.

As Sir Garnet intended himself to cross the Prah on the 15th, and hoped to reach Coomassie in ten days after that date, it is evident that he left Captain Glover alone as long as he could, and that if Glover was to go to Coomassie at all, he must start at once. He summoned the native chiefs, read them the despatch, said that the general's orders must be obeyed, and called upon them to follow him to the Prah. The chiefs replied that the Awoona war was of more importance than invading Ashantee, and they refused to go. The truth is they had wanted from the first to make war on Awoona, and not to make war on Ashantee. They had therefore utilised Glover. He had been paying them money, giving them powder and arms, and assisting them with his steamers and Haussa contingent, not to carry out his wishes but their own. It is much to Captain Glover's credit that he did not hesitate to obey his orders, and this fidelity gained him his reward. He crossed the Prah on the appointed day with something less than a thousand Yorubas and Haussas, and took the village Obogo.

There he was forced to remain some days, waiting for stores, ammunition, and reinforcements; for without a larger force it would have been imprudent to venture further into the country. At last he was joined by some Croboes and Akims, and he pushed on to the banks of a river called the Anum. There he had a skirmish, routed the enemy, and broke up a camp. But he was not opposed in force; and this was fortunate, for the Akims would not fight. However, they were useful in plundering plantations and destroying small villages. There were two Christian companies, converts of the Basle Mission, who attended prayers every day to the ringing of a bell, and fought bravely enough. Captain Glover's orders were to march on Juabin, the second city of the kingdom; but it seems he was not strong enough to do so.

His attempts to open up communication with Butler were not attended with success. He was still on the Anum River when two Haussa runaway slaves brought him the news of the taking of Coomassie. He then pushed on, meeting with no opposition, and arrived at a village which was, as he supposed, seven miles from Coomassie. He sent Captain Sartorius with twenty Haussas to join the General and receive his orders. Sartorius rode seven miles. The country now became populous. There were many villages. All the people ran away as he approached; in one village only a man fired at him. Night came on and Sartorius bivouacked upon the way. The seven miles were really fourteen. The next morning he was told that the king and his young men were weeping over the ruins of Coomassie and raging for revenge. On rode the brave Sartorius. He came to Coomassie, and passed through the still smoking ruins of the town. No one was there, excepting two Haussa slaves searching for plunder. They told him the white men were one village on ahead. Sartorius rode and rode, passing the ashes of village after village, and seeing no one but a wounded man by the way-side. Finally he found the general at Fomana. Such was the famous march of Sartorius—fifty-one miles with only twenty men through the heart of the enemy's country.

While he was at Fomana the chief of Adansi (who had been much oppressed by the king) requested permission of Sir Garnet to migrate into the Protectorate. This was accorded. It was rumoured that the Chief of Becqua had a similar desire. The Chief of Juabin tendered his submission. Messengers came in from the king begging Sir Garnet to stop Glover's advance, and promising to pay a thousand ounces of gold as first instalment of the indemnity. Sir Garnet would not detain the regiments; but courageously remained at Fomana with the native troops. In four days the gold was brought, with a request that the treaty should be sent to the king. It was signed and sent to Cape Coast about a month afterwards.

In the meantime Captain Glover followed up Sartorius, passed through Coomassie, and went down to Cape Coast. Just as the king had sent after Sir Garnet begging him to stop Glover, so he sent after Glover with a present of gold on a salver, asking him to send home the King of Akim and about two thousand of his men who had been left at some village on the road. Captain Glover sent back the gold, but complied with the request. However, he afterwards heard that the Chief of Juabin had invited the King of Akim to his town to discuss the migration of the former to Akim. So it seemed that the Ashantee kingdom was about to be dissolved.

Thus it will be seen that Captain Glover's expedition completed the work which Sir Garnet Wolseley had been forced to leave in an unfinished state. Without Captain Glover, the commander-in-chief would not have taken home either treaty or gold. He has reason therefore to rejoice that he ordered Glover up to the Prah; while on the other hand Glover should be grateful to Sir Garnet; for had he been left to his own devices on the Volta, he would have had no share in the glories of the Ashantee Campaign.

CHAPTER 22

The End of the Campaign

In this work I have applied to Sir Garnet Wolseley's brilliant success that searching kind of criticism which is usually reserved for undertakings that have failed. I have not glossed over or palliated a single error which he committed during the campaign. The application for a railway—the concerted and disconcerted movements in the bush—the weakness displayed at Abrakrampa—the inflated Proclamation—the neglect of the Transport—the Sarmatian telegram—the sacrifice of Captain Nicol—the various errors in diplomacy—the vacillation at Coomassie—all these have been fully examined and exposed. I shall be charged with errors of judgment, but at least my judgment has not been affected by any prejudice of a personal kind. No one can be acquainted, however slightly, with Sir Garnet Wolseley and desire to attack him. I must also observe that in many cases I have not expressed my own isolated opinion but the opinion of the army.

It may be said that I have given undue space and prominence to the errors of the general; to which I reply that these errors if treated in detail may serve as warnings to other commanders. It may pain Sir Garnet to be accused of having sacrificed Nicol, but the revelation of the fact may save other men's lives; and Sir Garnet in this case does not deserve that the truth should be concealed, as he at Ordahsu repeated the order which had already borne fatal fruit. In cases of civil tumult at home, it is better that soldiers should be killed while the riot act is being read than that an attack should be made prematurely on a crowd.

But when a general invades an enemy's country, and that enemy a nation of savages noted for their treachery, he is guilty of actual wrong if he orders his men to seek contact with the enemy, nay, even to seize a village, yet not to fire unless attacked. Generals who give such orders should walk in front of the column and see how they like being face to face with a band of savages who have not quite made up their mind whether they shall fire a volley or not. Then as to the transport question, what I have said may serve to warn generals that this is a 'detail' which in such expeditions requires their personal attention.

Anyone reading Sir Garnet's despatches would suppose that the transport had at one time given him some trouble, but that he had triumphed over the difficulty, and that it was the bad weather which made him run into Coomassie and out again like a ferret in a rabbit-hole. That is the way history is written; but I have shown how Sir Garnet's early neglect of the Transport vitiated the whole expedition, delayed the regiments on the march, caused some sickness, deprived the army of troops which were afterwards urgently required, and finally hastened the return from Coomassie, making it almost resemble a retreat.

It is for the good of the service that this breakdown of the control should not be passed over; and I believe it will be found that the more closely the combatant and commissariat departments are united, the more efficient an army will be. I have seen enough to convince me that the art of providing food for an army is not less, difficult than the art of manoeuvring an army in the field, and not less essential to success against the enemy. I am inclined to believe that a commander-in-chief will always be deficient unless he has had some practical experience in matters of transport and supply; or at least he ought to know as much of general principles in that department as of general principles in engineering and artillery.

It is also my duty to bring more into relief than I have hitherto done the achievements of General Wolseley and the high qualities which he displayed. The difficulties under which he was placed at the outset of the campaign were of a most strange and complex character. In the Abyssinian Campaign Sir Robert Napier knew from the first what he had to do. He had to carry an army to a place called Magdala in Abyssinia. The enterprise was difficult, but it was not ambiguous. On the other hand, Sir Garnet, who on account of the climate had much less time at his disposal, was sent out to the Gold Coast to look about him and see what was best to be done. He was not to ask for European troops if he could help it; he was not to invade Ashantee if he could help it; he was not to burn Coomassie if he could help it.

That is what he calls being 'untrammelled by instructions.' Had he been sent out purely as a general to make war against the Ashantees, and to wring the neck of that power if he could, no doubt he would have fixed his mind from the first upon Coomassie, and devoted himself to the transport and the road. He knew when he first arrived that he might go to Coomassie, and probably would, and there- fore it behoved him to make preparations. But it is not in human nature to throw one- self heart and soul into probabilities. It was this uncertainty as to what his future movements would be which embarrassed and weakened Sir Garnet as a general. Added to which it was not an ordinary war. He always seemed afraid of doing too much; he feared public opinion, which when he left England was languidly hostile to the war; he did not understand that public opinion had changed in the course of the war, for the British people, though averse to begin a combat, like to fight it out: when once arms have clashed and blood has been spilt they want no parleyings. But Sir Garnet was led by his instructions to regard the Ashantees, not as a foreign enemy, but rather as Maoris and Caffres; natives who had rebelled, not without justification, and were not to be conquered too completely.

It is not therefore just to institute a comparison between the Abyssinian and Ashantee Campaigns; but when the regiments had come out, and Sir Garnet had determined that he would take them to Coomassie, he displayed high talents for organisation and command. In no campaign have British soldiers suffered so few privations. Despite the transport difficulty, there was not a day in which they received anything short of their rations excepting in the dash upon Coomassie; and so liberal were the rations that it was but a slight privation to make four days' rations do for five. The man who fell out of the ranks from sickness had never to wait long for a hammock and a doctor, and was soon housed in a hospital hut. From Cape Coast Castle almost to Coomassie a good road had been made, and at intervals of eight or ten miles were comfortable camps, or fortified posts, containing stores and medical comforts, and capable of resisting an Ashantee army.

The postal service was admirably arranged; letters travelled at the uniform rate of four miles an hour. It took no more than a day and a half for the mail-bag to travel from Cape Coast Castle to Coomassie. But as it is more difficult to describe health than disease, so it is more difficult to define excellence than to indicate error. The success of Sir Garnet can best be explained by negatives. He never exposed his troops to hunger or needless exposure; he never allowed any quantity of stores to fall into the enemy's hands; in battle he never was in want of ammunition, though its expenditure was always extravagant; to sum up all in one phrase, during five active months he never suffered a disaster.

It is impossible to praise too highly the conduct of officers and men in the expedition. Many officers were of necessity precluded from going to the front, and it was this cause alone which produced anger and bitterness during the campaign. One officer threatened, if he was ordered back, to send in his papers and go on as a civilian. Another engaged in the transport disobeyed orders that he might be 'in' at the taking of Coomassie. Some went almost crazy with rage and disappointment. Many volunteered to serve as non-commissioned officers in the native regiments. Sub-Lieutenant Bradshaw, R.N., concealed the illness of which he died, and would not at first seek medical attendance, fearing to be put in hospital.

That was not the only case of the kind. The men showed a similar spirit. When there was the deadlock in the transport, the Highlanders volunteered to convey loads from Mansu to Sutah, and the Rifles imitated their example. The 23rd were especially keen. I have seen more than once a sick man by the wayside, with haggard face and exhausted eyes, begging and praying that he might not be sent to the rear. 'I can go on, sir; indeed I can go on if I rest here a little while.' The Naval Brigade was always full of merriment and joy. There was an utter absence of disorder, crime, or insubordination. Though the soldiers clearly did not like fighting in the bush, and were always looking forward 'to get them in the clear,' they all behaved admirably. For my own part I shall never forget that day when on the slopes of Amoaful I fought side by side with the soldiers in the ranks, and I shall always think of the Black Watch with a kind of affection.

The staff and special service officers who went out with Sir Garnet in the *Ambriz*, or who followed in the next steamer, are entitled to the highest praise of all. They were the pioneers. Some died, some were invalided home, and nearly all of them had suffered much from the climate before the march to Coomassie began. They created native regiments and native artillery, and made the Queen's highway to the Prah. Fortified posts sprang up under their hands. They fought the enemy at a disadvantage. Wood, Russell, Home, and Rait, with their young officers, went into the interior soon after their arrival on the Coast, and remained there till Coomassie had been taken. Similar work was achieved, and similar privations were endured, by the little band of English officers attached to Glover's expedition.

On February 19th, Sir Garnet entered Cape Coast Castle, passing under a triumphal arch erected by the merchants and the natives. The

Fantee women painted themselves white, and waved green branches, singing hymns of welcome and triumph. As the troops came in morning after morning, the women received them, saluting the soldiers, the carriers, and the hammocks of the wounded. The native regiments were paid off and were sent back to their homes. Some of the Bonnys and Ophoboes were seen strutting about the streets in ladies' hats with feathers, and patent leather boots. In a few days the great troop-ships steamed off, and became specks on the horizon; Cape Coast Castle resumed its ordinary aspect. But the telegraph still connected that town with Prahsu, which was garrisoned by the 1st West.

As I sat in my little room with my face turned towards Europe, and wrote my last letter to the *Times*, with what joy I bade *adieu* to the scenes of the campaign—its days of monotony and weariness—its sickness and anxiety. The episodes which I have selected to describe in this book did not fill the same space in our lives. The days of excitement were few and far between. I had to pass weeks of inaction, and was always haunted by the fear that, when the long-hoped-for time should arrive, sickness would prevent me from reaching Coomassie. But now all was done, all fear of failure at an end, and I strove to forget the forest, and to think only of the Land beyond the Sea. For all the pictures of the forest that came back to my mind were sombre and sad. Great gloomy trees shedding darkness; creepers coiled round them like serpents; fungi feeding on their flesh; pools of green water; sloughs of black mud, yielding, when stirred with the foot, a sickening stench. And then I saw, as in a dream, long lines of dark figures toiling wearily with burdens on their heads, and dead bodies lying by the path, and wan-faced soldiers by the wayside, waiting for the hammock ambulance, and the man with the red cross upon his arm.

But now when I look back upon the past other scenes rise also before me. I see the bright bivouac fire, and faces lit up with a ruddy glow, and the rough table, and bottles upon it containing the rations of rum, and the barrel hospitably proffered as a seat. I remember those pleasant conversations under the night-sky of Africa. I remember the days of honourable toil. Friends and companions of the bush, from most of you I parted without the farewell shake of the hand: let me give it you here. Our ways in life are different; many of you I shall never see again. But I shall follow your fortunes with interest, and doubt not I shall see them crowned with distinction, such as your seniors have already obtained.

Brave in battle, cheerful in hardship, patient in sickness—such I can testify are the virtues that you have displayed. I return from the Ashantee Campaign proud of my country and proud of its soldiers. I have learnt that the spirit which animated the bowmen of Agincourt and Cressy still lives, glowing and warm, in the ranks of an army which is drawn from the lowest classes of the people. I have learnt that chivalry is not dead, and that valour, goodness, courtesy, compassion for the weak, tenderness to the fallen, the passion for adventure, the love of romance, and need I add, devotion to the fair, are still to be found harmoniously blended and combined in that modern knight—the English Gentleman.

CHAPTER 23[1]

The Future of the Gold Coast

Sir Charles Adderley has stated that the Ashantee invasion was due to the Liberals being in office; he might as well declare that Goschen caused gales in the Channel, or that the wheat harvest was withered by the malignant influence of Lowe. The state of political party at Coomassie may have had something to do with the invasion; but none could have done more than Lord Kimberley and his servants on the Coast to avert war, if it could have been averted by concession. All events have their proximate causes. The invasion of 1873 was proximately due to the transfer of the Dutch and English settlements in 1867, which led to the cession of all the Dutch settlements in 1872. But it should never be forgotten that while these events were taking place we were actually at war with Ashantee, and the cause of that war, which commenced in 1863, was the refusal of Great Britain to surrender two Ashantee fugitives, one of whom was a runaway slave. Had the Dutch and English settlements never been exchanged, had the Dutch always remained upon the Coast, there would have been an Ashantee invasion all the same.

If not today, it would have been tomorrow. The true causes of the war must be sought for at Coomassie—in the ambition of the Ashantees. In the beginning of the century they conquered the native tribes which now form our Protectorate; they made the English their vassals and their tributaries, they ruled upon the seaboard. Little by little the English power growing on the Gold Coast wrested these conquests from them, and they were driven back across the Prah. But they have never ceased to hanker after the lands they abandoned by the Treaty of Maclean. As if that treaty had never been made, they have always

1. This chapter was written before Lord Carnarvon presented his scheme for the future government of the Gold Coast.

spoken of Denkera, Assin, Wassaw, and Akim as theirs. They have even spoken of Cape Coast Castle as their own, because it had once paid them tribute, and of the Fantees as their slaves, because they once conquered that people. Hence at various periods—the Fantees say every ten years—they have crossed the Prah, sometimes making mere raids, sometimes with organised invasion.

Elmina belonged to Ashantee by virtue of conquest in Denkera, as Cape Coast Castle by virtue of conquest in Fantee, and Accra by virtue of conquest in Akim. When Ashantee lost Denkera, Fantee, and Akim, it lost all claim on these three settlements, and the notes or stipends previously paid. The Dutch, however, continued the stipend for reasons of policy and trade; therefore Ashantee appeared to have some shadow of claim upon Elmina; and it cannot be denied that the Elminas preferred the Ashantee rule to the British flag. They consented, it is true, to accept the British flag; and the King of Ashantee withdrew his claim. But the fact remained that the Ashantees wanted Elmina, and the Elmina natives wanted Ashantee. Under these circumstances, why should not we have made the Ashantees a present of Elmina? It would have gained us the friendship of the most civilised nation on the Coast, and it would have been in accordance with the wishes of the people to whom Elmina and its district belonged.

This sounds very plausible; and as Lord Kimberley may yet be arraigned before the tribunal of public opinion for not having adopted this just, wise, and politic measure, I shall describe what would in that case have occurred. The reader must bear in mind that this would have been before the conquest of Ashantee, at a time when our government was weak—when it was unable to prevent the Fantees from waging war against Elmina, their ancient enemy.

In the first place the Ashantees would wish to occupy Elmina. But how were they to get there? The road lay through Denkera. The king of that country might reasonably object to an Ashantee army passing through his dominions. Disputes would have arisen; and the Ashantees would declare that Elmina was no use to them unless they had a road of their own, or in other words, unless they also possessed the countries lying between the Prah and their port. This in the first place would have brought about a war.

However, let us imagine the Ashantees peacably established at Elmina. The king would appoint a viceroy, as the King of Dahomey appoints a viceroy to reside at Whydah. This official would levy port dues on the shipping, take his royalty on the trade, extort from the merchants, loans, fines, and loving contributions. If Elmina belonged to Ashantee, as so many have asserted, and if we gave it up for that reason, we could not put any restrictions on their government; and if we attempted to do so there would be war. Nor could we interfere with the customs of the Ashantees. In that ancient settlement, which the Portuguese and the Dutch had governed during nearly four hundred years, human sacrifices would be restored on a grander scale than in the ancient days.

The town would be given back to barbarism. The Elmina people themselves would be oppressed. Then it cannot be supposed that the Ashantees would become less exacting and imperious when such an important concession had been made them, from fear (as they would imagine) of their majesty and power. There would be quarrels with the Fantees. Slaves taking refuge in Cape Coast Castle would be deanded from the British Government. But it is needless to discuss impossibilities. The project is a mere dream. When Sir Charles Adderley and others proposed that the King of Ashantee should be given Elmina, as the King of Dahomey has Whydah, they wrote about things they did not understand.

Well now that palaver is finished. The King of Ashantee has given up by treaty his shadowy claim to Elmina, and the natives of that town having been convinced that we are stronger people prefer us for their lords. It is probable that Elmina will be made the seat of government; it is more healthy than Cape Coast Castle, and has a better landing-place; an essential advantage on a surf-ridden coast. If it be made the capital we shall have no more loyal subjects than the people of Elmina.

The true cause of the war was the, imperial ambition of the Ashantees; and the weakness of our Government gave them encouragement, hope, and provocation. At one time a poll-tax was levied on the tribes of the Protectorate, but no settled system was ever pursued for the regulation of the road to Prahsu, and the protection of Ashantee traders from stoppage and blackmail. When I visited the Coast in 1868, with the intention of going to Coomassie, I was advised to choose the Assinie route, because the Assins would not allow me to pass through their country to the Prah. It is now no longer their country, as regards government. Sir Garnet Wolseley has not only conquered Ashantee, but also Fantee. Never again will the natives under our protection have a war of their own against our desire, as with Elmina in 1868; never again will they cut off the heads of peaceful Ashantee settlers under the walls of the castle, as in 1873. There is now a road from the Prah to Cape Coast; garrisons will be established at Prahsu and Mansu, and when the Ashantees come down to trade they will meet with no obstacle.

If on account of their ancient alliance with Elmina they choose to trade in that town, no one will prevent them; but they are a shrewd people and not very sentimental; they will buy goods wherever they are cheapest. Much has been said about a certain 3 *per cent*, claimed by the Fantee brokers from the merchants on all goods sold to Ashantees. The merchants refused to pay and the Fantees broke into riot. It has been gravely asserted that this was one of the causes of the war; and Mr. Pope Hennessy took side with the natives *versus* the merchants. Such stupidity is really marvellous. Why should the Ashantees go to war because the Fantees were refused 3 *per cent?* Had that brokerage been paid, it would have been put on the price of the goods, and the Ashantees would have been the losers—which they understood very well. The demand was a relic of the old middleman system which the Fantees enjoyed in the days when they ruled the factors of the Royal African Company. It should be the policy of the government to discourage all interference of Fantees with the Ashantee trade. Let the Fantees make palm-oil, which is the produce of their country, and leave the Ashantees alone.

It is impossible to say whether the Ashantees will dare to invade our Protectorate again. Of this at least we may be sure—that the way to secure peace is to show them that we are prepared for war. We can raise an African army of Haussas, Kossoos, Bonnys, and Opoboes. With a little time and care Mandingoes might be obtained from the Gambia. Even the Fantees make good soldiers enough if properly drilled and disciplined. But it is most essential that such irregular troops should be well officered. It was the character of the officers which proved fatal to the Gold Coast artillery, and has always done much harm to the West Indian regiments. The native regiments of the future should not be regiments of refuge for line officers who have run into debt, or for young men who cannot get into the regular army. Special arrangements of promotion and pay (and these are justified by the dangers of the climate) should invite and reward volunteers.

It is generally allowed that had the Ashantees been armed with the Snider it would have gone badly with us in the recent campaign. They are not marksmen it is true; but marksmanship is not necessary in the bush. As I heard a rifleman observe, 'A bad shot is just as well off as a good one.' It is all shooting in the dark, and the Ashantees aiming low could do as much execution as the experts of the Rifle Brigade. Now as they must always greatly outnumber our troops—for the untrained Fantees never will fight—it would be idle to deny that the future has its elements of danger. Sniders are already articles of trade in the Cape Coast Castle factories, and have, to my knowledge, been purchased by the Fantees of Annamboe. Whatever the Fantees have the Ashantees will have sooner or later.

I found that my hammock-men perfectly understood the percussion-cap muzzle-loading Enfield; and the Ashantees have begun to purchase these weapons. I believe that the natives of the Gold Coast are in a state of transition as regards their armament, and that before many years have passed the old flint-lock with its charge of slugs will have disappeared, like the bow and arrow and the spear. However, all innovations are difficult and slow; every sportsman will remember how long it was before breech-loaders displaced muzzle-loaders in England; and therefore government might, in this case, interfere with effect. The sale of superior weapons should be prohibited; and perhaps the sale of powder and arms should be monopolised by Government, a system which works well at Natal. The Ashantees are placed at a great disadvantage in this—that their base is the sea. They cannot purchase powder and guns without coming down to the settlements; but unfortunately one of their ports is Assinie, which belongs to the French.

It would be of great advantage to obtain Assinie and Grand Bassam, which are no longer occupied; and as the French are in want of the Gambia, which lies in the midst of their possessions like a freehold in a manorial estate, possibly an exchange might be effected. If not, the following arrangement might be made. The French, who are often at war with the natives of the Senegal, wisely prohibit the sale of powder and arms to the natives, who obtain them from the Gambia. If we prohibit the sale of powder and arms in the Gambia, which would be to our advantage as well, the French would prohibit in return the sale of powder and arms at Grand Bassam and Assinie.

Had Sir Garnet been able to feed his troops, he would have remained a few days in Coomassie, and comfortably housed his men, as at Fomana. Glover would have joined him on the 12th or 13th. Then had Glover been allowed to remain for a time in occupation of the town——and to this I have reason to believe that thorough-minded man would have gladly agreed—the Gamans and other tribes to the north would have poured over the country and down to the coast. The Ashantee monarchy, which is now in a tottering condition, would then have been broken, and I am unable to agree with those who think it would have been a misfortune. By means of that despotism, the Ashantees have been made a superior people in war; but that is not of advantage to their neighbours or to our trading interests. There seems to be a common belief that the Ashantees are the most civilised people of Africa; that they alone have an organised government, and so forth.

Such, as an African traveller, is not my experience. The Moslem tribes to the north of Ashantee doubtless resemble the tribes of San-gara and Bouré on the Niger, whom I found living in walled cities with schools, mosques, and a municipal form of government resembling the 'communes,' or independent cities of the Middle Ages. The despotism of Ashantee is injurious to trade, for the king is the chief trader in the kingdom; the gold-mines of the country are neglected; in Coomassie the inhabitants do not care to raise live stock (as Mr. Kühne informed me) lest their property should be seized by the people of the king, who have license to rob as much as they please. It would have been preferable for ourselves, for the neighbouring tribes, and for the Ashantees themselves, that the monarchy should have been destroyed, or reduced to a nominal chiefdom.

In that case the Ashantees would have been able to work their gold-mines without paying all the nuggets they found to the king; and their country would have become a thoroughfare; the traders of Gaman would have come to the sea As it is, we must make the best of the affair. The King of Ashantee should be paid a stipend by the year, the amount of which should depend on the amount of gold-dust brought down; and he should also be tempted by a royalty to allow the Gamans to pass through his land—a stipulation, by the way, which should not have been omitted in the treaty. An expedition might also be sent to Sallagha, upon the Volta, to invite traders to visit Addah and Accra; for probably the Ashantees are no longer strong enough to stop the road at such a distance from their capital.

As regards the important question of government in the Protectorate, all such elaborate schemes as that of a Fantee Confederation should be avoided. The result of such schemes would be to place power in the hands of a class of *mulattoes* called 'Scholars,' who serve as go-betweens, and cheat both the English and the natives. Let there be in the first place a strong government, and then let it grow. Time and circumstance will show what laws are the best to be enacted. The chiefs of Wassaw, Denkera, Assim, Akim and other tribes can continue to govern their people, but at Cape Coast Castle there should be a Court of Arbitration and Appeal. Those natives who dread the expensive law-suits of their country can bring their case by mutual agreement before the Judicial Assessor. Those who are plundered and ill-treated by their chiefs can appeal to the governor for protection. Slavery must be abolished in the settlements, but not as in the West Indies.

When Dr. Madden went out as commissioner in 1848 he released a number of slaves at Accra. They overwhelmed him with their gratitude, but came to him in the evening for their dinner. When he declined to provide that repast, they cursed him and returned to their master. It would be absurd to establish a domestic inquisition and to insist on all slaves being turned out of doors. But the Court of the Judicial Assessor must no longer take cognisance of slaves as property, and the liberty of slaves must be unrestrained. If a slave chooses to leave his master, the law must protect him from being taken back against his will, or being in any way detained.

Those slaves who are ill-treated, or have the ambition to be free, will thus have the power of taking their liberty whenever they please. Those who are content to remain in slavery can do so, and these will form the majority. In most cases the African slave, so-called, is a poor relation clothed and fed by his master, running messages and doing a little work about the house. If he labours for money, as canoeman or carrier, he receives a portion of the wages. The Bonnys and Opoboes who served in our army were all of them slaves; two-thirds of their pay went to their chiefs, and a third to themselves. The Ashantees have always been in the habit of bringing down slaves to sell; the people with gashed cheeks who are to be seen in every household on the coast were prisoners of war taken by the Ashantees from the tribes of the north. This traffic must of course be suppressed, and all runaway slaves from the interior will be made free at Cape Coast.

The government of the Gold Coast has been of late years subjected to the governor-in-chief at Sierra Leone. This arrangement I presume will now be done away with. To rule a country which extends from the Assinie River to the Volta, and beyond it to Jella Coffee and Quitta—to open up communications with the tribes of the interior—to watch the encroachments of Ashantee—is quite enough work for one man; and for this work will be required men of no slight ability.

In conclusion, it is my belief that this Ashantee War, which would bring us as everyone said neither glory nor gain, has not been inglorious, and may in time be the means of largely profiting our trade. But we have fair reason to hope that this war will be the means of bestowing perpetual peace over vast regions hitherto subject to periodical invasion. In no great space of time this war I fully believe will have saved thousands of human beings from death, hundreds of villages from destruction. If not, it will be because the war was not carried out to the full, and the evil power too mercifully treated. It cannot be denied that there have been wars which were blessings to mankind. There is a Party of Peace who protest against war merely because it is war; that is just as rational as it would be to protest against a well-proved kind of operation intended to cure a man of a painful disease. The operation may fail through want of skill, or it may be so indifferently performed that the disease after an interval breaks out again.

But no rational being would deny that the operation in itself is beneficial. But the Peace Society cry out, 'See what a sharp knife he has got! O dear, look at the blood! What a barbarous shame it is that human beings should be laid upon a table and butchered like this within sound of church bells!' Such is the style of reasoning which these philanthropists employ; but a little common sense is sufficient to refute them. Here are the Ashantees, who for nearly two hundred years have been making war upon their neighbours almost without cessation. If not making war on the Fantees, they are making war on the Gamans, or the Kreepees, or some other unfortunate neighbour. In six weeks an English Army puts it out of their power to make war any more. Is that a proceeding opposed to the principles of peace?

I do not assert that the operation has been perfectly successful. I wish the knife had gone in a little deeper; but still it was a dexterous performance, and, if it be followed up with judicious applications, may save our Gold Coast for all time to come from the pain and suffering caused by Ashantee.

Appendix

Catalogue Raisonné of Special Service Officers and others engaged in the Gold Coast Expedition.

This list, chiefly compiled from personal knowledge and without assistance, is of necessity incomplete. This applies especially to the officers of the Naval Brigade, and to those Special Service Officers who came out late in the day, and were employed in the Transport service. I have not attempted to specify the services of officers in the regiments; each one had his appointed duty and each did it well. But the duties of the Special Service Officers were individual and singular, and it is useful to enumerate them.

Adams, Surgeon, *Simoom*. Distinguished himself at Essaman.

Allan, Lieutenant, R.M.A. Assisted to bombard Elmina. Made good rocket practice at Essaman. Invalided.

Atkins, Surgeon, *Ambriz* passenger. Attached to Russell's Regiment Went to Coomassie, and was more often in action than any other medical man.

Aylmer, Lieutenant, 43rd Regiment Wood's Regiment Commanded the post Essiaman beyond the Prah. Baker, Major, 18th Royal Irish. Assistant-Adjutant and Quarter-Master-General. Acted also as Chief of the Staff for a considerable time. Went to Coomassie. A most industrious and efficient officer, both at the desk and in the field.

Baker, Captain, Brother of the above. Succeeded Captain Thompson as Inspector-General of armed Fantee Police; organised the post-office runners. Went to Coomassie. This officer, who is much beloved by his men, will remain on the Gold Coast, holding his present appointment.

Bale, Surgeon, R.N. Glover's Expedition. Died near the Prah.

Barnard, Lieutenant, 19th Regiment. Glover's Expedition. Drilled Haussas and Yorubas; several times engaged with the enemy. Went to Coomassie.

Barton, Lieutenant, 7th Fusiliers. Russell's Regiment. Went to Coomassie.

Bell, Lieutenant, R.E. This, young officer highly distinguished himself by untiring industry and by cutting bush under fire.

Blake, Captain, *Druid*. Commanded the Naval Brigade. Invalided at Prahsu and afterwards died.

Bolton, Lieutenant, 1st West India Regiment. Special Service Officer, and passenger in *Ambriz*. Did very great service in raising the Winnebah and Mumford company for Russell's Regiment, and afterwards did much good work in transport service.

Brabazon, Captain, late Grenadier Guards. Served with Butler's Expedition, and afterwards in transport service. Captain Brabazon it is said will re-enter the service.

Brackenbury, Captain, R.A. Assistant Military Secretary. An officer of well-known reputation and literary abilities. Late lecturer at the Royal Academy, Woolwich. Joined the Red Cross movement in the war of 1870, and obtained the Legion of Honour and the Iron Cross. Distinguished himself at Essaman. Went to Coomassie; always energetic in the field.

Bradshaw, Captain, *Encounter*. Explored the Prah; took part in land expeditions.

Bradshaw, Sub-Lieutenant, R.N. Died in the bush.

Bromhead, Captain, 24th Regiment *Ambriz* passenger. Russell's Regiment. More frequently in action than any other officer. Obtained a thousand carriers from Abrakrampa in the time of need. Went to Coomassie.

Buckle, Captain, R.E. Major Home's right-hand man. Killed at Amoaful.

Buller, Captain, 60th Rifles. D.A.A. and Q.M.G. Appointed Chief of the Intelligence Department; but his talents are best displayed in active service. Went to Coomassie.

Burnet, Captain, 15th Regiment Russell's Regiment Defended Quarman, he being under fever at the time.

Butler, Captain (half-pay), 69th Regiment. Author of *The Great Lone Land*, and *The Wild North Land*. Was sent soon after his arrival to Western Akim, and remained in the interior throughout the campaign. No man could have done more than he did; few men could have done so much.

Cameron, Lieutenant, 19th Regiment. Glover's Expedition. Drilled Haussas and Yorubas. Went to Coomassie. Suffered much from the climate.

Charteris, Lieutenant the Honourable, Coldstream Guards. Distinguished himself at Essaman. Died on board the *Simoom*.

Clowes, Lieutenant, 30th Regiment. Wood's Regiment.

Cochran, Sub-Lieutenant, R.N. Sent to Esseboo in October to raise fighting men. In both skirmishes near Dunquah.

Colley, Lieut.-Colonel, 2nd Queen's Own. Services detailed in the text. Went to Coomassie. Assisted at the defence of Fomana. A benefactor of the expedition.

Commerell, Captain, V.C., C.B. Commodore of the West African Squadron. This officer, who is much beloved in the navy, narrowly escaped death from wounds received in an ill-judged expedition up the Prah.

Crease, Captain, R.M.A. Distinguished himself at Essaman. Inventor of excellent filters used in the expedition. Invalided.

Crosbie, Lieutenant, R.M.L.I. Naval Brigade. Went to Coomassie.

Dalrymple, Captain, 80th Regiment. Sent to the Wassaws. As in the case of Butler, ordered to attempt an impossibility.

De Hoghton, Lieutenant, 10th Regiment Russell's Regiment.

Despard, Captain, R. M.L.I. Did much in transport service and present at taking of Amoaful.

Dooner, Lieutenant, 8th King's Own. *Ambriz* passenger. Russell's Regiment Went to Coomassie.

Douglas, Lieutenant, 7th Fusiliers. Wood's Regiment.

Evans, Lieutenant, R.N. Explored the Prah under Captain Bradshaw. Went to Coomassie.

Eyre, Lieutenant, 90th Regiment. *Ambriz* passenger. Wood's Regiment Killed at Ordahsu.

Fegan, Staff-Surgeon, R.N. Went to Coomassie, where he discovered a very curious document, the journal of a Fantee prisoner.

Festing, Lieut-Colonel, R.M.A. Repulsed the Ashantee attack on Elmina, June 13, 1873. Improved the defences of the settlements. Created the post Dunquah; twice fought the Ashantees in the neighbourhood, and was wounded on each occasion. Commanded Prahsu. His services require no comment.

Ficklin, Sub-Lieutenant, R.N. Died in the bush.

Filliter, Lieutenant, 2nd West India Regiment. Did good service under Festing at Dunquah, and afterwards in transport service.

Fisher, Surgeon, R.N. Present at the affair of Ampenee, and went to Coomassie.

Fox, Staff-Surgeon. Much service in the bush. Went to Coomassie.

Fremantle, Captain the Hon., *Barracouta*. The Gold Coast Expedition owes much to this officer, who has not that nervous dread of responsibility which is the bane of the naval service. At Elmina, being then senior naval officer, he placed himself and his men under Festing's command. Though wounded at Essaman, he went through the whole work of the day; and he went both times with Sir G. Wolseley to Abrakrampa.

Furse, Captain, 42nd Regiment. Special Service Officer and *Ambriz* passenger. Went to the Gambia for soldiers without success. Joined Wood's Regiment, and went to Coomassie.

Gifford, Lord, Lieutenant, 24th Regiment. At first organised and commanded the company of Winnebahs in Russell's Regiment; afterwards commanded the scouts, with what success everyone knows.

Godwin, Captain, 103rd Bombay Fusiliers. Commanded the Annamboes in the first action near Dunquah. Severely wounded and invalided home.

Goldsworthy, Deputy Commissioner, Glover's Expedition, late 12th Lancers. Has been for some years in colonial appointments on the Coast. Commanded the Accras against the Awoonas on the other side of the Volta, was wounded and had his horse shot under him.

Gordon, Lieutenant, 98th Regiment Was making the Coomassie road when Sir G. Wolseley arrived. Appointed to the command of Haussas in Russell's Regiment. Went to Coomassie.

Gordon, Lieutenant, 93rd Regiment. Raised the Kosso contingent at Sierra Leone. Russell's Regiment. This excellent officer was invalided.

Gore, Surgeon-Major. Was also invalided after doing much good work. He was three or four times slightly wounded.

Grant, Captain, 2nd West India Regiment. Distinguished himself at Abrakrampa, and went through the whole campaign.

Grant, Lieutenant, 6th Regiment Russell's Regiment. Had command of scouts for a time. The first officer to cross the Prah.

Graves, Lieutenant, 18th Royal Irish. *Ambriz* passenger. Wood's Regiment and afterwards in transport service. Went to Coomassie.

Gray, Lieutenant, R.M.L.I. Died in the early part of the campaign.

Greaves, Colonel, Chief of the Staff. Succeeded Colonel McNeill. Went to Coomassie.

Grubee, Captain, R.N., *Tamar*. Severely wounded at Amoaful. Went to Coomassie, and marched into Cape Coast Castle at the head of the remnant of the Naval Brigade.

Hare, Lieutenant, 22nd Regiment. Attached to the Royal Engineers. Went to Coomassie.

Hart, Lieutenant, 31st Regiment. Russell's Regiment. Made a military survey of the whole road from the Prah to Coomassie.

Hearle, Lieutenant, R.M.L.I. First sent to Denkera; then attached to Engineers. In the extreme front at Amoaful. A modest hard-working young officer.

Hewett, Captain, V.C. Commodore of the Squadron. Went to Coomassie. Co-operated cordially with the general.

Home, Deputy-Surgeon-General, V.C, C.B. Present at Essaman and in other bush expeditions. Invalided. This distinguished officer made all the medical arrangements for the march to Coomassie. Displayed powers of organisation which almost amounted to genius.

Home, Major, R.E. Superintended the making of road, bridges, &c, from Cape Coast Castle to Egginassie, near Amoaful. Slightly wounded at that battle, where he was in extreme front. One of the first into and last out of Coomassie. A benefactor of the expedition.

Huyshe, Captain, D. A.A. and Q.M.G. Made a military survey of road from Cape Coast Castle to Prah. Went on missions to native chiefs. In the first action near Dunquah. Died at Prahsu.

Irwin, Staff-Surgeon. *Ambri'* passenger. All invalids spoke with gratitude of Mr. Irwin's attention to them on board the *Simoom*.

Irwin, Lieutenant, 1st Foot. Wood's Regiment. Also served under Festing.

Jackson, Surgeon-Major. *Ambriz* passenger. Present at Essaman. Went to Coomassie.

Jekvll, Lieutenant, R.E. Engaged in setting the telegraph. Invalided.

Jerrard, Lieutenant, 8th Regiment Engaged in the transport.

Jones, Lieutenant, 2nd West India Regiment. Severely wounded at Dunquah. Defended Quarman under Burnet.

Knox, Lieutenant, R.A. Served under Rait in the Haussa Artillery.

Lang, Sub-Lieutenant, R.N. Employed on mission to native chiefs.

Lanyon, Captain, 2nd West India Regiment. Gave up the post of private secretary to Sir John Grant, the Governor of Jamaica, that he might join his regiment when the war broke out. Acted for a time as Colonial Secretary, and afterwards appointed A.D.C. to Sir G. Wolseley. Invalided at Prahsu.

Larcom, Commander, R.N. Glover's Expedition. Went to Coomassie.

Lazenby, Major, 100th Regiment. Employed in mission to native tribes. Invalided.

Lees, Captain, late 23rd Regiment. Was called up from Lagos to administer the Government of Cape Coast Castle during Sir G. Wolseley's absence in Ashantee. A most experienced and talented official.

Loggie, Acting Inspector-General of Police. Distinguished himself at Elmina, where he was wounded, and also fought against Ashantees when they first invaded Fantee. A man of remarkable courage.

Low, Surgeon. Accompanied Butler's Expedition.

Luxmoore, Commander, *Argus*. Severely wounded in the disaster on the Prah. Present at Ampenee. Invalided after Amoaful, in which battle he commanded a wing of the Naval Brigade.

McCalmont, Captain, 7th Hussars. A.D.C. to Sir G. Wolseley. This officer, who showed much dash in the Red River Expedition, had the misfortune to be invalided at an early date.

McGregor, Lieutenant, 50th Regiment. Joined Butler's Expedition.

McKellar, Surgeon, R.N. Fought on the side of the Fantees when Ashantees first invaded the country. Highly spoken of by the natives.

Mackinnon, Surgeon-Major, C.B. Succeeded Dr. Home as P.M.O. Dressed wounds under fire. Went to Coomassie.

McNalty, Surgeon. Attached to Headquarters. Went to Coomassie. I have to thank him for curing me of dysentery.

McNeill, Colonel V.C., C.M.G. Chief of the Staff. Severely wounded at Essaman. Invalided home.

Maltby, Sub-Lieutenant, R.N. Went to Coomassie.

Mann, Lieutenant, R.N. Went to Coomassie.

Mann, Lieutenant, R.E. Invalided. Was subjected to an unusual amount of hard work and exposure.

Maurice, Lieutenant, R.A. Private Secretary (Colonial) to Sir G. Wolseley. Author of the Wellington Prize Essay. Distinguished himself by activity in the field at Abrakrampa and Becqua. Went to Coomassie.

Maxwell, Lieut.-Colonel, 1st West India Regiment. Acting Administrator of the Gold Coast after Sir G. Wolseley's departure. Died.

May, Midshipman. Went to Coomassie.

Methuen, Captain the Hon., Scots Fusilier Guards. Wood's Regiment. Commanded a post beyond the Prah.

Moore, Captain, 80th Regiment. Accompanied Dalrymple's Expedition.

Moore, Lieutenant R.N. Glover's Expedition.

Mosse, Surgeon-Major. Distinguished himself in a yellow fever epidemic at the Gambia, and is highly experienced in Coast disease. Attached to Wood's Regiment. Went to Coomassie.

Mundy, Sub-Lieutenant, R.N. Died of wound received at Amoaful.

Nicol, Captain, Hampshire Militia. Went to the Bonny and Opobo Rivers and obtained two good fighting companies. Served in Russell's Regiment. Killed at Borborassie.

Noel, Lieutenant, R.N. An officer of great talent and energy. Distinguished himself at Amoaful.

Paget, Captain, S.F.G. Joined Butler's Expedition.

Palmer, Lieutenant, R.A. Served in Rail's Haussa Artillery. Present at Amoaful.

Parke, Surgeon, R.N. Glover's Expedition.

Peile, Captain, *Simoom*. Took part in bush expedition.

Pipon, Lieutenant, R.N. Went to Coomassie.

Pollard, Lieutenant, R.N. Employed on missions to native chiefs.

Pollock, Lieutenant, 21st Regiment Wood's Regiment.

Ponsonby, Sub-Lieutenant, R.N. Glover's Expedition.

Rait, Captain, R.A. Created the Haussa Artillery. Went to Coomassie.

Rawson, Sub-Lieutenant, R.N. Distinguished himself greatly in transport service. Wounded at Amoaful. Went to Coomassie.

Richmond, Lieutenant, 50th Regiment. *Ambriz* passenger. Wood's Regiment. Commanded post beyond Prah and afterwards invalided.

Rolfe, Lieutenant, R.N. Naval A.D.C. to Sir G. Wolseley. Went to Coomassie.

Rowe, Surgeon-Major. Through the Ashantee War from the very beginning to the very end. Sent on a mission to Assin to see if it was an Ashantee invasion. Fought on side of Fantees. Present at Elmina affair. Joined Glover's Expedition. Made

Chief of the Staff. Went to Coomassie.

Russell, Major, 13th Hussars. Commanded a native regiment Defended Abrakrampa. Led the advance the greater part of the way through Ashantee. Went to Coomassie.

Russell, Captain, 14th Hussars. Commanded at Akrofum and cleared out villages in neighbourhood.

Russell, Captain, 12th Lancers. A.D.C. to Sir Archibald Alison. Went to Coomassie.

Sartorius, Captain, 6th Bengal Cavalry. Several times engaged with the enemy. His famous march described in the text.

Saunders, Lieutenant, R.A. *Ambriz* passenger. Rait's right-hand man and a most deserving officer. Died after his return to England.

Thompson, Captain, Queen's Bays. Inspector General of armed Fantee Police. Sent on a mission to Wassaw. Invalided and died at St. Vincent.

Townshend, Lieutenant, 16th Regiment. Russell's Regiment. Died.

Turton, Surgeon. An active officer. Went to Coomassie.

Van Der Meulen, Lieutenant, 50th Regiment. Wood's Regiment.

Waters, Surgeon-Major. P.M.O. Sierra Leone, and well known in respect to sanitary improvements. I saw him in the extreme front both at Amoaful and Ordahsu.

Wauchope, Lieutenant, 42nd Regiment. Russell's Regiment. Afterwards A.D.C. to Colonel McLeod. Wounded at Ordahsu.

Wells, Lieutenant, R.N. Distinguished himself at Elmina and Abrakrampa. Died of yellow fever going home.

Wilmot, Eardley, Lieutenant, R.A. Killed near Dunquah.

Wood, Lieut.-Colonel, V.C., 90th Regiment. Commandant of Elmina. Commanded a native irregular regiment. Wounded at Amoaful. Went to Coomassie. Many times in action.

Wood, Lieutenant the Honourable H. 10th Hussars. A.D.C. to Sir G. Wolseley. Went to Coomassie. Took home the despatches as special messenger.

Young, Lieutenant, R.N. Wounded at Tacorady.